ROBIN SPIELBERG

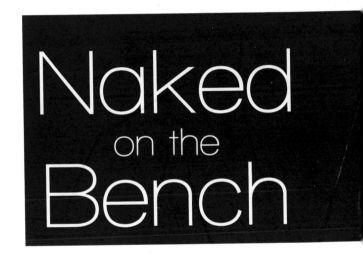

Naked on the Bench

My Adventures in Pianoland

A MEMOIR

Cover design: Kenneth O'Banyoun
Artist photo: Larry Kosson

©2013 Spobs Music/Robin Spielberg
All Rights Reserved

ISBN: 0970563353
ISBN-13: 9780970563354
Library of Congress Control Number: 2013909521
Spobs Music Incorporated

Dedication

To Larry, for understanding the spaces in between the notes are the most important part of the music.

A Note from the Author

Everything that happened in this book is true, but some things might not be so true. They are true to my memory. Some names have been changed to protect the innocent (as well as the guilty)

CONTENTS

PART V — NAKED ON THE BENCH

PART VI — IT'S ALL IN MY HEAD

PROLOGUE
SECRET ROOMS, SECRET DREAMS

The dream was so real, I felt compelled to check the piano afterward. In the darkness of the night I slipped downstairs, careful to place my weight on the left side when I got to the third step and again on the seventh on the way down. Those were the ones that creaked. My mother was a light sleeper. I moved my ten year-old body down the stairs by holding on to the chestnut wood banister. When I got to the bottom, I leaned against the doorframe that led to the living room. After my eyes adjusted I saw the Knabe baby grand in the corner, its curve facing me. Gently, I walked over to where the long piano lamp chain dangled from the ceiling. I pulled it, and the lamp, which hovered over the keys, sprang on, illuminating the beautiful eighty-eight. The brightness of the light made me squint. To my amazement, the mark wasn't there. I felt along the piano's curve. It was smooth, no ridges, and no signs of any patching whatsoever. I turned off the light, feeling a little perplexed, and went back upstairs to the bedroom I shared with my sister, hoping to fall asleep and dream it again.

In the dream I am playing the piano, working on a lesson for the following Tuesday. As I play, I hear a rattling sound. I stop playing. The sound stops. I continue playing, and the rattling starts again. No doubt a pencil has fallen inside, I think. I stand up and pull the piano desk forward so I can look inside the instrument, past the hammers, but I don't see anything unusual. I put the desk back down, back away and sit on the bench like before and there is the sound again. Rattle rattle. Then the sound of the clock chime. I look up. The clock reads 4:10. Funny, it is not time for it to chime. I stand up once again; I am drawn toward the sound of the chime and the rattle. The strange sound seems to be coming from the side of the piano. And then I see it. I can't believe I hadn't noticed it before. On the curved side of the Knabe baby grand is a small panel. In my dream it is obvious that I am supposed to push the panel in. As I place my hand on the small square panel, the square panel moves *into* the piano. Amazing: I can push it in. I do. I push it as far as I can. Where does the wood go? There is now a perfectly cut square on the side of the piano. I crouch down so I can see inside. There is a whole room in there! *Inside the piano.* Another room to the house. There is furniture inside, and books, and a long corridor that looks like it leads to more rooms.

Like Alice in Wonderland I put my head in, but instead of a scary ride down a rabbit hole, I simply emerge on the other side fully sized. I am greeted by the warmth of a fireplace, soft incandescent lighting, and the grandfather I have never met. My grandfather is sitting in a rocking chair smoking a pipe. It smells sweet. He puts his newspaper aside to look up at me and smile. I long for him to speak as I have never heard Rubin's voice, but his eyes go back to his paper. With a gentle and inviting wave of his arm he indicates I should look around. So I do.

The house is familiar, although I have never been quite here before. It is clearly our house, but these are secret rooms. Rooms you can only get to *through* the piano. The bookshelves are made of dark chestnut; they match the woodwork of our home. They are lined with music, but I don't stop here to explore any of the books, as enticing as that idea is. I want to see how many rooms there are and just how long the corridor is. Just as I turn to explore, a chime sounds and I know that means I have to go and practice. In a blink of an eye I am back on the piano bench, but the music I am playing takes on a whole new meaning now that I know about the secret room.

"You have to know when to push," my grandfather says without speaking. He hears my question even though I don't ask it aloud. I want to know how I can visit the room at will. I try and I try over a period of several weeks, but with no success. I long to dream of the room, to go inside. I think about it intensely when I lay my head down each night, but the dream doesn't come again for a long while. And then it does.

When it does, I am practicing a Beethoven sonata, only this time I am not completely focused on the music. In the back of my mind I am waiting for the sound of the chime and the sound of the rattle — the signs the panel is appearing. I have to practice sufficiently first. This I know. Someone is listening. Someone is waiting to see if I should be rewarded with a visit. And then, rattle rattle. Chime. The clock reads 4:10. Eagerly I stand up and look for the panel. I don't see it right away and feelings of extreme disappointment and despair wash over me. I run my hand along the curve of the piano pressing on the wood. My hand travels along with the grain until I feel it at last: a tiny, almost imperceptible seam. Without hardly any effort at all, the panel pushes in. This time I don't need to stoop down to look inside to gain access. I just put my hand in and then my arm and the next thing I know...

I am inside. My grandfather is not sitting in the rocking chair. The fireplace is not lit. I am alone. I walk over to Rubin's chair and sit down. I want to feel what it is like to rock in his chair. The newspaper on the side table is folded into fourths. I am unable to read it. The type is faded and blurry. I rock in the chair for what seems like a long while. Music begins playing from another room, but I dare not get up from my chair to explore; I don't want to disturb my grandfather's practice. He is playing the flute, working on a cadenza. I listen to his playing and feel so very happy to have the chance to finally hear him in person. He repeats a run over and over until a loud chime silences the flute. I close my eyes, only for a moment to take in its ring. When I open them I am back in my bedroom.

"If you push too hard, you won't be able to come in," he tells me, his thoughts burning into my head. This made total sense in the dream. Not so much when I am awake.

Every time I visit the secret rooms there is something new to see. An oil painting. A green leather chair. A Russian coin on the floor. A hand-knitted blanket, deep sea blue and grass green. It is understood I am expected to come to rest in the chair. This is the "learning chair". If I sit here long enough, I am sure to learn something important. I explore the new things I find and when my curiosity is satisfied, I retreat to the chair, enveloped in the cinnamon clove smell of the pipe that lingers in its brown velvet padding. Sometimes music plays in the other room, the room I have not yet been in. Sometimes it's piano music. Sometimes flute music. On rare occasion, an entire orchestra is in there. The room must be very large, I think. I enjoy everything I hear so very much. All of the music appeals to my sensibilities. It is such a treat to sit here and listen without interruption. I know I am not supposed to applaud. These are not performances. This is life. You don't applaud life; that would mean you were a spectator. You live it, and in the dream, I live the music.

"You are learning just how to apply the right amount of pressure," my grandfather Rubin says. "This is what is meant by a musician's 'touch'. You might not understand it now, but it is everything."

I am twenty-one when he tells me this and I haven't been playing piano much. "It's a pressing down and a pressing up," he explains in the dream. "Don't ask me how I know this because I am not a pianist. I just do." This advice doesn't mean much to me at the time, but in the very real piano rooms of New York City it begins to make sense. Sometimes I am required to be the wallpaper of the room, sometimes the focal point. You achieve either by applying just the right amount of pressure, energy, feeling into the music, into the piano keys.

My dream visits to the secret rooms inside the piano become more and more infrequent in my adulthood. The dream comes to me in one of its forms maybe once every few years. Each dream reminds me there is always something new to see inside the piano. Inside the secret rooms I read, I daydream, I listen. There is great wisdom in these rooms and when I leave, some of it is imparted to me. There is never anything technical to learn, but it is challenging nonetheless and I always leave needing rest. It is in these dream visits that I learn more than any piano lesson could teach me. Music is all about breath, relaxation, flow, ease and focus. There is music in the silence, in the spaces between the notes.

And now that the dream has stopped coming completely, I begin creating secret piano rooms of my own to retreat to in my waking life. My discoveries in these rooms, a flower, a broken heart, an adorable kitten, are all worth expression in music. They are the discoveries and observations that make my heart sing. I sit on benches everywhere and conjure up their music in my secret heart, and eventually record their melodies on CD. These become my life's soundtrack, but more importantly, my way of remembering my life. If I try too hard at a composition or to emulate someone else, no doubt the song will not flow. I learn I need to apply just the right amount of pressure to myself in terms of balancing discipline, practice, patience and dreams. I hope my grandfather would approve.

PART I
LOOKING FOR MY DOOR

THIS BUSY LIFE

My parents arranged it so I could play all night. They set me up with a pile of games, toys and puzzles before they went to bed. I had already put on my pajamas, brushed my teeth and said my goodnights. Now it was time to go into the living room. While my parents, my sister and the world slept, I worked at jigsaw puzzles, punched through patterns on my Lite-Brite, manipulated Play-Doh, played with Colorforms. It was dark, it was a little scary; it was lonely. I ventured into the bedroom I shared with my sister. I was forbidden to wake her up, but if I was lonely or bored enough like I was tonight, that's exactly what I would do. It was no use though. She just wanted to sleep.

"Hey Eileen, I think they're are asleep. Wanna play?"

"No."

"Why not?"

"I'm sleeping. Go away."

It didn't make any sense. I was offering her time to play in the middle of the night without adult supervision whatsoever. We could do anything we wanted. We could dance. We could make up songs. We could put on a show. We could play with her imaginary friend "Shoppie". But no. For some reason completely incomprehensible to me, she preferred to sleep. Something must be terribly wrong with her, I thought. Maybe she had some sort of sleeping sickness. I wandered in the dark back to the living room thinking of what I could do next to pass the time.

Our black and white television displayed gray bars on every channel when I dared to put it on, but the bluish glow was of some comfort, so on most nights, turn it on I did even though my parents told me that was a waste of electricity and I would be running up the bill. There was always a choice of coloring books next to the pile of games, and so in the wee hours of the morning, I'd end up with one of them on my lap, the box of sixty-four Crayolas at my side. I kept all the colors in the exact same order as they were the day I first opened them, and I had a special crayon sharpener to keep them new looking. If one were to break, it would be a complete disaster, and I would need to save up for a new box, so I was very careful. I sang to myself in the room of television blue light and colored until everyone finally woke up and the world was back to normal again.

Once or twice a week a teenager on our street would "keep an eye on me" at the park. My mother instructed her to make me run, in the hope I would wear out and require a nap at some point in the day.

"Mary Ellen, if you want me to run, you'll have to chase me," I told her.

"Your mom didn't say anything about having to chase you. Just run. Three times around the park."

"Well, that's no fun," I said. "I'm not going to do it."

Exasperated, Mary Ellen would say with no enthusiasm whatsoever, "Okay, I'm it. Go," and we'd run. And run. How much fun that was. I was so fast in my new white Ked sneakers, she couldn't catch me even though she was a teenager and much bigger. I ran and ran and laughed as I ran. It was so much fun to be chased. In all the months Mary Ellen babysat me, she never once caught me.

My sister and I had a red portable record player. This, along with our small play-by-numbers organ, was our prized possession. We'd put on the LP of *The Adventures of Peter Pan*, which we both had memorized. We'd recite all the parts, marching in a circle in our living room as we acted out the play. My sister was a very good Captain Hook. I daydreamed about what I would do if I was ever made to walk the plank — how I would escape. My plan was to swim underneath the boat and hold my breath for a really long time until the ship sailed away and Hook was convinced I was done for. Then I would swim a hundred miles to shore. I was four and Eileen was six. We listened to the record so often she could recite the entire play, playing all the characters, and that is exactly what she did for her first grade class. My mother and I came to Mrs. Muransky's classroom to watch her do this. The class arranged their chairs in a circle and my sister stood in the middle. Her 45-minute one-woman show was a big hit. Afterward everyone wanted to know how in the world she was able to remember all that. I wondered how someone could ever forget it. Peter Pan was the most amazing story ever in the history of the universe. Everyone should be required to learn it. Someone had to teach these kids something worthwhile. I was determined to recite the play for my kindergarten class later in the year. Maybe it would inspire them to do something worthwhile in their spare time instead of playing with stupid dolls.

There was always so much to do at our two-family house. Outside, the cracks in the sidewalk were filled with anthills to look after and explore. Weeds with little pink seed heads grew in between the sidewalk slabs. They sprouted a long stalk of green bead-like seeds that turned pink. You could twist these off and put them into a cup. Someone had to collect all these. And then we had "caps" from the candy store. If you took a rock and scraped the bump on the strip it made a surprising pop. If I was lucky and didn't get a dud, the rock broke the surface of the gun-powdered bump, and a little plume of smoke would rise up that had the most fantastic smell.

The Sears catalog was very very big. It was almost too heavy for me to carry myself. When it was placed on the kitchen table with a pen beside it that was my mother's signal that I was to start "The Sears Job". The Sears Job was my job, and my job alone. It entailed me going through the entire catalog to select items for each member of our family: underwear, socks, tops, pants, coats, hats, mittens, dresses, shirts, skirts, shoes, belts. I really don't know why my mother couldn't do this job herself, maybe she was just too busy, but I admit the job grew on me, and over time I began to look forward to the arrival of each new catalog. Alone at the kitchen table, I carefully selected items that I thought each person would like and could use. I'd pick colors, sizes; I'd create outfits. I'd select the items for my mother to purchase by putting a pen mark in the little square box next to the item, dog-ear the page, and then move on. It took days to go through the catalog. When I got a little older I moved on to household appliances and gift items like jewelry, bath soaps, toasters. I never once questioned why the items I selected never showed up at our house. Once my job was done, I moved on to the next task. There were so many.

There was the little play-by-numbers organ I mentioned earlier. It was in the dining room. If my mom was singing in the kitchen I had a very important job to do. I had to learn the song she was singing on the organ. She didn't tell me to do this. She didn't have to. I just knew that was my job. She'd be singing "You're Just too Good to be True" and I would figure out the melody line and then find the chords that would match. The chords were realized by pressing these accordion-type buttons on a left panel. I loved hearing the difference between the major and the minor chords. The major chords sounded pretty, happy; the minor chords were sadder and sometimes very dramatic.

We also had a few songbooks for the organ that used a number system to help us identify the notes and chords. The songs were Americana: "Beautiful Dreamer", "I've Been Working on the Railroad", "Oh Susannah", "Goodnight Irene", "On Top of Old Smokey", "There Is a Tavern in the Town". I didn't know how all these amazing songs ended up in one single book. We were so lucky to have it. After all, these were really the only songs anyone needed to know. How did my mother even find a book like this? There was a store in Irvington called Major Music and I thought that was where she got it, but I couldn't be sure. She didn't drive. I memorized all the songs in the book and hoped that my mom would notice so that she could find another book for the organ, although I didn't know if she'd ever be able to find one as good as this one. This book had everything in it.

Twice a week I went to what my mother called "Library School". We walked the three blocks to school, or rather, my mother walked while I skipped ahead. Once there, the children sat on little chairs in a circle while the librarian read us stories and taught us songs. My mother would browse for books to borrow while we sang "I'm a Little Teapot," "The Itsy Bitsy Spider", and "Row Row Row Your Boat." No one sang as loudly as I did. Maybe the other kids didn't know they were really in a show and needed to perform their very best each week? I never found out. Some kids mumbled the words unenthusiastically, others didn't sing at all, and some managed a meek and mild rendition of the week's repertoire. It was mind-boggling really. Pathetic. We were in Library School for Pete's sake. This was serious business. You were supposed to go over all the songs during the week until you knew them, mastered them, and could sing them with clarity and with solid vocal projection. It was embarrassing. I was embarrassed for them. I did my best to encourage the others, but there was only so much I could do.

Thunderstorms during the summertime were the very best. The house had an overhang that protected the small gray porch and when a storm was coming on I would beg my mother to come outside with me to play. She would tell me that this was the best time for a good nap. She had no idea what she was talking about. If you sat on the porch while the storm came through you could feel the weight of the air and how it changed. You could feel the wind against your skin, hear the rustle of the leaves in the trees. Best of all, you could smell the rain when it finally fell. I would count the seconds between the lightning strike and the sound of the thunder as the storm arrived and left. There was so much to do when a storm was coming. When a thunderstorm was brewing, I would race downstairs with my coloring books and crayons so I could sit on the porch and color while the storm set in. It could rain and rain and rain; there could be a torrential downpour and I wouldn't feel a drop. I was safe on the porch watching the rain wash away the horse dung on the street left by the horse-drawn wagon that still delivered milk to who knows who in our neighborhood. It was a bit strange that the guy with the horse and wagon came through — he was left over from another century — but I liked the sound of the cloppety-clop of the horse hooves on our street even if the man never stopped to let me pet his tired old horse, and the horse always seem to poop right in front of our house.

I did so many jobs all day long and kept myself occupied day and night, so it came as a surprise to me when my mother complained to my father over dinner how difficult I had been during the day.

"She doesn't stop," she told my father for the hundredth time with a sigh. "Why can't she just sit with a doll for a while, or take a nap? Eileen isn't like this."

"Dolls are stupid," I'd remind her. They don't do anything."

My mother had bought me a Besty Wetsy doll who did, well, *you know*, after you gave her a lot of water through a toy baby bottle, but big deal. The novelty of that didn't last long. And Eileen only liked to play games with me on rare occasion; that is, when she wasn't busy with her stupid Barbie dolls, reading a book or sleeping.

"Well, we should bring it up to Dr. Vaiken at her next appointment. Maybe he'll have a new suggestion," my dad said.

Last time we went to Dr. Vaiken's office we had stopped on the way home for a Bozo the Clown inflatable "hit 'n punch". When inflated, Bozo was as tall as I was and no matter how hard you hit him, he bounced right back up to standing position. It was amazing. Left, right, right, left. I could punch Bozo all day and he was never down for the count. I was told that if I ever felt angry or frustrated about something, like not being able to jump rope as well as my sister, I should just punch Bozo for a while and I would feel better.

It didn't seem right, punching Bozo. After all, he didn't do anything wrong. But punch away I did. When I was sick and tired of punching, I'd sit in the black office chair on wheels that my parents used for card games so my sister could unravel skeins of wool my mother had bought at Woolworth for her latest knitting project. My job was to sit perfectly still in the chair as my sister wrapped the wool around and around me, tying me to the chair. After the skein was completely unraveled, she would sit beside me on the couch and take a break. Then she'd revolve around me to make a ball of wool. Sometimes I would delight in turning the chair around and around so she could make the wool ball without walking around the chair. She got dizzy easily and she didn't like it. I got dizzy too, but I liked it. Enough rotations and the floor would spin in this wacky way and I could no longer tell which way was right and which way was left. I'd have to stop until the world righted itself again. This took a few seconds and then when my system caught up to reality I would start spinning again.

"Robin, stop spinning. You'll get dizzy," my mother would plead.

"It's fun, mom. You should try it," I'd tell her.

"Can't you just sit for a few minutes until this ball of wool is made? Just be *still*, will you?"

What she was so upset about I never found out. It was just a little spinning to pass the time, to make the job more fun.

My father told me to listen to my mother. I told him I didn't want to. Apparently this response was considered "talking back" and that was not allowed. I questioned that.

"*What* is talking back?" I asked innocently enough. "I'm just saying I don't want to."

"*That* is talking back. Who the hell do you think you are?"

Well, that was a dumb question if I ever heard one.

"Robin Spielberg! That's who I am!" I said.

My father got up from where he was sitting to give me a smack, but I ran away.

Even though this was the stupidest question in the entire world, he sure did seem to ask it a lot.

After the doctor examined me I was told to sit in the waiting area and my parents were escorted to the doctor's office where they spoke in private. The waiting room was filled with games and toys for little kids, not for big four-year-olds like me: cardboard picture books, simple puzzles, dolls, and a few wind-up toys that had seen better days. I sat and stared out the window and watched the doctor's son play basketball in the driveway with his friends.

My parents didn't speak on the way home, but I overheard them later behind their closed bedroom door arguing about something. I knew it had something to do with that doctor's visit, and me but that was all. I was fine. I was healthy. That much I knew. Why did they sound so concerned behind those closed doors? Why was my mother crying?

My father wanted a bigger family. Maybe next time they'd have a boy. My mother said she could handle another child like Eileen. But what if it turned out to be like me? Busy? No, she couldn't take that risk.

It wouldn't be until many years later that I discovered Dr. Vaiken had prescribed tranquilizers for me. I don't remember being drugged at dinner, but to hear my mother tell of it years later it sounded sad indeed. Suddenly the bright-eyed, always-laughing, always-moving, inquisitive child she knew stared into space, eyes glazed over, silent at dinner. After two nights of this she tried the doctor's second suggestion and started taking the tranquilizers herself. Why waste the bottle?

Listening with my sister Eileen (left) to the story of Peter Pan on our record player Irvington, NJ circa 1965

AUNTIE - LANE

My maternal grandmother died before my mother's twentieth birthday. Her sister lived and worked in Florida as a schoolteacher. My great-aunt Elaine taught Spanish, English, math, penmanship. On school breaks she traveled the world, and her apartment in Miami Shores was full of figurines and furniture from her journeys. She wrote us letters that were long and full of her memories of her travels, excursions to the opera and of her experiences as an educator in Miami. Sometimes she would include a program from a concert she attended, highlighting or circling the parts she thought I would benefit from reading. Sometimes she added samples of penmanship from students before and after they studied with her. The differences were astounding. I began writing letters to her when I was in the second grade and it always thrilled me to get a letter back, telling me to keep up the good work and to keep up with my piano lessons.

Aunt Elaine drank two glasses of milk per day, had a great knowledge of the arts and lived her life according to Miss Manners. She was a devotee of Jack LaLanne, the fitness guru of the '60s and '70s. Each day she would spread a white flat sheet on the floor and exercise to his television program. My mother used to joke that if Aunt Elaine ever married Jack LaLanne then her name would be Elaine LaLanne. She repeated this joke whenever Jack LaLanne's commercials aired and we'd all laugh.

When Aunt Elaine visited us, which was for about a week every other year, my mother told us we had to act like the perfect family. Prepping for Aunt Elaine's visit took weeks. My mother wanted my father to pick her up and twirl her around at the door when he came home from work just like on the 1950s TV shows. She was to greet him with "Hello dear!" in her best Mrs. Cleaver voice. My mother was to wake up early and make a wholesome breakfast — no more instant breakfast mixes! — And my sister and I had to be on our very best behavior. I wasn't exactly sure what this meant, but I guessed it involved not fighting with one another, and obeying our parents without any fuss.

All four of us picked up Aunt Elaine at the airport. There she'd be, all 4'11" of her in her Jackie Kennedy-esque size 2 fitted suit with matching hat. Her luggage could be identified by the red ribbons she tied around their handles. We were to greet her with enthusiasm, but not with too much enthusiasm. A proper greeting involved pecks on both cheeks and expressions of gladness. We were to watch our grammar and not use our hands to express ourselves when we spoke; this was considered by my aunt to be improper and "common".

In the morning when Aunt Elaine put out a white sheet on the living room floor, we were expected to join her for stretching exercises.

I loved Aunt Elaine's visits. I loved exercising with her. I loved the creams she used on her hands and how she wrapped her hair in a net at night. Sometimes she put some of her pink lotion on my hands. It smelled like roses.

My mother, I would learn years later, was very stressed during these visits and most unhappy. Because my mother did not have a mother of her own for most of her life, hearing any criticism from a relative was foreign and difficult. And Elaine, with her years of experience as an educator, did not hold back when it came to voicing how she thought my sister and I should be raised — from our studies to how we were disciplined, to what we ate. She also saw it as her duty to correct grammar and what she deemed as unsightly mannerisms. This would include everything from nail biting to uttering the sound "um" while struggling for a word while speaking. Everything was under scrutiny during her visits and my mother did not stand up for herself. She never talked back to her aunt, at least I never heard harsh words exchanged. She simply waited for the visit to end and spent nights crying herself to sleep. I grew up feeling guilty for loving Aunt Elaine so much because she made my mother so sad.

Aunt Elaine told me stories from the great operas and read to me from mythology books. She told me tales about mermaids, and these were my favorite, although I never understood them completely. "Why would men crash their ships into the rocks just because a topless mermaid is combing her hair?" I would ask. Aunt Elaine explained that men would be lured and distracted by the mermaid's beauty. It still didn't make much sense to me, but after Aunt Elaine left I began dreaming of mermaids and fantasizing about starting a mermaid collection of figurines the way my mother collected Lladro.

I am eight years old and I am dancing for Aunt Elaine in the living room, recounting my ballet lesson from the week prior. She knows the French names for all the ballet positions and movements. I sing for her. She knows the words to all the songs. We take walks. Aunt Elaine knows the name of every flower, every tree, by its common name and by its scientific one.

When I tell Aunt Elaine how much I love my cat she corrects me. "One cannot love a cat. A cat is an animal. You can say you are *fond* of your cat; that would be correct." I try saying this in the privacy of my room, but somehow telling Pummy, the black and white alley cat I would have for nineteen years, that I was most fond of him sounded pretentious. I hug him tight at night and whisper that he is the best cat in the world and I love him oh so much.

Other Aunt Elaine-isms intrigue me. I practice sitting on the couch, or sofa (as Elaine would have it) with my hands neatly folded on my lap. I try to have a conversation with my great-aunt this way. It is very difficult.

"You all talk with your hands!" she exclaims. "It is so common! One must sit calmly during conversation and use one's voice for expression, never the hands. Your mother talks with her hands and she looks like a Jew from Brooklyn." My mother *is* a Jew from Brooklyn, I think. What is wrong with that? I suppose, everything.

While walking down the street to the mailbox with Aunt Elaine, she tells me the secret to good posture.

"Imagine an invisible string attached to your chest bone. It goes straight up to the sky, lifting you up, just like a puppet on a string. Walk lifted in this way and you will never suffer back problems like most Americans."

Aunt Elaine says that music is very important and that I should practice my piano lessons well. She tells me that if I ever become serious about a career in music that I would have to take up an unusual instrument like the oboe or bassoon. "Too many women play the piano," she says. "There is too much competition and not enough jobs and you'll never have a career of it." She also tells me that I should marry a rich man and that it's just as easy to fall in love with a rich man as a poor one. Aunt Elaine is not married. When I ask my mother why this is so, she tells me that Aunt Elaine had a husband once, named Jim, but one day he and my aunt had a big fight. My aunt locked herself in the bathroom and would not come out. He begged and begged her to, but she would not. Jim gave up and left and had not been heard or seen since. I imagine at night when Aunt Elaine is visiting, what it would have been like if she had not been so stubborn and had only come out of the bathroom when Jim asked her to; if they had only kissed and made up. (Later in life I would learn that poor Aunt Elaine discovered Jim in bed with another man, and locked herself in the bathroom until his lover could get his things together and leave.)

When I am eight our family visits Aunt Elaine in Miami Shores. It is my first plane ride, and when I get off the plane the air feels moist and heavy. We are clearly in *another* place. Aunt Elaine's apartment is full of antique furniture, big mirrors, lots of breakables, and pink linens are on the tables and beds. I sleep in a room by myself on a twin bed with a pink chenille bedspread. When I tell Aunt Elaine that I miss Pummy, our family cat, she brings a china cat to my room that is black and white just like Pummy. This comforts me. She places it on the bedside table and I look at it and hold it for a while before she shuts off the lamp. I like Florida. I eat coconut for the first time. It tastes good, but when we walk on the streets that are lined with coconut trees I worry that one will fall on my head.

A few months after my tenth birthday, Aunt Elaine sends us her very large Hammond organ. It was in her apartment, but she has arthritis now and doesn't play it anymore. This is the real deal: two tiers of keys, lots of pedals and drawbars. My mother is annoyed for a little while that the organ arrives without any warning, but soon she finds an organ teacher to teach my sister and me. The teacher comes once a week to give lessons after supper on Thursday nights. I am already studying piano which helps, but this instrument is surprisingly different. We take lessons for a few years, but since we are Jewish we are not introduced to church hymns and non-secular organ music. Instead we learn classical organ pieces and manage to find pop books for the organ. When my friend Tamar comes over she begs me to play the theme from *Hawaii Five-O* on the organ. It sounds just like the TV show. I learn to play pretty much every television theme on the organ after that.

We sell the organ when our interest wanes a few years later. We also sell our spinet piano in the dining room and buy a Knabe baby grand piano from Altenburg's in Elizabeth, New Jersey. The piano's action is stiff and it hurts to practice for long periods of time. Aunt Elaine tells me in her letters that this will make me strong. She is not offended in the least that we sold the organ; she only tells us how happy she is that we were able to use its value to purchase a finer piano. I am relieved she is not angry.

I send cassette tapes of my piano lessons to Aunt Elaine and she always responds with great enthusiasm. As time goes by her handwriting grows messier and her concerns change. She sends Polaroid photos to my mother of her treasures. The photographs are of antique side tables, dishes, chairs and ruby thumbprint glass. She wants my mother to have all these when she dies. On the back of each Polaroid she writes what she thinks each item is worth, where it was purchased and whether or not my mother should sell it or keep it. We never do get to Florida again to visit, and when my aunt dies I am disappointed to learn my mother sells her condo without a thought. I had envisioned family vacations in Miami Shores. She keeps the ruby thumbprint glass, a few tables, mirrors and china. My mother invests Aunt Elaine's schoolteacher savings and makes several interesting investments over the years. One is a car wash in Wayne, New Jersey. Another is a medical latex glove line. None of it makes sense to me, but apparently these financial decisions help my sister and I secure good college educations.

I sometimes wonder what Aunt Elaine would think of the career I have carved out for myself. I wonder if she would have been disappointed had she learned I spent time as an actress and played piano in piano bars. Maybe my music wouldn't be "classical enough" for her. Or maybe she would have felt proud that I composed music, and managed to be successful in the world of piano and didn't have to play the oboe after all. Who knows? I do know I am grateful for her encouragement and love, her commitment to me and her caring across the miles. Thanks to her, I can still walk around the house with a tower of books on my head and never drop a single one. I even have a few mermaid figurines in a section of my garden I call "The Mermaid Garden". I know the name of every flower, plant and tree that grows there.

WHERE'S THE ORCHESTRA?

O ur family moved from the upstairs of a two-family house in Irvington, New Jersey, to a suburban house in Maplewood, New Jersey when I was five years old. Our new house was only two blocks away from the elementary school. Although my sister and I were only two grades apart, I have little if any memory of us ever walking together to school. Instead I walked to Clinton School accompanied by the orchestra in my head and sometimes my friend Jill.

Now let me tell you a little something about the orchestra in my head. It supplies a consistent yet ever-changing soundtrack to my life. It accentuates the high points, mourns the low ones, and sings funny Road Runner type motifs during life's most embarrassing moments. Thing is, as a kid I didn't know all this was only in *my* head. I assumed that everyone had a persistent music score accompanying his or her life's journey.

Our school encouraged orchestra participation in the third grade. In preparation for this, each student was given a "sound test" in the second grade.

An older white-haired man with black-rimmed glasses appeared in our second grade classroom one afternoon. He carried with him a black thick hard-shelled briefcase. Standing in front of the class, he placed the case on the table in front for us all to see.

"We're going to play a hearing game," the man told us. He snapped open the case to reveal a reel-to-reel tape machine just like the one my dad had at home.

"On the piece of paper Mrs. Runyon is handing out to you, you will write down the answers to the questions I am about to ask.

I will play two tones on this tape, one after another. All you have to do is write down whether the first tone is higher in pitch or lower in pitch than the second. Let's do one for practice."

The man pressed the play button on the machine and middle D on the piano keyboard was sounded. Then two seconds later a D an octave higher sounded.

"Who can tell me which pitch was higher?"

Was this a joke? One girl raised her hand and answered correctly.

"Great! Let's try another one. Now this one is going to be a bit more tricky."

Pressing the play button again revealed a treble clef F-sharp followed by a G just a half step higher.

"Anyone?"

No hands went up.

"Well, that's a hard one. Let me play the two tones again. Listen carefully and then raise your hand if you can tell me which one is higher in pitch."

Several hands shot up, but the boy who was called upon gave the wrong answer. I sat with my mouth agape, in complete and utter shock. What was wrong with everyone?

"Okay, well, you get the idea," said the music man. "There will be a series of fifteen tones. Write 'H' if the first note is higher than the second. Write 'L' if the first pitch sounded is lower than the second. Ready?"

He had to be kidding.

Instead of writing "H" or "L", I wrote down the proper names of the notes. Several of my classmates moaned and protested during the test, and asked the music man to sound the pitches several times before guessing their answer. It was as if he held up an orange and an apple and was asking the class to tell him which one was the apple. Something was wrong. Terribly wrong. I found the entire experience upsetting.

Two weeks later the school's music instructor put a violin in my arms. Being an instrument without frets or keys, it required its player to have good intonation. I didn't want to play the violin. I wanted to play the flute.

I had been told that my grandfather Rubin played the flute, a silver one. He died November 20th, exactly a year to the day before I was born. I had heard stories about his days with the NBC Symphony from my grandmother and my father and how he played for a famous conductor named Arturo Toscanini. He also played for the Metropolitan Opera and had a flute solo, which he wrote himself, cadenza style, for an opera called *Lucia de Lammermoor* or something like that. He was the flute in *The Magic Flute*. I imagined my parents would be proud of me if I gravitated toward this instrument.

"Absolutely not," my mother said. "You will need braces at some point and you can't play the flute with braces on your teeth."

"But why not?"

"The violin is better."

What I didn't know then was that Rubin's brother, my great Uncle Herman Spielberg, had been a first violinist for the NBC Symphony. As substitute Concertmaster he had earned a great deal of respect from his peers, from the Maestro himself, from the audience. He also earned a great deal more money than my grandfather.

Herman Spielberg and his wife Irene bought my father his bar mitzvah suit because Rubin and his wife couldn't afford one. So much for the magic of the flute. It was an instrument for the impoverished. The violin held more promise.

My parents didn't hire a private violin teacher and it never occurred to me that they would. I showed up to rehearsals with the school orchestra and did the best I could. The music teacher corrected my fingering and I seemed to blend in with everyone else who had been taking private lessons just fine, but I didn't care for the instrument much. It was stupid. It required that you play one note at a time, most of the time. Apart from the occasional instruction to "pizz" or pluck the string with your third finger, it was an empty experience compared to the piano.

In seventh grade I was placed in the second violin section of the orchestra, still cruising along on my musical intuition, but just starting to fall behind from the other kids who had private lessons. By the end of the year I convinced my parents to let me drop out so I could be in the choir.

I kept the violin in my bedroom in its case, under my bed. I played it in the privacy of my room whenever the mood moved me, which was not often. The string section in my head sounded far better than anything I could reproduce on the instrument and I focused my attention to the Knabe baby grand in the living room.

When I played the piano, I often imagined an orchestra playing along with me. Timpani, brass, strings. I gave the flugel and English horns solos. I let the oboe weep. I encouraged the bassoon. I comforted the cellos and applauded the flutes in my mind as I played my lessons from the John Thompkins books and vocal selections from Broadway musicals. It certainly made everything sound better, having the orchestra with me, but now and then I allowed myself to step out in a solo on the piano. When the orchestra was silent I felt pretty vulnerable and exposed, but sometimes silencing the players in my head was the only way I could express the truth of the piece.

My sister claimed I drove her nuts by humming at the table when we ate our meals. It was only when she screamed, "Stop it!" that I realized I had been humming. I slowly became aware by looks and stares that I often hummed out loud. I sang to myself on the way home from school, making up songs about the kids who made fun of me, writing laments for the crushes who didn't know I existed.

It never once occurred to me that I might have any special "talent" or "gift" in music. I figured everyone could make up melodies, name notes by name upon hearing them and sound good on their instruments if they wanted to. Most people probably just didn't want to, that was all.

Sometime in high school it dawned on me that perhaps I was a little different than other kids in this regard. I realized music wasn't swirling in the minds of my friends drowning out conversations and making it difficult to concentrate in class. I concluded I had some sort of mental illness and that it was best to keep it to myself.

Music: a natural release. I entertained myself by composing songs, writing phony commercials, arranging and rearranging Chopin's waltzes and Mozart's sonatas. My parents liked to come into the living room after dinner and sing songs from Broadway musicals. My father had a beautiful whistle, my mother, a clear soprano voice. They sang "If I Loved You" from *Carousel*, "I Have Dreamed" from *The King & I*, "The Impossible Dream" from *Man of La Mancha*, and "Ten Minutes Ago" from *Cinderella*. I loved these songs and made up arrangements using the chord patterns in the vocal selection scores.

But nothing I played in my living room ever compared to the

orchestra in my head. It entertained and amused me. It inspired me more than anything. What a shame no one else could hear it.

During one of the early summers with the Atlantic Theater Company, I worked on a play called *Women and Water* by John Guare. Part of his "Lydie Breeze" trilogy, this play took place on the island of Nantucket during the Civil War. It was an ambitious play for our young theater company (The Atlantic Theater Company) to mount; our resources were few and our time limited, but we were committed to the beauty of this play and to telling its story.

Guare had visited the company in Vermont as a guest artist and was inspired to entrust us with his play. We were studying drama and working on acting technique all day with David Mamet, William H. Macy and Gregory Mosher, and about as serious as you could get about creating *the* New American Theater.

Felicity Huffman was selected to replace Madonna on Broadway in Mamet's play, *Speed-the-Plow.* All the girls in the company were given the chance to audition for this coveted role, and it was terrific news that one of our own got it. Felicity had to leave for New York immediately to rehearse. As a result, Mary McCann stepped into Flicka's role as the lead in *Women and Water,* and I, into Mary's supporting role. I was thrilled. I played the role of a southern woman whose husband was off in the war. I remember having a rifle as a prop in the play and using it to protect my son played by Steven Goldstein (now an opera singer, director, actor and professor). I think at some point I wound up dead on the stage in an elaborate struggle. My friend Melissa and I also played male soldiers. Our costume mistress, the talented Laura Cunningham (now Laura Bauer), managed to find blue military uniforms and boots. She researched the emblems that needed to be sewn on to our hats. We hid our curls under our caps and smudged our faces so we could pass as male soldiers in the field. In addition to these roles, I was asked by Steven Schachter, the director, to compose and execute the music for the scene changes.

We had an upright piano available. Steven Goldstein played trumpet. Another company member, Clark Gregg, played snare. Karen Kohlhaas played flute and Margo Grib played the fiddle. I spent that summer researching sea shanty songs and songs from the Civil War era, and I also composed a few of my own. I took this music assignment very seriously and spent a lot of time daydreaming the music of this play. Since the play spoke of a "new world" and a hopeful utopian society, I called my theme to *Women and Water* "Memories of Utopia". The trumpet part was accompanied by snare and piano and then the fiddle and flute joined in a piece that was brave, bold and eventually triumphant. Our cast loved it, although I imagined the piece with a 60-piece orchestra and was never quite pleased.

A recording engineer in Vermont helped the Atlantic Theater Company mount a number of radio plays and often volunteered to help with our sound needs. After rehearsals we'd go to the studio where he worked, White Crow Audio. Douglas was determined to help me get the sounds out of my head and onto analog tape. There was a synclavier in the studio — a sampler and synthesizer that could create hundreds of orchestral sounds. We worked the entire summer on "Memories of Utopia", often into the night, and I came away with a tape that was very close to the music in my head. It was a very satisfying endeavor. We used all 48 tracks available to us. I learned how to play drum machines and create edits. Time went quickly at White Crow Audio. That is when I discovered that studio time was like no other time in the world.

Years later, a day after my daughter's first birthday, a flood in my Montclair, New Jersey, basement would destroyed the utopian tapes and all the pencil-written scores I had created for the orchestra members who would one day play it. I was sad, but I am comforted by the fact that I still have the song. It's in my head.

At our first piano, Maplewood, NJ

YOU ARE HERE

When I was eleven our parents took us on a trip out west to visit national parks. We were not the type of family that camped or "roughed it". We stayed in motels and bungalows, some of which happened to be set in the woods. This was rustic to my parents, who were both Brooklyn natives. Any neighborhood without a sidewalk was considered rustic to my parents, but we didn't mind. My sister and I were not particularly fond of the idea of sleeping in a tent; we didn't like spiders.

We flew from Newark, New Jersey, to Denver, Colorado, rented a car, and proceeded to get lost all the way to California. We stopped in gas stations and rest stops along the way, where my dad would get out of the car, ask someone for directions, nod as if he understood exactly what the attendant had told him, and then get back in the car only to wind up in the same spot twenty minutes later.

Once we pulled over at a rest stop that had a huge map display of the area. There was a big red arrow pointing to a spot on the map that read "You Are Here". My dad studied the map. My mother complained that we were lost yet once again. My mother was the one charged with holding the Triple A Trip-Tik maps, but never did any navigating since she couldn't put her head down to read them in the car while the car was moving; that made her carsick. My father turned to my mother and said to her calmly that we were absolutely, positively *not* lost. He proved this by pointing at the red dot on the map that said "You Are Here".

One of the things we liked to do while on vacation was shop for souvenirs. Our parents let us pick out one thing from each vacation spot. We were supposed to choose something that would serve as a reminder of the trip to that particular place. We could pick out a magnet that said "Grand Canyon" on it, or a "Go Climb A Rock" mug from a souvenir shop in Yosemite. A keychain that said "It's nice at Bryce" in Bryce Canyon, Utah, caught my eye because it had a rabbit foot attached, and for some reason at that age, I had a thing for keeping a rabbit's foot in my pocket as a lucky charm. (Gee, thanks, Gilligan). In Casper, Wyoming, there were racks and racks of t-shirts. My eye targeted one that was shocking pink (my favorite color at the time), and what a bonus! It had a cat on the front. Did I mention I love cats? In addition to the "Casper, Wyoming" in bold funky letters on the bottom, there was a slogan on top of the shirt. It read, "Everyone Needs A Little Pussy." Perfect. Size small. Mine.

I brought the shirt up front to the register so my dad could pay for it. He took one look at the shirt and said, "You are not buying that. Put it back."

"But why not? It's perfect! I love cats and it's pink! And it says everyone needs to have a cat! I can wear it in the pool so I won't get sunburn."

"Robin, pick something else. I said put that back."

But I insisted and wanted to exert my will. I always wanted to exert my will when my dad set down rules without explaining them. It wasn't fair at all. He said I could buy a shirt. Why not this one?

"I've brought my own money with me," I told him, while walking over to another cash register.

"Go talk to your mom. She'll tell you why."

I found my mother looking at clip-on earrings on the other side of the store. My mother never pierced her ears so she wore clip-ons, and she was always losing them, so she always needed new ones. I held the shirt up to me and showed my mom how cute it was. Without even blinking, she said, "Oh Robin, don't you know that 'pussy' is another name for vagina? Put it back."

What?? !

I must have looked astonished, because she put down the earrings she was holding and in a hushed tone so no one could hear, she elaborated.

"Pussy is another name for vagina. Only men use that term; it is a bit vulgar, but it is what it is. You have to put that back."

I couldn't understand why men would call a woman's private part a cat. That made no sense. And what really didn't make sense is that the shirt now read, in my mind, "Everyone needs a little vagina." What? Why would everyone need a vagina? That made no sense.

For the rest of the trip I stuck to magnets and key chains. But part of me still wanted that shirt. Even if some people thought it said vagina on it.

The Grand Canyon, The Grand Tetons, Yosemite, Bryce Canyon, Salt Lake City, Death Valley Desert, Los Angeles, Muir Woods. We got lost at all of these places, bought souvenirs, played Ping-Pong, took pictures, nursed blisters, swam in dirty hotel pools, and got very carsick. My sister was a sulky teen and couldn't be bothered with family portraits or lame swimming pools. Not having a partner in crime on this trip, I sang to myself quietly on the tours through the canyons and woods, the piano keeping me company even though there wasn't one around for miles. In my head I could still play through my lessons and Broadway show scores, and that I did. When my mother sang in the car songs like "I Have Dreamed" from *The King and I*, my sister would cover her ears, but I listened, only pretending not to like it.

My father's father was a professional flutist, which might have explained my father's uncanny ability to whistle with perfect intonation and with gentle vibrato. His whistle was simply unbelievable and rivaled the sound of any flute. When my mother tired of singing, my father would whistle everything from pop tunes to commercial jingles. We'd drive from place to place with the sounds of my parents singing and whistling. We even sang commercial jingles. We especially favored that one from Burger King about holding pickles and lettuce and making special orders that wouldn't upset the staff.

Everything turned into a song with my parents around. If they were having an argument and my mother said, "I don't want to talk about it anymore," my father and I would burst into singing the song we had written just for that particular declaration (which came often). It never failed to make her laugh.

> *I don't want to talk about it anymore!*
> *I don't want to hear about it anymore!*
> *Wah, Wah, Wah....*
> *Scooby doobie doo....*

There was a song for not wanting to talk about it. There was a song for going to the Maplewood Pool (*it's very cool, it's better than school, there are lots of rules*).

There was a song for the cat:
Pummy's a beautiful cat.
Fluffy soft and nice and fat.

A very smart kitty
And boy he's so pretty
Now what do you think of that?
What do you think of that?

There were songs I wrote in my head about the forgetful Yellowstone waitress, and one that my mother wrote about us leaving so many things behind on this trip. The famous title "I left my heart in San Francisco" was transformed into "I Left My Shoes in Yosemite". How else could one possibly remember all the things that happened on our vacation if we didn't write songs about them? The only reason I remember to this day that the eggs in Jackson Hole, Wyoming, were inedible was because of a remark my mother made while perusing the menu. We had a terrible meal the night before in the same restaurant, but it was the only game in town. After reading the breakfast menu, she said, "Let's order eggs. I mean, that has to be a safe choice; what can you do to an egg?"

The eggs were god awful, and so the song "What Can You Do To An Egg" was born in my head.

We ended our national park tour in California. My sister, mother and I all threw up driving up Big Sur and we toured Hearst's Castle in a post-nauseated Dramamine-induced daze. My father drove in circles around Los Angeles and kept ending up on Santa Monica Blvd. I collected a lot of rocks on this trip and my suitcase was weighed down with them on the flight home. My father, when he lifted the suitcase into our rental car said, "Gosh Robin, what do you have in here, rocks?" And I said yes. He thought I was kidding. I wasn't; I had a rock tumbler and I couldn't wait to polish up these babies. My sister bought pretty turquoise jewelry on the Navajo Indian Reservation; I collected rocks.

All these years later I can still hear the music of the national parks, and I can still tell you where I found each subsequently polished stone that is nestled in the vase above my sink. But damn if I ever found that cat tee shirt again.

PART II
ENTER STAGE RIGHT

BEHIND THE FOURTH WALL

A lot of people ask me how I came to be a composer and pianist. Believe me, it wasn't an intentional career path; I had dreams of a different kind growing up.

When I was five years old, my sister was in Mrs. Muransky's second grade class and I was a happy camper in Miss Cadodi's kindergarten. By the time the second grade play was ready to be staged in the spring, our family was making plans to move into a house of our own in Maplewood, New Jersey, that summer. It was exciting and it was sad. I was five, and my best friend Judy had already moved with her family back to Peru, so it was mostly exciting.

The lights dimmed in the wooden-seat auditorium. I sat with my mother in the middle of the theater and the play began. It was incredibly good, but what was truly amazing was my sister's performance on that proscenium stage. Somewhere toward the end of the play, my sister took to the stage all alone in a pool of light. There, with the accompaniment of Mrs. Muransky's piano, my sister sang the school song, "Hail Dear Mount Vernon."

It went like this:
Hail dear Mt. Vernon
School of our youth
Known for your teaching
Of knowledge and truth
Now we are leaving you
Parting is sad
But we'll remember

The good times we had
Do not forget us
As we move on
Just keep on smiling
After we're gone.

I didn't know my sister would have this solo. Her voice was strong and clear and she moved about the stage toe-heel, then heel-toe. She meandered in little circles as she sang, the spotlight following her every move, her eyes cast downward. I was awestruck.

I saw Mrs. Muransky after the play in the second grade classroom where parents were reunited with their stars. I told her I thought the play was the best thing I had ever seen in my entire life. She answered, "Next year, I arranged to have you in my class too. We'll have so much fun." I began to cry. Mrs. Muransky didn't know! No one had told her!

"Dear, what is the matter?" she asked, as the group of children and parents walked down the stairs from the classroom to the school lobby.

"We're moving!" I blurted. "To Maplewood! To a house! I have to go to a new school. I won't be in your class!"

I felt terrible giving her this news that would surely devastate her after experiencing such joy with the play.

"Oh I see. Well, good luck. We will miss the Spielberg girls." Her hand let go of mine and she moved away to accept flowers from one of the parents, her arms outstretched.

When we got home, I asked my sister who had taught her all that choreography to "Hail Dear Mount Vernon" and she said she didn't know what I was talking about. She claimed she had stood still on the stage and sang the song. "Not true!" I told her. "You had dance moves." She denied this to the point of tears. I guess she was *supposed* to stand still and she thought I was making fun of her. She was probably wandering aimlessly around the stage while singing, but I thought it was brilliant. Her movements were so perfect for her wandering thoughts and conflicted feelings about leaving Irvington and our dear Mt. Vernon. She didn't get the compliment. We had a big fight.

"Mom! Robin is making fun of me!"

For my sixth birthday we went to the Papermill Playhouse in Millburn, New Jersey, to see *Sleeping Beauty*. I invited six girls from my class. I don't know where they found a real prince and real princess to be in the show, but they did! Right during the climax of the play, when the prince comes to wake Sleeping Beauty with a kiss, the most unusual and amazing thing happened. The fourth wall disappeared.

Prince faced the audience and asked if there was anyone out there in the audience who knew how to wake the sleeping princess. The lights in the house came up and a few hundred little hands shot up. Then kids began yelling right to the prince.

"Kiss her! Kiss her! Kiss her!"

"Oh," the prince said. "You think I should *kiss her* to wake her up?"

"YES!!!" we all shouted. "YES!"

"I think there is only one person in this audience who can help me, and that is a birthday girl named *ROBIN SPIELBERG*!"

WHAT???

"Where is Robin? Will Robin please come up here and help me wake the sleeping princess?"

My mother, smiling and beaming, stood up and helped usher me out to the aisle. I was in such shock I don't remember leaving my seat. Before I knew it, I was not only on the stage, but also in the arms of the prince. He picked me up. I was wearing a poufy party dress and I was worried my underwear was showing.

While I was in his arms, the prince said, "Robin, the audience thinks we should kiss the sleeping princess to wake her up. Do you agree?"

I nodded, tugging on my party dress trying to get my panties covered. Was I wearing white ones or yellow? Together, with the handsome prince still holding me, we leaned over. I touched my lips to the cheek of the beautiful blond sleeping princess, and then the prince touched his lips to hers. Her eyes began to flutter.

"I think it's working!" he declared. The audience cheered. I was released below the lip of the stage into the arms of my waiting father. When he put me down I ran back to my seat. The play resumed, but I don't remember anything past that moment of being held by the prince. My face felt hot. He picked *me*. How did he know it was my birthday? How did he know my name?

The magic of the theater had me at hello.

When I was thirteen, my father came home with the LP to *A Chorus Line*. Every night after supper, the record would play while we all listened in the living room. This was a ritual we practiced with many LP's: *Man of La Mancha, South Pacific, and My Fair Lady*. When we had memorized the score to *A Chorus Line*, my father bought tickets to the show. It was my first Broadway musical. I had the vocal selections songbook and sang Lopez's song, "Nothing" every day, acting it out to the living room wall. My sister's favorite was Maggie's solo where she sings about her father asking if she'd want to dance with him in the living room. She sings that she would *loooove to!* It was lyrical and beautiful. It was hers.

I sat wide-eyed in the first row mezzanine of the Schubert. *A Chorus Line* was magic. It was real. It was life. No set. Just a white line across the stage where the actors stood, facing the unseen director. The show with all its brilliance and emotion pierced right through me. Everything rang so true — the pains and the triumphs of each individual vying for a job in the chorus. I cried at each rejection, my heart sang with each win. I knew what I wanted to do when I grew up. I was going to "get the job" just like those actors in *A Chorus Line* and tell my own story. I would be an actor on the stage. I would be one of the ones who would be "chosen" to shine. Pick me, pick me, pick me.

"I want to go to Stagedoor Manor," I announced the following year. I had never been to camp before and I don't remember who told me about the acting camp in Loch Sheldrake, New York, but I was convinced I *had* to go there. The kid from *Zoom* went there. All the soap opera kids went there. It said so in TV Guide. Anyone who was serious about becoming an actor went there. I had to go there.

We visited and my parents said okay. Well, my dad said, "Who the hell do you think you are?" and then he said okay. They were worried I would get homesick. But the summer of my fourteenth year, we all drove to upstate New York to move me in to my new home for four weeks. My roommates Holly and Valerie seemed nice enough. Holly had an amazing soprano voice and was destined to get the leads in all her high school musicals. Valerie was a "serious" actor. I didn't know what I was. I just wanted to be a star.

Everyone at Stagedoor took dance classes, voice lessons, acting classes and talked a lot about Stanislavsky. It was mostly over my head and I didn't shine. That was left to the older, more experienced campers. They smoked; they called our French acting teacher Jacques by his first name. I was in the chorus of *Follies* when Jacques was telling one of the actresses to play the part in a more sexy way. I didn't know what he was talking about. She was singing about Paris and he said in his European accent, "You want to fuck Paris. You want to be Paris. Sing it like you want to fuck." All I know is that his instruction worked. Suddenly she was on fire. Her boobs seemed bigger. Her hips swayed.

She sang, "*Ahhhhh PAR---EEE!*"

"Yes! Yes!" he shouted. His compliment burned through her, turned her cheeks pink, made her boobs grow even bigger and her voice rang through the theater. She leapt from the stage and she threw her arms around him. He swung her around. It was all pretty shocking. My favorite part of the play was the number "Waiting Around for the Girls Upstairs". I imagined myself in as one of the gals upstairs getting ready for her big date.

Glen, one of our teachers and camp counselors, was in his last year of college and he wrote a musical called *All The World Is A Stage*. One day during rehearsal (again, I was in the chorus), I showed him a few songs I had composed. His eyes widened.

"You *wrote* that? That is truly amazing, Robin! Maybe one day they'll do one of *your* plays here at Stagedoor Manor!" His play was not memorable in the least, but on opening night we had a big circular cake that said, "All the World's Is A Stage" on it in green script. It was delicious.

In *The Me Nobody Knows* I was given a short solo. I practiced it over and over and over again so when I sang it for the show my parents could hear me way in the back of the barn. Maybe next year I would get a bigger part if I just did those few lines well.

But there wasn't going to be a next year. My roommates complained about me. Apparently I had bad dreams and shouted in my sleep. My family had been in a car accident the year before and I dreamed about it over and over again. My nightmares woke up my roommates. Instead of being sympathetic, Holly complained to the heads of the camp. After all, she needed her beauty sleep and her vocal chords needed their rest. Maybe I was not emotionally mature enough to be at Stagedoor Manor.

Sad as I was about that, inside I agreed. There was a lot of kissing, Newport cigarettes and curse words at Stagedoor. There was even pot, but that was just a rumor. There were broken hearts and politics and nasty rivalries. They were all beyond me. I was a spectator, an audience member at that camp. It was all so foreign to me: the way these people hugged, cursed, related to one another. They hung out outside by the stage loading docks smoking, cursing, kissing and joking. I was left wondering how you could fuck a city. I admitted to myself that I wasn't quite ready for my spotlight, but I could be any minute. I could taste it.

In the spring of tenth grade, Harriet Holzer told me she was going to Phillips Academy in Andover, Massachusetts, for the summer. They had all kinds of cool academic programs, and if you went there, it would look great on your college applications. Andover, a rival of Exeter, was a fancy prep school/boarding school. John F. Kennedy Jr. went there. Spontaneous games of Ultimate Frisbee (invented at *my* high school, thank you very much) broke out on the quad, students sat with books of Shakespeare and Proust under trees and read to one another, in between discussions of the politics in South Africa of course. It sounded sophisticated. It sounded grown up. I sent away for a summer catalog.

In between the Advanced Calculus and Latin course descriptions, one popped out. Classical Theater. Could I convince my parents to let me take this? My mother thought I should take a writing class. My father thought a political science curriculum would be best since he was convinced I was going to be a lawyer one day (I argued so much with him and won so many times, how could that *not* be my path?) The Classical Theater curriculum combined the study of Bertolt Brecht's work (which culminated in a production at the end of the summer), a monologue class, a technical theater class, one 20th century American play (another production) and set construction. With my Stagedoor Manor experience on my resumé and my acting club activities at school, I completed the application and essay and got in, 1-2-3.

Thank you, Harriet Holzer, wherever you are. It was the best summer ever in the history of summers. I lived in a big house that served as a dorm called "Double Brick". I roomed with Joan, one of the smartest girls I had ever met. She was from California and her dad was an airline pilot. She couldn't believe I had never tasted an avocado and told me that I must come to California — there were orchards filled with them. All of the girls in this dorm were smart, smart, smart and fun, fun, fun. No one smoked. No one cursed. No one said nasty things. Everyone was kind, supportive and loved school. I was home.

One day while dancing in our room, we noticed a loose floorboard. We knelt down to examine it and voila! It flipped up to reveal a secret compartment.

"Cool!" said Joan. "I bet the kids who live here store their keys and money and stuff in there for safety. How neat." I agreed.

The light board in the black box theater was manual. Laura Kuhn and I operated it together for the Brecht play. We climbed up the fifteen thin metal ladder steps to the booth during tech to learn the cues. The cues were complicated and sometimes we needed all four limbs to pull the levers to make the light changes. We giggled and bonded up there in that booth while the chorus chanted below us. Laura told me a few things about boys. Things I didn't know. Like they enjoyed having their ears nibbled on. She also explained to me in great detail what a blowjob was. She gave very technical descriptions of the male anatomy. I was so grateful. Laura thought I was such an innocent. I told her not so. I kissed Barry Green behind his garage in the sixth grade after all. I knew a thing or two.

I was awarded the part of the English eccentric in *The Man Who Came for Dinner*. My parents came to see the play. I had a ball playing up the melodrama. My favorite part was being locked away in a sarcophagus and taken away off stage. One night it was so hot everyone was convinced I had passed out in there because when they opened it up stage left to let me out I didn't come out right away as usual.

My classmate Jenny had a beautiful voice and her dream was to land the lead in *Pippin* the next year at her high school. When I told her I played piano she latched on to me and every spare moment we had from the demands of the theater program, we went to the music practice rooms to work on her audition. She had brought the *Pippin* score with her to Andover. I tried to convince her to sing "What I Did For Love" from *A Chorus Line*, but nothing doing. She was going to sing "With You" from Pippin for her audition. Jenny had the most beautiful voice. I hope she got that part.

Eddie was one of our student teachers and a great dancer. He knew all the old dances and taught me how to jitterbug. I was small and light and got thrown around in the dance to my heart's delight. Up, down, in between Eddie's legs, over his back, around his hips. I loved it. We danced until the sweat poured down our backs. We didn't care. We danced after the sweat poured down into our shoes, and our arms were so slippery we had to towel them off so we could hold on to one another and dance some more. Every week the music played in the dance hall and every week I jitterbugged and Charlestoned, thanks to Eddie's tutelage. Jenny and I had big crushes on Eddie. He took turns dancing with both of us, but as the night wore on, he'd dance with me most. I was lighter and easier to toss around. Eddie liked boys and couldn't be won over. We tried anyway. We left love notes in his mailbox signed "guess who" and promised to nibble on his ear if he gave us a kiss, a real kiss. We didn't get kisses from Eddie, but he did give us candy bars now and then from the commissary.

In the theater department, we studied *Long Day's Journey Into Night* by day, and built cubes for the Brecht play set by night. You have no idea how hard it is to build a perfect cube. I was a disaster. Measure once, cut twelve times. That was me. But somehow I finally made a perfect cube and passed the class. Laura finished hers the first day (it figures — I heard she went on to get an MFA from the Yale School of Drama) and was free the rest of the week to work on monologues.

Suzy, our monologue teacher, called me into her office the last week of the summer session. She wanted to tell me something. She told me that she thought I was incredibly talented and should pursue a life in the theater no matter what. She said John F. Kennedy Jr. wanted to be an actor more than anything in the world, but his mother would not let him. I should do what I wanted to do with my life and not let my parents or anyone else sway me if a life in the theater was what I wanted. Then she made me promise not to tell my parents that she said that. She had my word on both counts.

ALL ROADS LEAD TO THE STAGE

We had a big theater department in our high school and in my senior year I was elected President of our drama club, The Parnassian Society. All of my friends were in it. Arts were so "cool" in our high school that the drama club was the biggest club in the school with up to two hundred members in any given year.

Some kids went on to fields in the arts after high school and achieved great success (Oscar winners Elizabeth Shue, Frank Langella, Grammy winner Lauryn Hill). I thought it would be great to go to a college with a strong drama department. My piano teacher at the time, Alan Wolfe, thought I should go to Conservatory for piano. My parents thought I should be a lawyer. What's a gal to do?

I opted for a Big Ten school in the Midwest, Michigan State. It offered pretty much everything, and while I took all the pre-political science major classes I promised my parents, I also took classes in communications, focusing on radio. I had a job as a DJ for the college station, WMSN and truly loved it, but once again found my way into the theater, or rather the theater found me.

Michigan was a lot colder than New Jersey, and some of my classes were clear across campus. The big field was nicknamed "The Tundra" for good reason. Although we weren't supposed to cut through the buildings, I found myself doing just that on a particularly cold day I just couldn't stand it. The building was the dramatic arts building, and on the callboard in the main hallway was a big sign that read, "OPEN AUDITIONS for THE DIARY OF ANNE FRANK". I looked at that sign and felt a deep longing.

I missed the camaraderie of the theater, rehearsals, dissecting a scene, learning my lines. Here I was happy in all respects in my new college life; but there was indeed a hole. I missed being in the drama club. *The Diary of Anne Frank* was a theater department production, but the sign indicated that the director was open to casting outside the department. I wondered why. Could it be they hadn't found their Anne?

I picked up the audition pages, or "sides" as the seasoned theater department kids called them, on my way through the building and signed up for the audition. So did sixty or so other girls, but after two, three, four callbacks, I was the last one standing and won the role I had only dreamed of a few weeks earlier. I was going to play Anne Frank.

Rehearsals were in the evenings and on weekends. Between my bi-weekly radio show on WMSN, "play practice" (as my roommate called it) and classes, I didn't see much of anyone. Our dorm had an upright piano outside the cafeteria and if the food line was particularly long, I sat down to play until the line dwindled. I caught up with my dorm friends then. My friend Annie who lived in the room next door liked to sing and had a lovely voice. She reminded me of Jenny back at Andover. Ironically, Annie loved the music from the musical, *Annie* and had the songbook in her room. Even more ironic, Annie herself was adopted! I played the song "Maybe" which spoke of little orphan Annie's longing to know her biological mother, and my friend sang. She sang it so beautifully; it made me cry.

On her birthday that year, Annie told me the freakiest thing while we were at the piano going through some songbooks I had brought along with me from home. She said she noticed an ad in the paper that morning that said something like this: "Darling daughter, have been looking for you. Please call me. Happy birthday." It listed Annie's birthday. Annie called the number. After speaking briefly with the woman on the phone, Annie was convinced she had been connected with her biological mother.

Annie wanted her friends around her when she was to meet Joyce for the first time. She was shaking with excitement, but also worried it wasn't a match and just some strange coincidence and she'd feel foolish. We waited in the lobby of Mason-Abbott Hall, by the piano, for Mystery Mom to show up. Annie sang "Maybe" and I sang "Tomorrow" and then Joyce walked in. There was no question. She was the spitting image of Annie. They hugged and cried. And then we all hugged and cried. Amazing that. To this day Annie and Joyce are good friends and have been in one another's lives from that moment on.

After being cast as the lead in *The Diary of Anne Frank* I cared little about my classes, or my major for that matter. We performed *The Diary of Anne Frank* in the 1500-seat Fairchild Theater to school groups and then to the public. It was my first time performing regularly in a large theater and instead of telling the director I was coming down with a cold during previews, I worked through it. I lost my voice completely by opening night and missed the opening and the first few shows, but I survived and so did the show, thanks to a wonderful gal named Susan who dyed her beautiful blond hair to brown and stepped into the role just for those nights. She saved me and, as I found out later on, I saved her. Apparently the department owed her big-time for not having to cancel shows when I didn't even have an understudy. She learned the entire part in a day, and in the years that followed she was granted several highly sought-after roles.

We performed five shows a week for a month and I was in my

element. I auditioned for *Man of La Mancha* next and then *Table Settings*, winning parts in both, but not winning many friends in the theater department. The girls in the department complained that a non-major was taking their parts.

Frank Rutledge from the department and John Baldwin, who directed *The Diary of Anne Frank* took me aside one afternoon. They said they wanted to talk to me. I felt scared. I thought they were going to fire me from *Table Settings*. Instead, I got some tough love and good advice.

"Robin," Frank started. "We were wondering...are you planning on switching into the department at the end of the semester? Because we'd love to have you, and not all the plays are going to be open to non-majors in terms of casting."

John began before I could answer, "Truth is, you are welcome here, it is true. But honestly, look around you. Most of the people in this department are never going to leave Michigan. You're from New Jersey. New York is in your back yard. We think you're talented and have promise as an actor. Everything you truly want is back home."

"So you're saying I should leave the school?" I didn't get what they were trying to tell me.

"No," said John. "We are not telling you to leave. But I was part of the Whole Theater Company in Montclair, NJ, as you know, Olympia Dukakis' theater company where you said you saw many plays...and there are so many more opportunities back east, more than we could ever give you here. Just think about it. You are welcome to our department, but I think — we think, everything you ever wanted is in your own back yard."

I knew they were right. I knew from the start that I was only humoring my parents and lying to myself with this political science major. What was I to do? I was invited to join the department, but also being encouraged to leave altogether. What to make of it? After rehearsal I walked back to my dorm, but instead of going to my room, I went upstairs to see Joel, who I had been dating. Joel was a senior who had majored in photography and engineering. He landed a job with Kodak in Rochester and was going to start right after graduation. I told him what had happened.

"Use my phone," he said. "You're a grownup. Call a conservatory. Call Julliard. See if you can get that audition Alan Wolfe recommended after all."

I called Information from Joel's dorm room phone. He had long distance. I asked for Julliard's number, but instead of asking for the music department, I asked to be connected to the drama department. The first semester was just ending, and as it turned out I had just missed the deadline for midterm auditions. I dialed 411 again and asked for the number to NYU's drama department. Auditions were in three weeks. I typed my letter of inquiry right then in Joel's dorm room, reserved a plane ticket using my own credit card (I had established credit while working at a shoe store during high school), and then called my parents and told them I had something important to discuss during break.

While I was typing my letter and putting together my acting resumé to send to NYU, Steve Winwood's "While You See A Chance" was playing in Joel's dorm room. We took it as a sign that this was the right thing.

"It's perfect, Robin," Joel promised. "You'll be in New York City, I'll be in Rochester. We can take the $29 flight on People's Express Airlines to see one another on weekends. I 'll even take your headshots. It'll be great."

My parents were less than thrilled about my wanting to

major in theater and the tuition for NYU was twice the price. I promised to figure out a way to pay the difference, but first I had to get into NYU.

The audition criteria called for an application, essay, letter stating reason for transfer request, and a monologue audition. The only monologues I really liked were the ones Johnny Carson did on *The Tonight Show*. Rather than go through plays and find text from a random scene, I decided to write my own. For my audition at 725 Broadway, I created a scene in which I was stuck in an elevator. I pretty much made it up as I went along. I think the word the Admissions Officer used was "refreshing". I can imagine how many versions of "Tomorrow" they had heard or monologues from *As You Like It*.

My looks, talent and demeanor had me placed in the Circle in the Square Theater School. I looked around me on the first day of class and realized I was surrounded by ingénue types who probably all had leads in their high school plays. Joel and I continued to date for a few months, but the travel became too much and we decided to call it quits. I had already completed all my required classes at Michigan State so I was now in the thick of the undergraduate drama major, taking classes in acting, scene study, dance, movement, voice, speech and Alexander Technique. Classes were uptown, midtown, downtown. I began to recognize my fellow students at the subway stations and we began traveling together to class, and making sure we were on the same subway cars when it got dark. We walked one another to our dorms in the village.

New York City was everything we knew it would be. Just one week into the school year and we all agreed: it was dirty, noisy, smelly, beautiful, bold, exciting, crowded, lonely, dangerous, alive, vibrant, depressing, joyous. There were so many possibilities. Where to start? You could dye your hair blue at 2am if you wanted to. Astor Place Haircutters was open 24/7. If you wanted to rehearse with your scene partner at 3am, that could be arranged. The city didn't sleep, and neither did we. We were busy. I loved it. It was challenging and exhausting, but it certainly wasn't boring.

When I wanted to have a mellow moment, I would wander into the store Star Magic. Star Magic was a retail store next to the 24-hour deli on Broadway off of 8th Street. Inside Star Magic I was in another world. As soon as the door closed behind me, I was transported out of the city. It felt like a planetarium, complete with twinkling lights on the store's ceiling. Through warm audio speakers ambient music played; it was New Age music that was dreamy, ethereal, and flowing. Bright halogen pin lights illuminated crystals in their glass cabinets. Amethysts, copper ore, citrine, topaz sparkled along with gemstone jewelry mounted in silver and gold. Pewter figures of wizards and sorceresses lined the glass shelves. Glow-in-the-dark stars, tarot cards, star maps, essential oils, kaleidoscopes, telescopes, books on astronomy: they could all be purchased here. My favorite was a tee shirt that depicted the vast Milky Way. There was an arrow pointing to the smallest spec on the shirt and next to the arrow it read, "You are here." *Yes I am,* I thought. I envisioned decorating my imaginary apartment with glow-in-the-dark stars, crystal balls and all the books on space and the stars that would fit from Star Magic. I was fascinated by everything in this store, but it was the music that really got me. Sometimes it was solo piano music that was played in here, the kind of music I would write when I was alone at the piano with no one listening. This non-classical, non-Broadway piano music touched me. When I had extra money I bought the cassettes of the music on sale at Star

Magic. It was the music of pianists Liz Story and George Winston, guitarists Will Ackerman and Michael Hedges. Simple. Beautiful.

The same music was being played in the Capezio Dance store in the West Village. I found myself wandering in there from time to time to try on dance skirts I didn't really need, but what I really got out of my visits there were a few minutes of musical transport as I browsed.

Besides my occasional visits to Star Magic and NYU's Coles Sports Center to swim, there wasn't a lot of outlet for the angst I felt in those early NYU days. I was taking the classes, I was following the instructions, but where was I going?

The few friends I had in other departments knew what their path was. Four years here, then four years in pursuit of an MBA and then a job at a firm. Or four years of pre-med, four years of med school, residency and then voila! You're a doctor. If I finished this program, who would dub me an actress? How would I know when I was ready? There didn't seem to be a clear path. Some people went into acting without the "proper" training and were successful. Others had years of training and were flipping burgers.

While it was discouraged, some of my classmates like Paige Hannah were taking acting jobs here and there and going on auditions in between classes. Paige's sister, Daryl, had already acted in a load of movies and was doing great. She was in this one film called *Splash* with Tom Hanks and that role landed her on the cover of all the magazines and the late-night talk shows. She was even dating Jackson Browne. Paige didn't want to be known as Daryl's little sister anymore. A reputable agency signed her on while she was still a student at NYU. Paige took me along with her on some of her commercial auditions so I could see what they were like.

Paige had straight red hair, freckles and blue eyes. She looked like a kid, not an NYU sophomore. When she landed a recurring role on a soap opera I hardly recognized her on TV. The makeup covered all her freckles and she was dressed in sexy outfits for the role. She had to leave school to do the soap full time. The teachers all shook their heads in disapproval when they found out the reason for her continued absence, but I think all of the students were a little jealous. *She got out of here. She's done with the guessing, and hoping and waiting. She doesn't need an acting teacher to tell if she's good. She's booked a real job. She's been validated.* Funny how we all marveled on how Paige got out when just a short time ago we were all consumed with how to get *in*.

More than anything, I suppose, I longed for the ever-elusive validation. Wasn't there some sort of certificate you could get after you played a certain number of parts that had ACTOR-CERTIFIED stamped across it? Was there something I could take with me to the real world when school was over as proof that I was "official"? I wanted to work as a stage actor, more than anything, and I wanted to experience that sense of belonging that came along with the teamwork of rehearsing a play. Other than the few department plays each year, our work in the world of theater was limited to classes where we mostly *observed*.

Our department needed a student government and I volunteered to represent our studio on the Tisch School of the Arts (TSOA) student council. My fellow council members included Jace Alexander, Daniel Sweeney (now known as D.B. Sweeney) and a handful of student actors with political tendencies such as myself. I started out as treasurer and had a hand in student council-funded projects. The following year I was elected President of the entire student body. This took up a lot of my time, but I loved it. I learned how to read budgets, allocate funds, write policy, and engage students by empowering them to participate in their department's activities. This position also gave me exposure to students in other School of the Arts departments such as film & television, musical theater, writing etc. We were all TSOA students, but until this time, I had very little interaction with anyone who was not a drama student. We were all so busy, that it was nearly impossible to meet anyone outside of the department. Our off-class hours were spent studying, rehearsing, building sets, or seeing a play.

The student productions produced under the auspices of the student council were daring and terrific. It was a thrill to be part of them. I acted; stage-managed and produced, and enjoyed those jobs equally.

And so it went. I went to classes, acted and sometimes starred in department productions. I was becoming a New Yorker. I did some good scene work and some bad scene work. I was involved on the student drama council and college council. I was busy, busy, busy and things seemed to be clocking along.

And then, just like that, I attended a guest lecture on a cold winter day and began to question everything I had learned up to this point. It was a scary thought, but I started to believe I had taken the wrong road to the stage. I remember the day. It was the day I met David Mamet.

In Vermont with the Atlantic Theater Company, July 4th BBQ circa 1985 at David Mamet's house

MAMET DAMMIT

"There is no such thing as talent," Mamet told us during his guest lecture at NYU. "I can teach a plumber to act. It is a skill, not a mystery, and has nothing to do with talent. Thinking about your dead puppy so you can cry in a scene is not the way to achieve truthful acting." And then he did something funny that is kind of an inside joke for all students of acting. He began running around the stage with his arms flailing and then asked us, "So, what was I just doing?" When no hands went up, he said, "I was *using the space.*" Hysterical laughter broke out in the auditorium. This one hit home. "Use the space," was a common instruction in our acting classes, one we were all used to hearing, especially if an actor sat in a chair for a long while to present a monologue in class or stood in a corner to work on sense memory. The instruction was to remind us that the entire space of the room was at our disposal and we should think of it as another "tool". Making fun of that instruction was sacrilege, but it was also hilarious.

A good deal of theater people came to lecture us as guests of the Tisch School of the Arts Undergraduate Drama program. Marvin Hamlisch, Stephen Sondheim, John Guare, André Bishop. But no visit was quite like David Mamet's. He said a lot of outrageous things and cast a spell in the room that was visceral.

In my training at the Circle in the Square Studio, we were taught "sense memory". We'd spend hours trying to conjure up the smells of imaginary coffee, relive the pain of our childhoods, crawl on the floor pretending we were crawling through mud and slime. All of this was, of course, in the name of becoming actors. Here was

David Mamet, a playwright, telling us we were wasting our money. All of it, and he meant all of these techniques, were complete garbage. I didn't know what to think, but I suspected there was truth in what he was saying. It was the Emperor's New Clothes. As long as we all followed the instructions and criticisms of our acting instructors, it would be okay, right? That's what we told ourselves. But the truth was no one could guarantee our success or lack of success in this field. No one could, David said, but us. He could teach us how to ready ourselves, or so he said.

Mamet ended his lecture with an invitation that sounded more like a dare: "Anyone who really wants to learn something about acting is invited to come to my house this summer in Vermont." A load of curious students signed up to do just that. Scott Zigler was one of them.

Scott Zigler was in the same studio as I was, the Circle In the Square Studio. He went to that summer session in Vermont and couldn't stop talking about it when he came back. There we were in the acting class of the legendary Michael Kahn at Circle in the Square Theater. I had just acted in a scene from *The Rainmaker*. It went terribly. My scene study partner and I were clueless when it came to directing ourselves in the scene. Michael Kahn shamed me in front of the entire class for not properly analyzing the script. I fought back tears as best I could. If anyone in the class was horrified by our teacher's admonishment, I couldn't tell. No one said a word. I wish I had been brave enough to have stood up and said "How *dare* you? How dare you talk to me like that? I am a *student*. I paid money to come here and *learn* from you. And you are not teaching me. You're shaming me. I didn't come here to learn to become a director. Directing this scene was hard. If you think I failed, help me make it better." But I didn't do or say any of those things. I was afraid. I listened to Michael Kahn rant and rave about how hard it was for him to endure such terrible scene work, and how *some* of us would probably not be returning the following year.

Deflated and humiliated, my scene partner and I returned to our seats as the next pair took their places for their scene presentation. My friend Pierre was in the seat next to mine. He put his hand in mine and gave it a squeeze. It made the lump in my throat bigger.

After class Scott found me in the lobby. "This class is bullshit," he said. "If you had taken the Mamet workshop, you would have known exactly how to have analyzed that scene and this would not have been such a struggle."

Again, with the Mamet crap.

Just the day before in Teresa's sense-memory class, Scott had challenged our elderly teacher, a grande dame of acting if there ever was one. She was talking to us in her slow post-stroke shaky, soft but deliberate voice about how remembering a pain from the past in order to do a scene in the present was crucial to acting with strong emotion. Scott raised his hand ever so politely and when she called on him to ask his question, he said, "In all due respect, this is pretty much a useless direction. You can't be in the moment and think about your past. It is not the actor's job to emote. If it were, we would be called emoters, not actors. Our job is to act. The important thing is to find the action of the scene, do *that*, and rest will take care of itself."

"And who told you that? I assume David Mamet?"

The class chuckled.

"Yes," Scott said. "He is absolutely brilliant. The playwright has it all there on the page. All you need to do is know your action; do that, and say the words on the page."

Scott was incredibly smart, cerebral, and blessed with

an analytical mind. What he said made complete sense. The concepts as he presented them were simple, yet challenging. It seemed you could learn this acting technique in five minutes and yet, it might take a lifetime to master. There was so much to it, and nothing to it at the same time. Teresa's technique seemed unachievable, mysterious. Some people could just cry on cue and others could not. Did that an actor make? I preferred the world where you did the hard work and, by doing so, would become a proficient actor. Not by chance. Not by luck. Not because of connections. Not by crying on cue. Scott encouraged me to interview for the next Mamet summer session. We had been rehearsing a scene together from Chekhov's *The Seagull* and he was so articulate about the essence of the scene. He learned all this in one summer with David Mamet? Scott said he was going to go back. I liked Scott. I liked his analysis of the scene. I signed up.

This time it was going to be harder to get in. Word had gotten out about the summer session and how brilliant it was. Everyone who had gone the previous summer wanted to return, and then there were all the new people who were late to the party. There were a limited number of slots. Mamet didn't believe in talent so there would be no auditions. There would be a test of another sort to determine who would get to go. Candidates were each given a list of questions to answer that contained riddles, hard-to-find facts and the like. This was pre-Internet so the task was difficult. That was the idea, that the task would be difficult. "Why do commandos lisp at night?" was one of the questions (A: because "s" is sibilant and the sound would carry in the night). You had to *think*. Then there was an interview.

David Mamet, William H. Macy and Gregory Mosher, the

artistic director of Lincoln Center Theater, were there at the interviews. They had known one another from their days together at Goddard College and had worked together in Chicago at the St. Nicholas Theater. I don't remember their questions in that interview. I don't remember my answers. I just remember being nervous and telling them that I really wanted to join them that summer, and that I wanted to learn a solid acting technique I could depend on. More than anything. I had managed to get cast in good roles in the department's plays. I landed leading roles in both *Night Music* and *Golden Boy* in the department's tribute to the Group Theater. I enjoyed a wonderful supporting role in the adaptation of Anne Tyler's book, *Dinner at the Homesick Restaurant*. But I knew something was wrong. I didn't know what I was doing. I was being cast based on my ingénue looks and personality. I guessed my way through everything. Directors sometimes gave me line readings and I used them to convey a certain emotion or intention I knew nothing about. For the most part, I made good guesses, and kept getting roles by acting on instinct, but I knew there was more to becoming a great actor than this.

I didn't hear back from the selection committee for the Mamet workshop and so I resigned myself to living in a dorm in New York City that summer. I had three jobs lined up. One at the Metropolitan Opera House where I was selling subscriptions by phone; one in the School of the Arts Dean's Office, and one as a transcriber of Braille notes for a blind student (I took classes notes for her and transcribed them on machine to Braille). At the end of June, two days before the Vermont summer session was to start, I got a call that there was a space for me if I wanted it. Someone who had been accepted had dropped out. I was an alternate. *Yes.* I packed my bags and got myself on a bus to Montpelier, Vermont.

I was scared, oh so scared, but in a delicious way that was full of anticipation, hope and promise of something wonderful.

It really would take writing a whole other book to describe the summers that followed, and maybe one day one of my former classmates will write one. For now, I will try my best to describe these times.

Life-changing.
Amazing.
Heartbreaking.
Eye-opening.
Revealing.
Difficult.
Vulnerable.
Life-affirming.
Dreamy.
Fun.
Satisfying.
Brilliant.

David Mamet, William H. Macy, Gregory Mosher and guests from the theater world joined us in Vermont for summers filled with acting classes, seminars and scene study. We worked hard. It was like army boot camp for acting students. The three most important requirements of the workshops were to be brave, to use our common sense and to exert our wills. If we practiced strengthening these three elements, we could achieve anything, including the most difficult of all: living in the moment on stage in front of an audience. There was nothing harder or more challenging. All instincts pointed to *planning* what would happen on stage. I had been guilty of rehearsing in front of mirrors for Pete's sake. And yet, to be truthful to the playwright and to the story of the play itself, one had to live in the moment on stage. It left one vulnerable. It was scary. It was appealing. Very appealing.

Because bravery can't be taught, the act of being brave was something we simply had to practice every day. We jumped from high cliffs at the quarry where we swam. We shot our hands up when David asked for volunteers. We accepted challenges before they were fully explained to us. Mary McCann and I even saved a guest actor from drowning once, when all logic and reason told us it would be impossible. I had just swum a very long length of a quarry. We shouldn't have been there. We had been trespassing. The guest actor, unbeknownst to me, saw me jump into the deep clear delicious water for a swim and followed, but got tired and began to struggle halfway across. Breathless and worn out from my long swim, I turned when I reached the other side, and leaned against a rock to rest before heading back. That is when I saw the actor who had been following me slip and begin to flail in the water. Holy shit.

Our fellow actors were far on the other side of the water. They couldn't see me, and I could hardly make them out. The drowning young man was just an ant in the water. *Don't think. ACT. Be brave, and you will be.* That is what my mind said. I began to swim back across, way before my body was ready, using my will to swim faster with every stroke. Thankfully Mary was swimming nearby and sensed something was wrong and joined me. She grew up on an island off the coast of Cleveland, Put-In-Bay, and was a water girl. Without speaking a word about trouble or needing help, we "played" with our friend, teaching him floating techniques, pretending nothing bad was happening and partially convinced ourselves we weren't in trouble. We took turns placing his legs around our hips and backstroked closer to the cliffs behind us in seemingly slow motion. When we reached safety, we started talking small talk about the water, the sky, the summer, the play we had been rehearsing, which ironically was entitled, *Women and Water*.

After driving the young man we had just saved off to his rented cottage, Mary and I burst into tears. It's a bond we three share to this day. The three of us know what happened that hot summer day, but I, for one, doubt I would or could ever have been that person to have swam back for someone twice my size had I not practiced being brave every day during that Vermont summer.

"The job of the actor is to make the difficult easy, the easy habitual, and the habitual beautiful," David told us. I wrote that down and highlighted it. "To act truthfully under imaginary circumstances should be fun," he said. "If it's not fun, don't do it. Choose another imaginary circumstance." That's in my notebook too.

Forming good habits was key. We worked on our bodies and our voices daily. Our exercise instructor was relentless. Our heads hit the pillow exhausted at the end of the day. To be an actor, you had to be strong physically, emotionally and mentally. Stamina was required.

We set up volleyball net. No one played volleyball going into the summer, but by the end of the summer you would never have known that. Teamwork was achieved, trust, flexibility. We had the most intense games and long volleys. We played softball too. Just because you hadn't done something before was no reason not to do it and to become good at it. I left that first summer feeling I could do anything I set my mind to. I suppose that was the point.

It was becoming instilled in us that we could and would

change the American Theater using the "practical aesthetics" we were practicing. We could create the theater in our hearts. There was no need to sit around in a casting office waiting for an opportunity. Within our group were all the writers, directors, actors and designers we needed. There need not be a mystery to become a theater artist. We could create our own opportunities. David had written something on the blackboard of the Vermont College classroom one morning that really hit home. It read,

WHAT'S STOPPING YOU?

It seems that at any given time an actor could have a thousand excuses as to why he didn't land a role. My agent didn't call me in for the role. The casting director didn't forward my photo/resumé to the director. So and so is friends with the director and had an "in". I had a bad audition. I was right for the part, but no one else saw that in the two minutes I was granted to audition. The casting director knew me from another job and never liked me because I had quit that job. On and on. And here David was telling us, that all of that was garbage. CREATE THE THEATER IN YOUR HEARTS. WHAT IS STOPPING YOU? Why wait for anyone else's PERMISSION?

In the summers that followed we knew something extraordinary was happening. Our friends back home made fun of us. When we tried to assimilate back into our respective acting studios at NYU (Circle in the Square, Lee Strasberg Studio, Stella Adler Studio, Experimental Theater Wing), we no longer fit in. We were accused of being in some sort of "acting cult". David Mamet was the guru and we had fallen under his spell. Shaken by the push back our studio teachers were getting from us, NYU was facing a true dilemma: what to do with these unruly upstart acting students who were rebelling against traditional acting techniques?

Rather than lose us or fight with us, the Practical Aesthetic

Workshop studio was formed at NYU as a temporary compromise so the unruly class could graduate. William H. Macy, who lived in Manhattan, rode his bike to NYU's Tisch School of the Arts each day and taught classes. David came in from Boston twice a week. Voice, dance and bodywork classes supplemented the new studio. Everyone was happy. Our Vermont group continued the work in New York under the auspices of NYU. I won't deny that many of us exuded a sense of superiority. The students in the other studios began to hate us and for good reason. We were a pompous group, but we also had good reason: we were the new face of the American Theater and we knew it.

Out of these workshops, the Atlantic Theater Company was formed. Our teachers, David, Bill, Lindsay (Crouse), and Greg were among its first board members. After graduation, we returned to Vermont in the summers, broke and jobless, to create summer theater for the residents of Montpelier and later Burlington, Vermont. Shel Silverstein, Howard Korder, John Guare, Peter Hedges, Craig Lucas, and many other playwrights gave us plays to workshop. We elected among us an artistic director, Scott Zigler, and passed a Constitution, which held all our rules of conduct, casting policies and bylaws. One of the Code of Ethics instilled in us from our very early days was to be early.

"If you're not fifteen minutes early, you're late!" declared Mamet on the very first day of class. Amazing how this changed everything. Class began at 8:30am. If you arrived after that time, even if you had a scene to perform for the class, you'd find the door locked. "Being late is a big 'fuck you' to your fellow actors. It is saying subconsciously or consciously that your time is more valuable than theirs. Don't be late. *Ever*," he told us. His rule might have scared some people but it made me very glad inside. Being the nervous type, I was usually early by nature and disliked waiting for late people. Late people made me *more* nervous...and resentful. Abiding by this one rule gave us all respect for one another instantly. No longer put in the position to judge excuses, we were free from judging one another. Whew. Is the subway running late a legitimate excuse? Is the alarm clock not working an excuse? Is being sick a legitimate excuse for being late? It didn't matter. It didn't come up. The door was locked at a certain time. Period. Amazing: we all managed to be there. Issue, gone.

It was more than a little ironic that practically the entire committee that volunteered to write that darn constitution was late to its first meeting and, as a result, got kicked off the committee. That left Clark Gregg and me with the task. Clark and I set to work and created a document that stood up for many many years. I didn't know it at the time, but writing the Constitution for the Atlantic Theater Company was probably my greatest contribution to ATC.

In 1986 the Company members decided to move to Chicago by a two-thirds majority vote. I had just settled into my West Village apartment with my boyfriend and started playing piano at The Limelight at night.

The Limelight was a dance club and my boyfriend was friendly with one of the managers. This manager ran the VIP room upstairs. Entry to that room was reserved for celebrities and power players. There was a piano inside the VIP room. I was hired to play from 11:30pm – 2:30am, which was perfect. My cocktail waitress job at the piano bar at the Clock Lounge (inside the new Marriott Marquis in Times Square) finished up at 11pm. It was impossibly dark inside the VIP lounge. Candles were placed all around the piano. I could see shadows of people but could barely make out their faces. Carly Simon stopped in. Mick Jagger was there. Madonna came by. Only the rich and famous were allowed entrance past those red velvet ropes. I was instructed to play rock songs on piano. I played "She's Always a Woman", "Stairway to Heaven", "Thunder Road", songs by Styx, REO Speedwagon and Jackson Browne. I wasn't on payroll, but that didn't matter. Money was folded and put in the brandy snifter on the piano. Sometimes I came home with a hundred dollars. One night I made five hundred. I was so happy to have this job, but was still thinking about moving to Chicago with the Atlantic Theater Company.

My boyfriend thought going to Chicago was a dumb idea.

"You already play with your acting friends in the summer," he said. "Why go to Chicago in the winter? Aren't there acting jobs here in New York?"

"Yes," I told him. "There are acting jobs here, but the Company is working on changing the face of the American Theater! We are going to be like the St. Nicholas Theater, or the Goodman; Chicago is the place to be to focus on that and no one wants to be distracted by what's happening in New York."

He laughed. Donny was thirteen years older than me. We had met at the Old Homestead restaurant where he was waiting tables "temporarily". He was just getting on his feet after a bad divorce. My friend Valerie DePena helped me get a hostessing job there on weekends. Donny and I flirted with one another at work, and then began dating. In 1986 we were living together on West 10th Street and it was getting serious. We were thinking about getting married.

Donny thought all of my Atlantic friends were dreamers and naïve. We fought about my commitment to the Company quite a bit. He thought I put way too much time into this "hobby" and I wasn't cast enough in the plays. I acquiesced. I didn't go to Chicago, but I mourned the loss a little every day.

My parents were not terribly supportive of the Company either. Fans of the big Broadway musical, neither one understood or appreciated Mamet's ear for writing, and they certainly didn't appreciate his mouth.

"What is it?" my father hollered. "You went to NYU a young lady, and came back from Vermont with a toilet mouth. Every other word is a swear word. Must be that fuckin Goddamn David Mamet Dammit!"

I have to admit it must have looked like I had changed a great deal during these summers, but to me, I was becoming more myself. The layers were being peeled away. Not only did I stop watching my words so carefully, I began to feel comfortable without wearing makeup. Perhaps this might seem like a small thing, but I had worn makeup since the eighth grade, convinced my looks were not good enough to go without it. I was the only girl in those Vermont summers who wore makeup to class each day. One day my teacher, Bill, asked me why. In front of the entire class. I couldn't answer. Wasn't it obvious? I *needed it* and the other girls did not. They were blond and tan and I was pale and freckled. He didn't ask the question to admonish or embarrass me. He just asked it out of curiosity during a "repetition exercise". This exercise, also known in the Sandy Meisner technique of acting, is meant to help you take your focus off of yourself. In it, you verbalize things you see or notice about the person sitting in front of you. My partner apparently never mentioned during the exercise that I was wearing makeup, so Bill, who had been monitoring our work, brought that up along with all the other things that had gone unnoticed. I began to wear less and less. During these summers I learned it was okay to be me. I began to accept myself, freckles and all.

After the Company had been in Chicago a few months I really began to regret my decision to stay in New York. I missed everyone so much. There were a handful of other Atlantic members who did not make the move for various reasons. They had NYU credits to finish up, or needed to work etc. I called them one by one to reconnect and to see if we could do some theater work together.

Karen Kohlhaas, Madeleine Olnek, Faith Luther, Margo Grib and I decided to do a play. We wouldn't and couldn't call it an Atlantic Theater Company production, but no matter. We would use all the skills we learned in our workshops and take the plunge right here in New York. Why not? What was stopping us? We pooled our money and rented the 18th Street Playhouse. Faith's friend, who worked at PBS producing *Sesame Street* wanted to work in the theater. She directed us all in a play called *Chamber Music*. We chose this play because it happened to have had a lot of parts for women. I went door to door in the neighborhood of the theater and sold program ads to businesses for $50 a pop. Karen did the program layout. Each of us took on a non-acting job as well: props, costumes, set, marketing. I was producer and ran the box office. We ran the play for five nights and actually made money when all was said and done and began thinking about putting together another play.

I visited my Atlantic friends in Chicago one weekend. We squeezed in a company meeting sometime between the play they were doing and a Tom Waits concert we all attended. There was a discussion about returning the entire company to New York, but no decision was made.

Eventually the Company did return to New York, with their Chicago lessons behind them. After a brief period of being outcast for not joining the Company in Chicago in the first place, I was welcomed back as an ensemble member. Clark Gregg was now the artistic director and he challenged my commitment. It unnerved me. For one, he said, I did not go to Chicago and two; I was playing piano all over Manhattan. Was that a conflict?

"That's ridiculous, Clark," I countered. "Does Melissa's waitressing job take away from her commitment?"

"Yeah, but none of us *care* about our waiter jobs. You clearly care about this, enough to want to have rehearsals scheduled around it."

And he was right. I cared all right. I wouldn't jeopardize my piano gigs for the world. Despite our work ethic and company bylaws, there was still unpredictability in the world of acting. Even if you were to be cast in a play, it was all so *temporary*. I hated that. The play would eventually close. The union piano jobs I earned were mine to keep unless the room went 'dark' (meaning the piano room removed the piano or no longer wanted music). This predictability was a comfort in a career path filled with so much turmoil, angst and unknown.

Without being conscious of it, I began applying all the acting technique and practical aesthetics I learned from Mamet and the Atlantic Theater Company to my piano world. I was always on time. Early even. I was prepared. I never had music on the piano desk. I memorized everything and made the difficult music easy through habit, practice...and eventually the playing became beautiful. It was only then that I dared play the music in public, after hours and hours of preparing and practice at home. I only played songs on the gig after I understood its essence and had chosen an 'action' for it as I had learned to do in David's scene-analysis class. For example I might play a piano piece as if I were saying a prayer for a sick friend, or play it as if I were avenging an injustice. I was indeed acting at the piano. The music was the script, the words. I learned them by rote. I played them in the moment. I was never bored, even when I played for ten hours a day. The real music was well beyond the notes, and often in the spaces in between. The music was in my intention.

When people ask me, and they often do, who was my biggest musical influence, I don't even have to think about it. It was Mamet. Yes Mamet, dammit.

In the dressing room of Lincoln Center during the run of the play "Boys Life" by Howard Korder

PART III
MY LIFE IN PIANOLAND

CRYSTAL FOUNTAIN

A room full of men in ties and jackets, and well-dressed women are drinking from glasses that clink; their cocktails are laden with perfectly round discs of ice. The lights are dim, the chairs are leather, and oil paintings and brass trumpets hung as sculptures adorn the walls. The mood is set. A Steinway grand awaits the next pianist to audition. An attractive, slender woman stands and approaches the piano, places her music before her on the music desk and begins. It is "Rhapsody in Blue". She plays perfectly, impeccably. Oh my God. I played "Rhapsody in Blue" in my late teen years. It took me six months to nail those thirty-one pages and I never had it polished enough to perform it in public.

After she regroups from the grand finish, she plays a jazz standard. I scan the room that is "Trumpets Restaurant & Bar" trying to figure out who here is a decision-maker, and who here is a guest. The room is not quiet; it whispers and laughs and is full of light conversation. After all, the job in question requires the musician to serve as background music, wallpaper; to add to the ambience of the room the way the flickering candles set on each table in their crystal bowls add a glowing, romantic perspective to each face it illuminates. The piano player is fantastic.

The man who asked me to come here, Harlan Ellis, is in a navy blue suit and tie. He did not tell me that other pianists would be playing this evening. I had assumed he called me here to try out the piano and perhaps have a hotel manager listen in, but no, this is an audition in the true sense of the word. He asks me if I want a drink, but I politely decline. My fingers feel cold and I feel a sudden urgency to run away, run away home; especially after hearing Miss Rhapsody in Blue Girl.

When the piano girl finishes, there is polite applause and then a man takes to the bench. He is handsome and proper looking in a tuxedo. No music on the desk. He plays a medley of jazz standards. His music swings and sways, it boogies, it strides. I do not play like this. I feel panicky. After a few minutes another woman approaches the piano. She plays many of the songs I know and that makes me feel better. Her touch is lovely; her music is enchanting. She should get this job.

And then Harlan turns to me and tells me I am next. "You ready?" he asks.

His face is warm, gentle. I wonder if I should faint if he would come to my rescue, or

pretend not to know me. I don't know him well enough to tell. I feel dizzy and queasy as the adrenaline courses through my body. But as I walk toward the piano, it doesn't seem like anyone is paying attention to me or to what I am about to do, so when my behind makes contact with the hard ebony bench I feel a bit more relaxed than I did in the velvet chair. I begin with "Soon It's Gonna Rain" from *The Fantasticks*. I play "Moon River" and then segue to C Minor for a pensive version of "My Funny Valentine", and then for no reason whatsoever, a Billy Joel song comes to mind. I play it freely, improvising a bit on the tune, and that puts an end to my fifteen-minute set. Polite applause from a few listeners, including Harlan. I want to go home, but Harlan insists I have a glass of wine and stay a while. I do, and several other pianists play for the next hour while Harlan distracts me with questions about my life at NYU, my acting ambitions, my boyfriend, and life in the city. He tells me about his family and the agency he works for, Jerry Kravat

Entertainment. When it is time to go home, I thank Harlan for the opportunity and shake his hand. He gives me a hug.

I am barely outside the hotel when the tears come. They are tears of relief, tears of humiliation, and tears of defeat. Instead of hailing a cab or going down to the subway, I walk home. My apartment is clear across town in the West Village, but I don't care. I walk and cry, the tears flowing fast, hot on my face. My coat is still on when I call Robin Goldsby to tell her what happened.

"What's wrong?" she asks. "Why are you upset?"

It all comes pouring out; I tell her everything. "Oh Robin, you don't know how humiliating it all was. Everyone was a little or a lot older than me. Everyone has experience. All of them played better. This was all a big mistake. I am so sorry."

It was Robin who first heard me play piano in the Clock Lounge of the Marriott Marquis in Times Square, so really, this was all her fault.

When the Marriott Marquis was being built in Times Square, I bumped into an actor friend on the way back from an audition. We saw a long line forming by the new Marriott and figured it was an audition for something. The Marriott footprint was huge and required that they knock down a Broadway theater. Their deal with the city of New York was that the new hotel property would include a brand-new Broadway house. Maybe this was an audition for something going on there? We got in line.

It turned out the line was an employment line, all right. For the Marriott. The Marriott was accepting job applications even though the property was yet to open. My friend and I had been so busy gabbing and catching up that we hadn't been paying much attention, and were at the front of the line before we had much of a chance to think about it.

We were both handed forms and pencils, and sat down to complete them. Why not? After name, date etc. there were several job choices. The instructions indicated to circle in which area the applicant had the most experience: housekeeping, waiter/waitress restaurant, bartender, bar back, cocktail waitress, front desk reception, retail cashier/gift shop staff, employee cafeteria, security, maintenance. I did a little cocktail waitressing at the Old Homestead Restaurant so that is what I circled.

I was called back, interviewed twice and hired to open the hotel. A few months into the job, when I had just finished clearing my tables I sat down at the piano. The lights were on bright, as the maintenance team had begun to vacuum in the distance. It might have been midnight or so on a weeknight. Early. Robin Goldsby had stepped into the ladies room after her last set, and I stepped over to the piano after months of feeling curious as to what it would feel like to play it. This was a Yamaha C7 grand, a brand-new piano that resonated beautifully and deeply when Robin G played it. Her music drifted all the way up to the 44th floor, the top of the atrium. As you rode up and down the big glass elevators the music either moved closer and closer or drifted further and further, depending on which way you were going in the vertical capsule. The top of her golden-haired head was visible even at floor 44 and then her lovely face by floor 10. She was elegant, statuesque, beautiful, impeccably dressed and her music was what enabled me to endure working in this lounge. Without her I was doomed. The job was tedious and ridiculous. The gals had to wear heels and long black skirts with slits up to the hip, a rhinestone belt, white silk blouse (acetate), pearls (fake), pearl earrings (again, fake) and a black cap with rhinestones that we coined our "monkey hats". Our feet hurt like hell at the end of the night; the floor was marble. But Robin G took my mind off of it all with her piano playing. Her music made my shift go faster. She played all the music I loved, including her own beautiful creations. I began to know them so well; I hummed them as I worked. Her left hand held fabulous rhythms while her right tinkled and flirted with the treble notes like sparkling water. I loved the way she played. I could listen to her all day. I did.

Now I was playing my own compositions on the hotel piano. I was delighted to hear them on this huge instrument. The piano sounded amazing. Robin G had been in the ladies room. When she came out she sat down to listen. I was still wearing my uniform.

"Have you ever thought about trading in that horrific cocktail waitress uniform for a job playing piano?" she asked.

"No," I said. "I wouldn't know where to start. I'm pretty much waitressing until I get an acting job."

"Well, I'm playing piano until I get an acting job. This is a whole lot better, believe me. Do you know a lot of songs? You need to know pop music, standards, some classical...what do you know?"

"I've never counted," I told her, as I continued to play, "but I do think I know a lot. Maybe five hundred?"

"From memory? No music?"

"Yes. Sure," I told her.

Robin beamed. "Well, what do you know? You told me you played piano, but I didn't think like this! Oh, I can't wait to call Harlan. He will love you. Keep playing." And then she called Harlan from one of the hotel's payphones and told him about me. And now...

Now I fear Harlan will be angry at Robin G's recommendation. I wasted his time.

"Listen to me, Robin," my friend says over the phone line.

"Let's go through the entire audition."

I sit down at my little kitchen table, my coat still on. I tell her about the Rhapsody in Blue Lady.

"Okay," says Robin. "Did she play with music on the piano desk?"

"Well, yes...come to think of it, she did," I say.

"Okay, she's out. Forget it. Next."

"Really?"

"Yep, really. Next."

"Okay, there was a jazzy guy who was really great."

"Okay, next."

"What do you mean, next? What's wrong with him? He was incredible!"

"Well, I don't think they want another jazzy pianist in a tux. The city is full of them."

"Um, well, there was a really good female player right before me."

I tell Robin G what she played, what I remember of her beautiful technique, her smart and oh- so-musical segues from one song to the next.

"Yeah...okay, but what was she wearing?"

What was she *wearing*? I do my best to describe the nondescript black bag of a dress and Robin senses my politeness when I describe her figure as not thin, but not really overweight.

"Okay, good. Now let's get to you. What did you play...and what did you wear?"

I tell her I wore my new Betsey Johnson black skirt with the red crinoline underneath and the top I found in the sale basket of the store that had a ballet neckline, a little poof in the sleeves at the shoulder. She seems to approve greatly of what I wore and played because she begins laughing and shrieking.

"My dear," she says. "You got this job!"

I can't help but think she is crazy when she declares this with such glee. I didn't even get to tell her what the people after me were like; I was talking to Harlan at that time and wasn't tuned in. I love my new friend for her confidence in me, but surely she is deluded.

She is also right.

Harlan called me later the next day to tell me that after two weeks of a trial period, I would receive a union contract and would need to join the American Federation of Musicians. I had just landed a great two-week job, better than cocktail-waitressing, better than temping. I couldn't wait to tell my friends.

Back at the Marriott's Clock Lounge the piano player who played a day shift at another hotel was complaining to the bartender. I was on line behind two waitresses waiting to give my drink order. It seemed Jay had lost his steady engagement recently at a place he'd worked at for seven years straight. He couldn't understand what had happened and he was fighting to get re-instated. He had put a few calls into the union.

Jay was kind of cute. I liked listening to his sets at the Clock Lounge and he was certainly not a creep; he respected all the girls in the lounge. As I placed my drink order or my six-top on my tray I overheard him telling the bartender, "…Yeah, and I hear they're replacing me with a girl of course. A *cocktail waitress* if you can believe that! Man." The bartender poured Jay a cup of coffee and gave a sympathetic chuckle. The laughter drifted off as I made my way to my customers. I couldn't believe what I had just heard. My heart began to race and the sinking feeling in my stomach was pure, unadulterated guilt mixed with recognition. I set the drinks down on my customer's table with a shaky hand. I had no idea I had just auditioned for *Jay's job*. The position, I was told, was an "open position", meaning it was currently not occupied. There must have been more to the story.

"Jay," I managed to say, a few days later when our shifts once again corresponded. "Remember you said that you used to work at the Grand Hyatt and that now they hired a young woman to play there? I overheard you say that. I wasn't eavesdropping or anything...I just heard you."

"Yes..."

Mustering up the courage I knew was somewhere inside me, I spilled it.

"Well, I thought you should know that *I* am that woman... I auditioned for the job. I had no idea this was a gig of yours or any of the circumstances. I'm real sorry."

Jay looked at me with incredulous eyes and wonder.

"I didn't know you played the piano...or that you had an agent for that matter."

"There's a lot you don't know about the girls who work here. See Diana over there? She's a cocktail waitress, but did you know she's also a real estate investor? She owns six properties so far. And me...I do this for extra money, but it is not who I am. You know. Anyway, I am sorry about your job."

"That's okay," he said with a shrug and a little bit of a sarcastic grin. " I already have plenty of things lined up. Hope you enjoy it — the job. It's a nice piano."

And then he walked away.

The Grand Hyatt sat above Grand Central Station and was a bustle of activity. Commuters stopped there for business meetings on their way to the subway or on their way to somewhere. The chairs were set up in comfortable configurations to encourage passersby to have a cup of coffee, read the *New York Times*, listen to the piano, take a meeting. The walls were marble, the lobby's columns brass; the sound of water was everywhere. An enormous block of marble that spanned more than forty feet across made up the famous lobby fountain. Situated about fifteen feet to the left of the piano, water cascaded over its tiers until dropping a good twenty feet to a basin below. The water gushed and poured in urgency. It was Niagara Falls in Manhattan.

It screamed a constant rush; not a soothing sound, but a hurried, stressed and immediate sound that kept the energy of the lobby moving, the waiters bustling, the visitors moving. The sound of the fountain motivated the people passing through to walk just a little bit faster, with a little bit more intention. There was no meandering to be done here. This was a busy place, a place where people had important things to do, important people to meet.

The fountain was the lobby's focal point, and it gave the impression the hotel was busy, even when it wasn't. The constant splash of water on marble drowned out conversation, glasses clinking, cash registers ringing, telephones, or the very lack of this activity; it drowned out silence.

It also drowned out the Steinway grand that I was assigned to play Monday through Friday from 11am - 2pm. My forty-minute-on/twenty-minute-off life was about to begin, was full of promise; the only obstacle was that darn fountain.

It was really loud.

When I started my set, I felt like I was playing inside the ladies room with ultra powerful flushing toilets, or a locker room full of showering athletes. I could hardly hear myself, never mind concentrate on the piano without having the urge to pee. All during my shift, the waiters and waitresses in the Crystal Fountain restaurant came by to tell me they loved my playing, that I was much better than the other guy who used to keep a metronome on the piano and performed to its constant click (so was *that* why Jay was let go?) I was amazed they could hear me above the falls, but they assured me the sound of the music carried throughout the hotel lobby, through the restaurant, through the football field of chairs, tables, elevators and off to the end zone where the reservation desk lived.

I complained to Robin Goldsby about the fountain when she asked me how the gig was going. Robin was a cocktail pianist with a degree in acting just like me, who'd had a steady piano gig since her teens. Like me, she was gigging while waiting for her big acting break to come. She was surprised at my complaint; I guess it seemed petty and silly.

"You have a *job*," she said. "You are a *woman* with a steady piano job in New York City. Do you have any idea how rare that is? Get used to the fountain!"

"But I can't," I protested. "It is a constant struggle. The sound of it is like the worst tinnitus...plus it makes me want to pee all the time."

"Tell you what," said Robin G. "You're writing some 'new agey' kind of music, so here is some 'new agey' kind of advice: Don't fight the fountain."

"What?"

"The fountain is not the enemy. The fountain is creating its own music. You can make music along *with* the fountain. Try it."

So the next day I took a deep breath and began performing *with* the fountain. Robin G told me to, and she was right about mostly everything, from what to wear at a piano gig, to how to respond (or not respond) to an unkind comment. And you know what? She was right. When I sat on the piano bench the next day, I made a point to *listen* to the sound of the fountain. Not resist it. Not hate it. Not judge it. Just listen to it. An interesting thing resulted in this exercise: the water rushing over the marble slowly transformed from a noisy nuisance to a musical symphony. I'm not kidding. It even invited me to join in, and so I did. I began improvising in the key of E-flat and let the notes flow along with the rhythms of the fountain. Up and down, drop and roll...arpeggios flowed forwards, backwards and inside out.

The next day I started my afternoon set with a version of this, and the next, and the next. One day, a businessman waiting for his appointment stood poised by the piano reading *The New York Times*. When I was done with my afternoon ritual of joining with the fountain, he approached me.

"What was the name of that song?" he asked.

"Oh, I call it...I call it..." I paused and looked at the restaurant next to me, The Crystal Fountain Restaurant, named for its own fountain inside, made of, you guessed it: crystal.

"I call it 'Crystal Fountain' and I composed it."

"Brilliant. Do you have it recorded?"

"Well no, but I plan on recording it."

What? What was I saying?

"Well, when you do, please let me know," he said. "Here's my card."

I tucked Mr. Businessman's business card between the desk and fallboard of the piano and smiled to myself. And so it went like that. Each day, I would start my set with "Crystal Fountain" and then play a popular piece. After the required twenty-minute union break, I would resume at 12:30pm, the height of the lunch crowd, with no clue as to how I would start set number two. This was intentional. I forced myself to improvise.

"Choose a key, any key," I'd say to myself. And I would. I would improvise in that key until a melody evolved and carried me away. Sometimes my creation was memorable and I could repeat it and recall it the next day and improve upon it; sometimes it was gone the moment after I played it, a fleeting piece of music never to be heard again. The melodic pieces were the most memorable and I worked on them every set for the first ten minutes. Then I began working on them the last ten minutes of the set. The twenty minutes in between were filler; I began to live for creating the perfect music to accompany the marble fountain's efforts. It was there to soothe people, but it was too loud, so I provided soft melodies to ease its force. It was there to provide energy and distraction, so I balanced it with subtlety and inner purpose.

Gradually, the 'people in chairs', as I called those who were waiting for someone, or killing time, or taking a break, or hiding from work, or waiting for a train, began to look up from their newspapers, appointment books and novels. They moved closer to the piano. They began to talk to me in between songs, asking me the name of this tune or that; and it was almost always after I had played an original creation.

Business cards began to line the inside of the piano and so I took them home at the end of each day and placed them in an empty fishbowl in my bedroom. I began humming my sets in my head before even getting to the Hyatt. I began playing my creations in my sleep, while cooking, while daydreaming. It became a relief to go to work and express all the music I had kept to myself for so long. It was always there; I just never gave it permission to emerge. The fountain provided the perfect opportunity for it to come forward; not as solo work (that would have been too scary) but as the perfect water-diluted soundtrack to what I witnessed from the bench: the older woman in the Chanel suit, elegant and experienced, the sad-looking man who I imagined was lovesick, the couple who sat together but didn't look into one another's eyes for fear of what they might find there. I wrote this music for them, but played it for me. And it changed me somehow. I was no longer 'killing time' on a piano bench as a job to support my fledgling acting career. I was doing something meaningful. At least to me.

It was on this piano bench that I felt the most *real*. Centered. In time I found myself going with the flow…on the bench and off.

I would play this piano for the next twelve years of my life. My shift was 11:30am-2:30pm, but I was often called upon to sub for the "power breakfast" player whose shift was 7:30am - 10:30am. Many of my days consisted of six hours of piano performance at the Hyatt, an acting audition or two, and a pre-Broadway or after-Broadway gig at another hotel. It was in these rooms that I began to compose the soundtrack of my life.

I held steadies at various times at The Plaza Hotel's Edwardian Room, The Sheraton Centre, The New York Athletic Club, and of course, The Grand Hyatt. I subbed at the Marriott Marquis, The Waldorf, The Hilton Midtown, and The Helmsley Palace. I was hired for parties everywhere else in between: the top of the Chrysler Building, The Water Club Restaurant, The River Café, The ballroom of the St. Regis. I played parties for New York mayors Koch, Dinkins and Giuliani, benefit events, weddings, and corporate holiday parties. I played until my arms were falling off. I subbed out gigs when I got cast in a play, so I could rehearse. When the play started to run, I resumed my daytime piano gig and then picked up evenings when the play was through.

Robin Goldsby and I covered for one another quite a bit. Instead of bothering Delma, the bookkeeper in the office of Jerry Kravat Entertainment, Robin kept her own small journal. It fit in her purse. In it, she wrote down how many hours we played for one another. When she was in her last month of pregnancy I covered all her shifts. Then I did a play for a while and she covered mine. In all those years not a single dollar changed hands. No matter what the gig or where it was, an hour of piano time was an hour of piano time. The only time either of us saw any money from all that switching around was when she left for Germany to start a new life and we knew there would be no more subbing, at least not on this continent. All the agents knew was that one of the Robins was playing the piano, and they stopped caring which one.

Malcolm Gladwell says in his book *The Outliers*, that to be good at something, anything, you need to devote at least 10,000 hours to it. That could apply to sports, computer programming, writing or music. In my case, my 10,000 hours of playing time happened under the radar while I was trying to be wallpaper, but nonetheless, those steady gigs allowed me to forget everything I knew about playing the piano and simply *be*. Over the course of time in these piano rooms, my playing, composition skills, arranging skills and technique emerged as uniquely mine, and would one day translate to recordings and the concert stage. But I didn't know that...yet. I was still chasing down a dream of another kind.

At my Grand Hyatt gig on Halloween, late 1980's

SWING

Inherited by father's terrible sense of direction, which is not a great thing if you are an artist who wants to go places. I got lost going to auditions. I got lost going to my classes at NYU. I got lost just about everywhere I went. But sometimes I discovered I was lost even when I arrived at my planned destination.

At the Plaza Hotel, that is how I felt every day: lost. I won the job after a competitive audition, and the requirements were simple enough. I was hired to play a few nights a week in the fancy schmantzy restaurant, The Edwardian Room. Ivana and Donald Trump now owned the hotel, and changes were being made. I was one of them. The harpist and violinist who had played in the Palm Court would remain, but not for long. Hotel rooms were being renovated, menus changed, ballrooms painted and re-carpeted. I had the Hyatt gig during the day, so the only time I had to sub out the Plaza job was when I was actually in a play, which was not often.

I loved that I had this job. I loved that I was in such an elegant setting, but I couldn't get rid of this nagging feeling that I didn't belong. The room was extremely elegant from its draperies to its silverware to its woodwork. The music coming out of the piano, which was backed against a wall on the left side of the rectangular room, was meant to be wallpaper. This job required quiet, gentle playing of familiar, classical and neoclassical music. This was the first gig I played where people seriously tipped even though I was instructed to play as quietly as possible. Each night the maitre'd would hand me a piece of paper or two with a song title written on it, wrapped around a twenty, fifty or hundred-dollar bill, and

I would panic, even if I knew the song. I wished there wasn't money involved. It was so uncomfortable. It felt so wrong.

Friends could drop by to hear me and visit at the Hyatt or Rainier's, where I worked on weekends, but not on this swanky gig. This hotel was filled with security and people in uniforms were able to sniff out those who didn't belong. I was from New Jersey, a 'bridge and tunnel person' to most Manhattanites. Surely, I thought, security would ask *me* to leave one day. On my break I called Robin Goldsby from the payphone adjacent to the chocolatier on the other side of the building.

"Hi Robin, it's me, Robin."

"Hey, what's up? Are you at work? How's the gig?"

"Terrible. Awful. I am an imposter of the worst kind. I keep getting asked to play songs I've never heard of."

"Like what?"

"Here's that Rainy Day".

"Oh, okay. Hang on." I held on for a few minutes while Robin got her fake book.

"Okay, it's in G, to B-flat to A-minor to D..." And then she hummed the melody. "Got that?"

"I think so. Do it again."

"Did you already get a tip?"

"Yes."

"Geez, I hate that. Pre-tipping. Lots of pressure."

Robin Goldsby, or Goldyhead as I came to call her later in our friendship, got it like no one else. Robin sang the melody to "Here's That Rainy Day" again into the phone a few more times. I didn't learn the bridge; there was no time. I'd pick up the song during the week and return with it truly polished, arranged and memorized by next week. For now, I'd have to muddle through.

When I returned to the piano I faked through my new song. The man and his female companion who had sent me the note and fifty, nodded and smiled in my direction. *Goldyhead saves the day once again*, I thought. There were a lot of nights at the Plaza like that.

Unlike the other places I gigged, there was no convenient place to take my twenty-minute union break at The Plaza. I would wander into the gift shop and look at the Eloise books, peek inside the chocolatier's shop and occasionally splurge on a five-dollar piece of tiny chocolate (but they were divine!) and end up in the elegant Plaza Hotel Ladies Room to wait it out. It wasn't that comfortable in the ladies room lounge area despite the fact that the furniture was French velvet and quite cushiony. I think it was the maids in French uniforms that made me feel out of place. I was the same as those maids, I thought. We were hired hands of the Trumps here to serve the guests and yet I was sitting down on the velvet sofa while the maid had to stand there and wait for a decked-out-to-the-nines socialite to finish washing her hands so she could hand her a towel. It was all so fakey-fake.

On my next break I called Robin Goldsby again.

"This place is freaking unbelievable," I told her. "You should see what this lady I saw in the ladies room was wearing."

"Tell me."

"Well, she's dining in the restaurant where I'm playing, and of course I was taking my break in the Ladies' Room..."

"Of course."

"And in comes this woman I had only seen in the restaurant from the waist up. It turns out the gray feathered dress she's wearing has feathers all over it. All the way down to the bottom. And she has on a little hat thingy with a feather that matches the dress."

"A fascination."

"What?"

"I mean fascinator. It's called a fascinator; the thing in her hair."

"Yes, yes, that's right."

"You should go back and play 'Fascinating Rhythm' or maybe the 'Feather Theme' from *Forrest Gump*.

Goldyhead always made me laugh.

"That's hilarious," I told her. "Yes I should. But really, what am I doing here? Why didn't they give this job to Earl Rose or someone like that? He knows more songs than I do. I really don't belong here. I mean, who do I think I am anyway."

"Don't be ridiculous. You're Robin Spielberg. You know plenty of songs. Plenty of them. They wanted *you*. I'm sure they're happy. If they weren't, Harlan would have heard about it by now and been asked to talk to you. By the way, I heard this rumor. A bunch of the male pianists in New York are going around saying that you, Napua, Debbie and me, must have slept with Harlan. That's why we have these jobs."

"You're kidding!"

"I'm not! Harlan told me."

"They are just jealous of us I guess. We do have great gigs. But we're good at what we do! How obnoxious. If anyone asks me point blank if we slept with Harlan to get these jobs I will tell them point blank that they are crazy. I will tell them that we did not sleep with him; we only had to give him blow jobs."

Robin G cracked up.

"That's right. That's what we should say."

"Assholes."

"Assholes."

"See?" Robin G said. "You said it yourself. We're good at our jobs. You *belong* there. So what are you wearing tonight?"

"Oh, I have on a black cocktail dress and some jewelry."

"What kind of jewelry and how short is the dress?"

I looked down. "The dress is just above my knee and I'm wearing my pretty but fake pearls and patent-leather black pumps."

"Perfect. You are perfect. You better go back. It's been twenty minutes."

Goldyhead always reassured me. She always knew what to say, and she had a million fake books.

When I passed by the lobby on my way back to the piano, the classical violin and harp music made me smile. The violinist was so old. So very very old, and yet so animated, so happy, so very much in his element. He belonged here. In the Oak Room, Michael Roberts was playing and singing jazz. Too bad I can't swing, I thought. Maybe I would fit in better if I did. Next break, another call to Robin Goldsby.

"Hey, it's me again. I think I figured out my problem. I don't swing."

"You don't need to swing. They didn't hire you to swing. Just be you. Play like you," she advised.

"I know. I know you're right, but I can't help but feel uncomfortable. I don't hear anyone in any of the piano bars who play like me."

"What piano bars?"

I hadn't told Robin G that I had been going around town to hear other pianists play. I watched Ted Rosenthal in awe. Winner of several jazz competitions, Ted also played at the Grand Hyatt with his jazz trio, which included Robin G's soon-to-be fiancé.

"This is what is adding to that Imposter Syndrome of yours," she said. "You have to trust yourself. You have to do what you do. No one plays the way you do and that's good. If they wanted someone like all the other New York tuxedo players they would have hired one."

But still. I was no good and I knew it and someone was going to find out. Someone at the Plaza no doubt who had handed me a hundred dollar bill. Maybe he'd go to the piano police and scream, "IMPOSTER!" She doesn't know how to play 'I'll Take Manhattan'! What pianist in New York doesn't know 'I'll Take Manhattan'? Out! Out with her!"

With the help of Robin Goldsby I was able to do what I called "fake jazz" on the gig. "Fake Jazz" is when you pre-plan your chord changes, runs and tempo shifts ahead of time but make it seem that you are improvising on the spot. Horrible this, but what to do when someone has written "Please play 'All of Me' on a cocktail napkin and you don't know how to swing the song on the spot? So you learn it ahead of time, come up with a few chord substitutions that sound "jazzy" and get through. You get through. I had about two-dozen of these at my fingertips, probably the least amount of any piano player with a steady gig in New York City, but it was enough for me to get by.

Goldyhead was right of course. I was hired for this job because of my neoclassical sounding originals and theater song arrangements. I eventually learned there was really no choice than to leave the real jazz to Bobby Short at the Algonquin. I also figured out that if you forgot the bridge to any jazz standard you could pretty much play the bridge from "Blue Moon" and no one would notice.

After a few months I managed to find my groove at the Plaza gig. I walked as Aunt Elaine had taught me: a string pulling me up from my breastbone to the ceiling. I was confident. I dared more and more every evening to play my own musical creations and was now being tipped as patrons left, as a thank you.

In the spring I called Harlan and asked him if he could find someone to sub for me at the Plaza that summer. I had saved enough money to go Vermont with the Atlantic Theater Company to work on a season of plays, and would need a sub for eight weeks. He called back the very next day with a response.

"Hmmm. This is odd, but the Plaza will not honor your request. Apparently Ivana said, if you leave you should not come back."

"Really? Howard Danziger is going to cover me at the Hyatt and they're fine with that."

"I'm just the messenger; Ivana said no."

I went to Vermont anyway, thinking that was an empty threat, but it wasn't. Mrs. Trump had meant what she said. I was so surprised by my feelings of loss. This was a job that had fed every insecurity about playing the piano I had ever known, and yet I mourned the loss of it. Somewhere in those six months at the Plaza I had found my swing. It wasn't the swing you heard in other New York piano rooms, but it was mine. I liked it, and that was good enough.

FIRST NIGHT/LAST PLAY

It was my roommate who saw it first: an ad in the *Montclair Times* announcing an "open call" audition for artists wishing to perform at the annual New Year's Eve event, First Night Montclair.

The First Night franchise began in Boston in 1976. Over the years, the celebration grew from an arts event centered on the Boston Common to a major citywide festival. First Night started with a parade, and as the evening progressed on the 31st of each year, throngs of people gathered to check out the music, dance, theater, film, and art exhibits. The evening culminated with fireworks at midnight. Events were held both outdoors and indoors, in parks and concert halls. One of the main goals of the organizers was to have art kind of "pop up" in unexpected places. Montclair was the first town to embrace the tradition in New Jersey, and my roommate encouraged me to audition to be part of the festival.

"I've only played one real concert before. I won't get in," I told her.

"Are you kidding me? You have a CD with a song called *Montclair* for Pete's sake! You composed a piece inspired by this *town*! You can certainly play everything on your record for the concert. They'll love you!"

The open call was held in the auditorium of the high school. When I showed up, auditions were already well underway. The auditorium was dark; the stage illuminated. I estimated about thirty people were in the house. A juggler was performing on the large stage under a white-hot spotlight to Led Zeppelin music. Next up was a string quartet. While the quartet set up, the house lights came up which gave me the opportunity to approach the man with the clipboard.

One thing I have learned in my acting adventures, is that if you are auditioning or showcasing, you need to find the person holding the clipboard. These are the people who know things. Important things. Things that can affect the success or failure of your audition. This man definitely knew things. He held the clipboard, which held a pad of paper, which contained a list. He had a pencil behind his ear. When he saw me coming he reached for it.

"You are?"

"Robin. Robin Spielberg."

"And?"

"Just me. And…piano. I play piano."

"It'll be about 45 minutes before we call you," he said without looking up as he scribbled 'Robyn Speilburg-piano player' on his pad. "You're welcome to have a seat and watch the other performers."

It was then that I realized that most of the people in the house were artists like myself, hoping for a First Night slot. It turned out the four people around Clipboard Man were the decision-makers: three men and a woman. Playing for the four judges was not a problem, but the idea of playing while other artists looked on made my stomach queasy. I decided to go home. Great relief swept over me when I closed the car door behind me in the cold dark night, but something stopped me from putting the key into the ignition. The relief I felt came with a price. The price was the knowledge that I was nothing short of a coward. Could I live with that? Yes. No. Maybe. The brave part of me knew I would be judged no matter what I did in life and I just had to deal with that. What was I running from? Wouldn't it be incredibly fun and wouldn't it just feel right to do a concert in Montclair where I was living and where

I had rehearsed for my first recording? It was a good match. Buck up, Robin, I told myself. I was already playing piano six hours a day in public in New York City. Ten minutes for a few people in a high school auditorium — why should that a big deal? Why was it so scary? Coward Robin told Brave Robin that failing would be very embarrassing. Brave Robin told Coward Robin it would be an error on the judges' part if they chose not to hire me. I was more than qualified to do a few 45-minute sets of music for a paying audience. Brave Robin won.

I re-entered the auditorium just as my name was being called. I walked down the auditorium aisle to the piano in front. The piano was an older grand, which was bright, but not particularly in tune. I began with "Soldier's Journey." I told the listeners I composed the piece at the beginning of the Persian-Gulf War. My introduction to "Montclair" was simple. Having lived in Manhattan for nine years, the open sky, lush trees and pond in the local park I frequented every day for a daily run was incredibly refreshing. I knew this town would be my home for some time. The tune's melody came to me on a visit to the park

and stayed with me long enough to complete the piece at the piano. I played it with all my heart. When I finished, the room erupted into applause. Clipboard Man didn't even wait for me to get up from the piano bench; he rushed toward me.

"You wrote that?" he asked incredulously.

"Yes. Yes I did. It's on my record even."

"You have a record?"

"Yes, yes I do!" I said, hardly believing it myself. "It just came out this past February. It's called *Heal of the Hand* and the local record store in town, Crazy Rhythms…they're the first store to carry it actually."

"Well that is just terrific. Thanks for coming in."

"My pleasure."

Brave Robin couldn't help but smile at Coward Robin on the way out the door. Coward Robin didn't quit though. "Yeah, well, you don't know anything yet. It seemed like it went well, but they might have just been polite to you. Don't expect a call anytime soon."

The phone rang the next day from the First Night office asking me if I could check out a few pianos in town, assess them, and then let them know which one would be the most suitable for my concert. Earning the spot in the line-up felt akin to winning the part of Anne in *The Diary of Anne Frank* at Michigan State.

I tried out a number of pianos in town and decided upon the one at the Montclair Art Museum. It belonged to a museum board member and I felt its temporary home at the museum was suitable for the kind of concert I wanted to do. The white walls of the exhibit space were adorned with Americana art. The acoustics and seating for 100 made it just right.

I went to work at the Hyatt the next day with a secret that made me smile. I was no longer just the piano lady in the lobby. I was a concert artist in the making.

I stopped over on the east side to the Betsey Johnson store in search of something to wear from my First Night debut. Most things on the racks were out of my price range, but I was hopeful because the two barrels by the cash register that contained clothing on sale were full this week. If you didn't know any better you could easily think these barrels were garbage pails — that's how rumpled and messy the bins were, but when I pulled out each article, a little treasure was revealed. A beaded belt. A rhinestone-trimmed glove. A black taffeta mini skirt with purple crinoline lining. And then there was my concert dress: a forest green floor-length dress made of velvet with a sweetheart neckline and spaghetti straps. Ten bucks. I didn't even need a bag; it fit in my purse. I rolled it into a ball and stuck it in inside out to protect the velvet and made my way to my second job on 66th Street and Broadway, a play called *The Lights* where I was understudy to the leading lady and bit part player.

The costume mistress at Lincoln Center Theater was thrilled with my find. After I modeled the dress for her in the theater's costume fitting room she pinned, measured and then clasped her hands together.

"Robin, you found the perfect dress. It is perfect, perfect, perfect, and I will make it even more perfect! You just need an inch taken up in the back, and the straps made a little tighter. It'll be ready by the time the curtain comes down tonight."

The Lights was a somewhat depressing play set in New York City. I had dyed my hair black for my small part and straightened my curls each night, which was a labor-intensive undertaking. The leading lady was quite vocal about not feeling well on a regular basis, which put me at the ready to go on at any moment, but the show ran for three months without her missing a performance. Unlike the previous Atlantic Theater Company production of a different Howard Korder play, *Boy's Life*, this play didn't make the audience laugh much; its message was more poignant, darker, and deeper.

During *Boys' Life*, the stage manager told us to tiptoe when we passed Patti Lupone's dressing room on matinee days. Patti was starring in *Anything Goes* upstairs in the bigger theater, the Broadway house, and often napped in between performances. My heart raced whenever I passed by her door. How I adored her. I knew she had worked on many David Mamet plays, and ironically was a favorite of the acting teacher I hated most, Michael Kahn. She had been in his ensemble, The Acting Company. Our paths did not cross during the run of these shows, but I think I woke her up a bunch of times talking with my cast mates on the way to the stage in my clickety-click high heels.

For most of us in Atlantic, *Boys' Life* was our first Equity contract and it was one big party. We goofed off, pulled practical jokes on one another, hid one another's costumes, and had water balloon fights. We joked and flirted with the chorus members of *Anything Goes* right before curtain. They lined the staircase to make their entrance at the Beaumont; we were in the basement en route to the wings of the Newhouse. My Atlantic girlfriends were all in the play with me: Théo Cohan, Karen Kohlhaas, Melissa Bruder, Felicity (Flicka) Huffman and Mary McCann. The boys were next door. Jordan Lage, Steven Goldstein, Clark Gregg, Robert Bella, Todd Weeks, Robert Ostrovsky, Neil Pepe. The girls shared one giant dressing room. There were showers in it and lockers! We had our own lighted mirrors and a few cots. How luxurious it all was after playing so many shows in dingy off-off Broadway houses. Flicka worked on needlepoint projects in between scenes on the sofa near her dressing table and taught me how.

One Saturday between the matinee and evening show, Melissa and I headed downtown to Macy's on 34th Street. We decided to buy some really *nice* makeup and wanted to be waited on at a department store. Who did we think we were? We tried everything and finally decided upon Chanel's Finishing Powder. We couldn't believe it. It cost a fortune. We split the cost and shared the powder. We placed it between us on our shared dressing table and for weeks kept asking one another, "Who do you think you are to be using $45 powder?" She'd answer, "I'm Melissa Bruder, a professional actress doing a play at Lincoln Center that's who," and I'd say, "I'm Robin Spielberg! I'm a professional actress too!" and we'd burst into hysterics. Fun times.

I was grateful to be working again at Lincoln Center on *The Lights*, but the experience made me sigh a lot. I had wanted the part of the lead pretty badly and coming so close did not inspire me. It was just depressing. Now with my upcoming concert and forest green dress, I felt hope in my heart once again.

There was an important truth I was discovering at this time but too scared to fully admit: I was not enjoying the journey. And I was old enough now to know that the journey was what the hokey pokey was all about. Acting in a play was terrific. I loved the theater company, its mission, and my theater friends. We had been through so much together. But the day-to-day journey of being an actor was not doing much for me. Voice class. Audition. Gym. Go see this casting director. Get called for that commercial. Callback. Wait. Gym. Voice class. Pick up sides. Prepare audition. Wait in hall with picture and resumé. Wait for call.

I wanted to live in a world where our Vermont life existed 24/7. In this utopia of acting worlds, we often wrote our own plays, took turns acting in them, producing them, servicing them with costumes, props and the like. But alas, this existed only in our Vermont world. New York directors did not want to hear about ensemble members "taking turns" in roles. They would cast as they pleased. When there was any discourse at company meetings, it usually was about this issue of casting.

Well, I couldn't sit in my apartment and *act*, but I was able to compose music and play the piano. Playing the piano didn't put me at the mercy of a casting director or producer. I didn't need someone else's "ok" to do it. Sure, I had to audition for the steady gigs, but even without a gig, I could still play, compose, arrange, and express myself, and I loved the day-to-day journey of composing, arranging, practicing and performing at a gig.

During the run of *The Lights*, I found myself going to Lincoln Center earlier and earlier. Sign-in time wasn't until 6:30pm. I began arriving by 4:00pm after changing out of my gig clothes from the Hyatt lunch job. I'd let myself into the dark dressing room in the basement of Lincoln Center, turn on the makeup lights, hang up my coat and piano dress in the locker, and begin my evening at the theater with more than the play on my mind.

The ballet room down the hall had a decent upright Yamaha, and I'd play it to work on new music that wasn't ready enough for playing at the Hyatt gig. Back in the dressing room I'd dream up ways to market *Heal of the Hand*, the CD of original tunes I had just recorded. I made lists of stores that I thought might want to carry it on consignment: book shops in Manhattan, that cute boutique that sold hats and scarves and soaps on Lexington. I looked through my bookkeeping log to see how many more copies I needed to sell in order to pay back the loan I took out for making the CD. I pored through magazines looking for photo shoot ideas for the album cover for my next project. I planned concert sets, striving for the perfect 45-minute musical arc. I checked music business books out of the library and kept them on the top shelf of my dressing room locker. I read up on copyright law, the ins and outs of music licensing, read through sample record company and publishing contracts with highlighter in hand. I learned about what music retail marketers did, what distributors serviced which stores. I was driven. I was obsessed.

Back in Montclair, I spoke with Joe over at Crazy Rhythms every Monday night, the night the theater was "dark". After a few minutes of giving me one-word answers to my questions, he'd eventually give in to my persistence and take me to the back room which was filled with books, music trade magazines, directories and CD demos. He handed me trade magazine after trade magazine, catalog after catalog to take home and bring back. Joe pretended to be annoyed with all my inquiries but I think he liked being treated as the expert he was. Joe taught me how distribution worked and which distributors carried which kind of music. He chatted about music artists and the mistakes they made with signing with this record label versus that record label. Joe gave me his opinion on everything about the music business, as well as contact names and numbers of people he trusted in the business whom I could call with his name as a reference in case I had even more questions.

"This guy works for Soundscan. Make sure you talk to him," he'd say.

"This guy writes for the Billboard charts. He knows the story."

"This company took over this company and there is a lot of bad blood there…don't call them until we know how that all pans out," he cautioned.

"You can find yourself a record company, but you already made your record. You don't really need one. Find yourself a good distributor, and now you're talkin. That's what you need. A good distributor."

It was the early '90s, and Joe still sold some cassettes and cassette singles in his store. He didn't use Soundscan and his cash register didn't use UPC codes; he did everything the old-fashioned way. He had a manual credit card machine and hand-punched the numbers into a separate terminal. Joe certainly hung on to the past in a lot of ways, but still knew a lot about the future of the music business. It would be another ten years before I understood what he meant about distribution being the most important part of the business. I was very focused on "the record deal"— that was what was shiny, glossy, prestigious, respected, revered. No one congratulated you for signing on with a distributor; but there were congratulations galore for those lucky musicians who scored record company contracts. I convinced myself that is what I needed.

"That might be what you want, but that is not what you need," Joe would say. "You're a smart girl. You could do well in this business just in the business side of things. You'll put it together."

Back at Lincoln Center I modeled the green velvet dress for the gals in the dressing room.

"Where are you going to wear it?" asked Kathleen.

"Oh! I didn't tell you? I'm going to play a concert on New Year's Eve!"

"Really? Where?" asked Kristen?

"For First Night Montclair."

"Montclair. Isn't that in *New Jersey?*" she asked.

"Yes — it's twelve miles outside the city, where I'm living now."

"Oh."

So they were nonplussed. But my heart raced every time I thought about the concert.

Kristen sat at her dressing table while the hair stylist for the show piled her hair on top of her head. An open tabloid magazine in her hands and stack of others to be read next were at her feet. How ironic that just a few years later Kristen herself would be in those very tabloids after become famous for her role in *Third Rock from the Sun*, and for gaining weight, losing weight, going to rehab, and writing a bold book about her recovery from addiction.

Flicka, on the other hand, seemed to "get it" even before I did. Back at the Circle in the Square acting studio she heard me tinkering around on the piano before our scene study teacher showed up.

Peter's claim to fame was acting in the *Fantasticks* off-Broadway for years on end in the role of The Narrator, and his scene class was something I looked forward to, because unlike Michael Kahn, he was kind to even the most untalented of us. It was an easy class and I welcomed easy on Thursdays at 2pm, because the rest of the week was so damn brutal.

"Where did you learn to play like that?" Flicka asked me when she heard me playing piano in the acting studio space before class.

"Oh, I've always played. I'm just fooling around."

"My God! If I played like that, I wouldn't be *here.*"

"What do you mean? Where would you be?"

"I'd be playing the piano somewhere instead of in this joke of an acting class."

I was astonished. Felicity Huffman was clearly one of the stand-outs in our acting group, and this was her assessment. She always told it like it was. She had the inability to lie, be fluffy, soft. You asked her a question, she gave you an answer. With all the bullshit in the drama department, Flicka was my go-to for the truth. She told you how it was. I filed away her opinion, not knowing what else to do with it.

Flicka went to the Vermont workshops too and we had become friends. Now we were together in a dressing room for the first time since *Three Sisters* in Philadelphia 1990. She was visiting us all backstage an hour before curtain and planning on seeing the show that night. She couldn't help but notice my mind was on anything but the play.

"What's all that?" she asked, pointing to my dressing table stacked with postcards.

"Oh. That. Those are just some postcards I'm mailing out to advertise my New Year's Eve show to some people."

"What people?"

"The people who signed up for my mailing list."

"What mailing list?"

Felicity always had a way of getting me to talk. On that night in the Lincoln Center dressing room, I sat with Flicka on the cot behind my dressing room mirror and told her that I had been playing piano during the day at the Grand Hyatt and that about 800 people had signed on to my mailing list in case I ever had a solo concert or new CD. I told her my secret: that I knew directors hated that I had a piano job; they wanted me to focus on the show, the show, the show. But I knew that all shows ended and the union piano gig was long-term and I loved it. While everyone else was taking an acting class, going to an audition, open casting call or taking a meeting, I was happily on the bench playing away to my heart's content. I was supposed to be playing the piano to help support my fledgling acting career, but something had switched. I looked forward to reporting to the bench and dreaded going to Lincoln Center. I pushed that reality out of my mind whenever it popped up but when I looked at Flicka that night, I just spilled it.

"I knew it," she said, rather triumphantly. "Your playing is beautiful. Beautiful. You're so smart to keeping doing it." She picked up my hairbrush and began fixing my hair for the show.

"If this acting thing doesn't work out for me," she said to my reflection in the mirror, "I think I'm going to be a hairdresser."

She finished my hair in a jiffy and then she was gone.

First Night was everything I had hoped it would be and more. The museum room was full. The piano was in fine tune. I played well and was so very proud of myself for fending off my doubts. I did it. What was truly great about that night is that it didn't feel like I was "performing" at all. I "played". Using the acting technique I picked up from my years with the Atlantic Theater Company,

I had selected an "intention" for each song. I was so committed to these actions while playing my music, that self-consciousness disappeared and freed me to play truthfully and in the moment. I made a note to myself to call David Mamet and let him know that this acting technique worked beautifully for music as well as for scripts. How lucky I felt. My parents were there, my boyfriend was there, my sister was there and my roommate was there. All of them beamed. My mother helped me sell copies of *Heal of the Hand* and *Spirit of the Holidays* in the lobby of the museum after the show.

Every New Year's Eve, for the next fourteen, (yes *fourteen!!!*) I would play in Montclair, NJ. There were two years I played on 12/31 that were not part of the First Night Festival, but as my own separate ticketed concert. Year after year the audience grew along with me, and by year fifteen, I had fifteen CDs on the sales table. My mother helped sell the CDs after the show, then my husband, and in 2008, our ten-year-old daughter helped sell them. Audience members made my concert their New Year's tradition. There was the man who came every year by himself and reminded me that he had "discovered" me first — playing a CD-signing event at the Borders Books & Music store in Wayne, New Jersey. There were my neighbors from Ridgewood Avenue who came to the show and back to my house afterward for food and cocktails by the fire. There was my mom who came each year with my dad, and after he died, alone, and then with her boyfriend, and then alone again. There was the piano technician David who worked his miracle on a piano that had been neglected all year so it could sing, even if just for a night. There were kids who began playing my music for their recitals and came with songbooks for me to autograph. Oh I couldn't imagine a New Year's Eve without playing piano in Montclair. The tradition continued even after I had moved to rural Pennsylvania. And then, there on my calendar, December 31, 2009 was blank.

"All gigs end eventually," said Robin Goldsby. "It was a good run. A long run. Something else will come along, you'll see."

For months I fought the notion that I wouldn't be playing a piano concert on New Year's Eve. I asked Larry to find something, anything to fill the date.

"What will we do? Watch the ball drop on TV?" I asked incredulously with a little belligerence in my voice as if this was all his fault. Interest in First Night was dwindling each year, the budget falling, and by 2009 the festival presented a handful of local events focusing on kids.

When I introduced my piece "First Night" to an audience in Boston that December 2009, I shared the inspiration behind the piece: the looking back one more time as the year comes to a close, the hopes we have for the future, the sentimentality that seems to take us all by surprise. And then I told them. This was going to be the first year since I was thirteen years old that I wasn't going to work on New Year's Eve. I wasn't going to play piano; I was going to be home with my family. Instead of the sympathetic tongue-clucking and sighing I had expected as a response, the audience erupted into applause. They thought this was a *good* thing for me and that I was happy. Audiences are smart. Maybe they knew something I didn't.

"You know that chocolate fondue set I bought at Costco?" I asked my husband on the phone that night. "We haven't used it yet. Let's invite Sue and Bruce over on New Year's Eve and use it then."

"Great idea. They'll love that."

"So will I. So will I."

I spent New Year's Eve away from the piano and the sky did not fall, the moon still rose, and yes, the ball dropped. I saw it with my own eyes.

Performing at First Night Montclair 2008

STEVE JOBS: MATCHMAKER

I was pretty much a mess after my breakup with my ex. We had dated for four years and married in February 1989. It didn't last long. I knew he had access to pot, and smoked on occasion, but was blind to his level of involvement or that he was actually addicted to drugs and alcohol. I had grown up in a house that was as dry as they come and just didn't pick up on the signs. My ex was a highly functioning addict, with a steady job and great sense of humor, but once we moved to Montclair, his behavior became odd. He'd leave the house at strange hours to "go get something" or "meet a friend". When I confronted him about partying too much or asked him where he had been, he told me I was becoming a bore, a nag, and wasn't any fun. It seemed that for months I was waiting for our marriage to start and then one day I realized that this *was* the marriage and it stunk. Counseling didn't help. He lied about his addictions to the counselor and so neither I, nor the counselor knew the truth. All I knew was that the person I married was hardly ever home. The guy I fell for because he was so well liked, and so much fun, was not the person I could build a life with.

My ex hit bottom when he lost the job he loved. I hit bottom when his former boss called me and told me I could stop covering up for him; it was over. I didn't know what he was talking about. As Paul told me about my ex's drug and alcohol problem and the ways in which it manifested itself at work, I sank to the floor with the phone in my hand in quiet disbelief. How could I have been so stupid? With the help of a friend, I organized an intervention and got my ex in a good rehab program. After a few relapses we decided to part ways. As much as I knew this was the right thing to do, I was still devastated. It wasn't that I missed him; it was the feelings of failure, deception, betrayal and utter disappointment that grabbed hold of me for the longest time.

My parents were never for our marriage, but were hardly celebrating now. I had spent the majority of my twenties with a cocaine-addicted alcoholic pothead who barely realized I played the piano and considered the theater company my "little hobby". I was single, lost and emotionally exhausted.

My friends thought I should move back to the city, but I viewed that as a sign of defeat. I loved this Victorian apartment that we had moved into, and the way it felt to leave the city and come home to Montclair. The place was spacious. If I were to move back to New York, I'd be just about able to afford an apartment the size of this apartment's bedroom. No no. I was going to stay.

I took the #33 DeCamp bus from Walden Place in Montclair to Manhattan each day to play my gig at the Hyatt. The piano kept me sane during that vulnerable time, and just like it did during the pain of adolescence, the piano gave me the gifts of understanding and peace when I sat on its bench. When I wasn't playing, I was overwhelmed with feelings of sadness, loss and despair. My friend Brett, who lived on the upper west side and worked in midtown, made it his business to visit me at the Hyatt on his lunch hour. He'd show up right before my break and take me for a walk down Lexington Avenue just so I could keep moving, and not be alone with my thoughts. It went on for months like this, not eating much, not sleeping much, just playing piano and taking walks with Brett, until I finally began to emerge out of the darkness. Thanks to Brett, the piano, and a good therapist, I began to understand why I married a man like

Donny, and what I needed to do to move on. I needed to not *find* the right person; I needed to *be* the right person.

It was a real challenge meeting my expenses each month so after I began to feel better, I started to look for a roommate. I began to date again too.

Ariane was a professional businesswoman just a few years older than me. She answered my ad in the paper, and we hit it off right away. She liked cats and even had one of her own, (although she'd be the first to admit it was the most unsociable cat in the history of housecats).

My new roommate was into technology. She had one of the first Apple computers and was always typing on it and discovering things. She spent hours on it.

"What in the world would I do with a computer?" I asked her. "I play piano. I don't need one."

"Oh, but look what you can do! There's a new thing called America Online. Have you heard of it?"

"No, what is it?" I asked.

"Well, come look."

And so I did.

It was all so new. America Online, or AOL as we came to know it, had fewer than a million users at this time. People were connecting with one another via their computers. There were these "forums". Ariane showed me the forums that were popping up for music. There were radio forums, piano forums, and NewAge music forums.

"Look," she said. "The DJs are posting their playlists on this radio forum. You can look at who's programming piano music and write them about *Heal of the Hand*. See if they want a copy to play on their station." I was sold.

I was dating an acting student named Tom. Tom worked a day job solving computer problems. In fact, when you called this 1-800 number in the back of a *MacWorld Magazine*, you were likely to get Tom on the other end of the line. Tom would tell me the funny things people called about during his shift each night. There was the woman who read the instructions that came with her computer reminding her to keep the keyboard clean. She called the 800 number and told Tom she had soaked the keyboard in the bathtub overnight and now it wasn't working. She wanted to know why. Then there was the secretary who called to say the cup holder on her Mac broke off. Tom spent a while trying to find out if any of the stores were offering special promotions for cup holders that attached to the machines and couldn't find any. After a while, he figured out she was using the CD-ROM drive as a coffee cup holder. She didn't know it was a CD-ROM drive.

It was all so new.

Macs were expensive, but Tom said they were by far the best machines out there and if I bought a used one, or even a broken one, he could refurbish it for me. I scoured ads in the back of the computer magazines and bought a secondhand Mac SE-30. If you were to look one up on Google you would see it was a compact machine, an "all in one" with a small black and white screen. When the machine arrived, Tom took the entire computer apart. It was in pieces on my bed for hours. Looking at that $2500 mess gave me a stomachache so I closed the door and let him get to work, while I made dinner. By the time dinner was ready, Tom had ramped up the speed of the computer, increased its memory and installed all the software.

It was exciting to have a computer of my own. I bought a dial-up modem and joined America Online. I opened an email account. Email was so new that there was no such thing as spam (yet). Each piece of mail was personal and important. I took Ariane's advice and joined music forums like rec.music.newage. I researched radio playlists. I connected with music directors and radio hosts and introduced them to *Heal of the Hand*. Before long, my music was getting airplay on many of the NPR affiliate stations. I called *Billboard Magazine* and told Ed Christian, a long time staff writer in the music business world, how I was using the computer to open the music market for myself. He wrote an entire article on this entitled "Indie Musician Connects with Radio Hosts Online." I was in love with my Mac. I came home from my piano gigs and went right to the computer to see what music I could discover next, who I could meet, what I could learn.

By the time I was dating Gary, I had a little web site of my own up and running. Gary was a pit musician on Broadway and was playing *Showboat* every night. He was fun and caring and kind, but there was one thing that was really hard for me to get over. He didn't like my music. He didn't come out and say it, but whenever I shared a new piece with him on his New York apartment upright, he would give me suggestions on how to make it jazzier. He gave me Bill Evans albums to listen to, Chick Corea, Pat Metheny, Oscar Peterson.

"Gary, I am not a jazz player," I told him. I was already shaken up enough by having jazz piano players all around me in the piano rooms; Gary didn't do much for my confidence. In his efforts to help me, he suggested I take some piano lessons. Gary toured with Ray Charles and was such a consummate musician, I began to believe that I did need some help, so I began lessons with a gal named Bobbi who also played a shift at the Marriott in the same lounge as Robin Goldsby. Bobbi taught me twelve-bar blues, and how to work a bass line, but when I incorporated these elements at work, no one stopped to give a compliment. I was complimented when I played my *own* music. After a few months, I stopped the lessons. When Robin found out what I had been doing she said I was nuts.

"You have a professional piano gig, Robin. You beat out all those Julliard students. You don't need lessons right now. If anything, just learn more and more repertoire and keep composing."

"Yeah," I said. "But you can always learn more."

"Be you. Be you. They want to hear *you*."

If only I believed that.

Ariane was going on a blind date. She met someone on an AOL chat room.

"What's a chat room?" I asked. "Is it a dating service?"

"No, silly," she said. "I can't believe you've been on AOL all this time and haven't gone into a chat room! Let me show you."

And then she did.

Ariane sat at my computer and opened up the long long list of chat rooms that were active. There were so many.

"Look," she said. "You can start here. This looks harmless. This is a chat room called New Jersey."

"So you go in here and talk about the state of New Jersey?"

She answered me with a hearty laugh.

"The people in this room all live in New Jersey. Just go in and watch what people type."

The moment I entered the chat room I saw there were about fifteen people participating in a conversation. Everyone was writing what they did for a living and what county they lived in.

"Go ahead," Ariane said, "Type yourself in," and with that, she went back to her room.

I typed in "Musician/Essex County".

Almost immediately a private response came in along the side of my screen. It said, "Hi, I am Photographer/Essex County."

"Cool" I wrote.

"What town?" was the reply.

I was a little nervous about saying, but this was an anonymous chat. My moniker was Spobs, a longtime nickname coined by Flicka. For fun Flicka had inverted everyone's first initials around. I was Spobin Rielberg. "Spobin" kind of stuck, and somewhere along the road it was shortened to just "Spobs".

The screen was staring at me. I typed in "Montclair."

"ME TOO!" came up on the screen. "If you ever need a photographer, come find me!"

"If you ever need good piano music to listen to while you take pictures, find me," I typed. "*Heal of the Hand* is in our local music store."

The doorbell rang. It was Dave to come take a look at our refrigerator. It had been making some really weird noises and it was so hard to get our super's attention, so I signed off AOL. He wasn't the kind of super to wait very long.

Ariane eventually got a new job with better pay and decided to get an apartment of her own. I was afraid I would be lonely, and afraid I wouldn't be able to meet the rent, but at the same time I was ready to have the place to myself. I turned her bedroom into an office. One night during my second month alone in the apartment, the phone rang.

"Hi," said the man on the other end. "I don't know if you remember me, but we met on AOL in a chat room."

Oh shit. How did this person get my number? Does he know where I live? What did I say online? I tried to recall my latest interactions on the computer and quickly decided I needed to get an unlisted number.

"Umm, who is this?"

"My name is Larry. I am the photographer in Montclair? I just wanted to tell you that I took your advice and I went into Crazy Rhythms and bought your CD, *Heal of the Hand*."

"Oh, cool," I managed.

"I love it. It's really great. I just wanted you to know that if you need anyone to take a photo for a future album cover, to consider using my studio. Let me give you my number."

"Oh, okay, "I said. This seemed pretty harmless and uncreepy so I opened up.

"I didn't actually do a photo shoot for that album cover," I told him. "I'm also an actor and so I used this headshot that Ron Rinaldi took in New York."

"Well, it is a really nice photo," Larry said.

"Thanks."

"Okay, well, bye."

"Bye."

That week Gary and I had this little spat. And no surprise, it was over music. We were driving; I was at the wheel, and we were on our way to dinner and a movie.

"What the hell are we listening to?" he asked, his hand already on the dial to mute the song.

"You don't like it? It's Matthew Sweet."

I had recently discovered Matthew Sweet and loved his album *Girlfriend*. The song "Divine Intervention" was on the player.

"It's crap. I can't believe you like this stuff."

"You know, Gary, " I said, "did anyone ever tell you that you were a music snob?"

"Yeah, I know. Different strokes. But really, Robin. You're smarter than this. This music is really crap," he said with a laugh.

And with that, he reached down and turned off the CD player and found a jazz station on the radio. I sighed a little sigh.

The next day Larry called again.

"Hey. Remember me?"

"Yes, I do. Larry, the photographer, right?"

"Yes."

"Well, what's up Larry?"

"I don't mean to bother you. It's just that...well, I wanted you to know that I've been listening to your CD *Heal of the Hand* in the studio nonstop. Everyone who comes in just loves it. I'm always searching for music that clients will like. Some like rock, some like jazz, some like classical — I haven't found anyone yet who doesn't like this. It's really great."

"Thanks."

"The reason I'm calling is, well, you should go to Crazy Rhythms and bring them more inventory. The guy there said they were on consignment and didn't know when more would be coming in. I sent clients over there and now the store is sold out."

"You're kidding! Wow. That's excellent. Thank you so much."

"You're welcome. Well...bye."

"Bye."

I restocked Crazy Rhythms the next day.

"Joe, soon I won't be stocking you up," I said with a smile on my face.

"Oh yeah? Why's that?"

"Because I'm now signed with North Star Music, and they'll handle it from now on."

"Never heard of them."

"Well you will. And they'll stock you up."

"What are they gonna do for you?" he asked.

"Six-record deal, Joe. They sell mostly to gift shops and untraditional music markets. They paid off all my debt from making *Heal of the Hand*."

"Sounds good, sounds good. Make sure you get a good distributor there."

"Well, they do both. They distribute."

"Never heard of 'em."

"You will, Joe. You will. They'll call you about stocking the holiday album I just did and the next one that comes out soon, *Unchained Melodies*."

"Okay then. I guess you won't need my research room anymore," he said with a little smile.

"Thank you, Joe. For everything. I learned so much from this store and from you."

"My pleasure."

Gary still couldn't believe I got a record deal and that my recordings were doing so well. "It must be a scam," he said. "I bet you won't see a dime from royalties."

"Oh, because you think no one could ever possibly want to buy my music? Is that what you think?"

He didn't answer. He didn't have to.

I got sick that month, really sick, and developed a kidney infection that landed me in the hospital for a full week. When I was well enough to go home, I felt very lonely in my apartment; it was hard not to be a little depressed. I felt weak and vulnerable and unloved.

Larry, my AOL acquaintance, called. I didn't tell him I had been sick, because I had the feeling he was about to ask me out.

There was this awkward pause in our conversation after we had said all we could have said about the weather. And then,

"So, do you have a boyfriend?" he inquired.

Good question. Did I?

"Not anymore, " I said. And I realized then I had just broken up with Gary in my head.

"Ever go to the movies?"

"Not recently," I said.

"Well, I really want to see that movie that is out now, *Quiz Show*. Hear of it? It's that John Turturro movie?"

"Yeah. I want to see that too."

"Sometimes I go to the movies alone," I admitted, "if I *really* want to see something."

"How about we go alone to this one...but together? Where do you live? I'll pick you up."

"Tonight?"

"Sure, why not?"

Yeah, why not, I thought. It was just a movie. A public place. Safe.

I didn't feel all that well. I had lost weight in the hospital and felt and looked pale. I couldn't bring myself to dress up for the movies. I tossed on a pair of jeans and a sweatshirt, pulled my hair back in a ponytail. I wasn't looking for a boyfriend. Not after Gary. But this guy seemed nice and having a new friend in town would be a good thing, I told myself. I gave Larry my address, and he arrived exactly at 7:00, just like he said he would. When I opened the door, he blurted out,

"Oh. You're little."

"Excuse me?" I said. "What?"

"I'm sorry. I was really nervous about meeting you in person. I mean, you are really beautiful. And the album cover is just your face. And for some reason I looked at it and figured you would be really really tall like a model or something."

"Well, I'm not. And you are taller than me. Not that that would really matter."

"Good answer. Shall we go?"

We rode to the movies in Larry's Nissan Pathfinder and while we both loved the movie, it wasn't the best first date. Going to a movie is kind of a dumb first date, because you can't really get to know your date very well sitting in the dark paying attention to a screen. Larry wanted to go out for a drink afterward, but I was still on antibiotics from my kidney infection so I declined. He drove me home.

Our second date wasn't that memorable either. In fact, I don't remember it at all. But I do remember October 14, 1994, the day of our third date. That was the evening the angels sang, the stars appeared, Cupid aimed and his aim was true. We went to a Christine Lavin concert at Outpost in the Burbs and then out to dinner at Lotsa Pasta, a restaurant that had opened in one of the old railroad station buildings in Montclair. I was so comfortable around Larry. He was unlike anyone I had ever dated: easygoing, confident. He was handsome and funny and he genuinely liked my music. When we were together, it seemed like we had known one another for years. We laughed at one another's jokes, we shared a spirit for entrepreneurship. I had launched my publishing company, Spobs Music Inc. in 1993 and Larry had launched his commercial advertising business that same year, Deja View Photography. We talked a lot about marketing and business as well as photography and music. He was a Mac enthusiast. When he showed me the studio he worked out of in his apartment, he put on the CD player. Playing was Matthew Sweet's album, *Girlfriend*. Need I say more?

I hadn't spoken to Gary since our little tiff a few weeks earlier. When he called to get together I told him I didn't think it was a good idea that we see one another anymore.

"What?" he said, completely flabbergasted. "Just because I didn't call this week? I was busy with *Showboat*. Eight shows a week, plus rehearsal. C'mon baby. You know I'm crazy about you. Come on over after your gig tomorrow. We'll work it out in bed."

"No, not because you didn't call. It's just not working out. You're *not* crazy about me. You might think you are, but you're not. I think you're just lonely. Gary, you don't even like my music."

"Oh, that again?"

"Yeah, that again. The music I compose is the essence of myself."

Silence.

"Goodbye Gary."

"I can't believe this. We're great together. Is there someone else?"

"Actually, yes." I told him about Larry.

"So now you're dating a fan? A stalker? You're that insecure?"

I hung up.

I felt tremendous relief when I hung up the phone, like I was giving myself a gift. The gift of not having a relationship with someone who would criticize and disapprove of my musical tastes and talent, whatever they might be. The gift of not having a relationship with someone who was jealous and not supportive, who put me down just to lift himself up. I was tired of being ducked under the water and held down. And now that I was experiencing what it was like to be floating, held up, the comparison was an epiphany.

When the record label freaked out that too much cleavage was showing on the cover shot for *Unchained Melodies,* it was Larry who photo-shopped the offending area with a smile. "You're a beautiful woman, and you have breasts. What is the big deal?"

"Well, there are a number of Christian bookstores that carry North Star's music; mostly because they carry so many Christmas titles. Apparently this is risqué to them."

"You've got to be kidding. Okay well then, we'll make you from a C to a B."

By mid-November I couldn't imagine a life without Larry. We were constantly together, finishing one another's sentences, sharing our days, telling one another our stories at night. The idea of going to Vermont over Thanksgiving without him with my trio to play at the Woodstock Inn Fair left me feeling empty.

"Take him along," said Byron. "My wife is coming, Chris's girlfriend is coming, and our manager is bringing her husband. There's plenty of room in the ski lodge they're putting us up in. Hey, he can even take our pictures!"

Larry loved the idea of coming to Vermont with us. The trio played all day at the fair and sold a load of CDs. Larry took photos. At night Larry and I went to the inn's sport center and swam, took saunas. We were going to meet everyone for dinner afterward. We sat on the sofa of the health club after we had showered and changed to put our belongings together in our gym bags. Larry told me he loved me. It wasn't the first time. We had shared those sentiments several times before, but this time was different. He said it with much intention. He grabbed my wrist and looked into my eyes. And then, in a very non-romantic, pragmatic way, he explained why he thought we really needed to be together forever. He said we should get married. It made sense, he told me. In fact his proposal was something like this: "Let's get married. It makes sense."

I loved his approach. It was so unexpected. There was no ring, no music, no fanfare. Just the two of us, post-workout, in our sweats, deciding to spend our lives together. After years and years of being courted by men who harped on beauty and talent (the former of which I knew would fade in time), it was so amazing to be with someone who didn't ogle and gush over me at every turn. When I got a compliment from Larry, I knew he meant it. He didn't tell me I looked beautiful every day; I could see in his eyes that he thought so. He didn't tell me if he preferred my hair curly or straight. He didn't question my need to be constantly moving, busy, doing, working. I was obsessed with playing the piano. He was obsessed with cycling. We were both perfectionists about our work and we loved having our own businesses. He accepted me for who I was. I could be myself around him. I never imagined in my little girl mind that one day I would get engaged to the man of my dreams wearing sweats without an ounce of makeup on. But there we were. He loved me, and I him. I said yes.

The concierge recommended we dine at the Barnard Inn to celebrate, which was about twelve miles from Woodstock, Vermont. We drove on our own down the windy dark road of Route 12; my trio members called the inn and had a bottle of wine sent over. It was the start of my new life. And really, come to think of it, all because of Steve Jobs. He invented that Apple Computer, which led me to going online, which led me to connecting with the love of my life. And that's not all.

Later Apple's iTunes service and the revenue it generated for my music opened up new markets for me and helped pay my rent for several years. Larry and I married the following summer on a very hot July day in 1995 that also happened to be his 31st birthday. We both still love Apple computers.

Falling in love with Larry 1994

DOING STUFF

Waiting around for things to happen is not a whole lot of fun and so I always find things to do. I like making lists and I like checking things off the list once they are done. Sometimes I even write things on the list that I've already done, and *then* check them off. That's cheating, but it makes me feel good.

One day I was making a list and it looked something like this:

1) Play at Carnegie Hall
2) Get my sheet music published
3) Play piano overseas
4) Do a 20-city concert tour
5) Take cats to the vet

I started with number one on the list. Who booked Carnegie Hall anyway? Who got to decide who played there? It would be fun to play so close to home and in such a beautiful and prestigious hall. I knew the old joke, "How do you get to Carnegie Hall?" (A: Practice), but it turned out that was not the only answer.

As my research unearthed, there were shows on the Carnegie Hall calendar that were being produced by the Carnegie Hall Foundation and all the rest were rentals and being produced by outside promoters. In just a few phone calls I was in touch with the person who controlled the calendar for one of the smaller halls at the venue, and she sent me a rental agreement. Now all I had to do was print tickets, organize a reception, get a box office number, come up with the hall rental money, write a press release, contact the media, and sell out the show. Cake. No one is born knowing how to do these things, but fortunately for me, I like "doing stuff" and learning how to do stuff, so it all worked out.

So the second answer to the how-do-you-get-to-Carnegie Hall question turned out to be, A: *You rent it.* There. Longtime mystery solved. I had always wondered and now I knew! My show was set for March 15, 1997. Jitters aside and a few "who do I think I am" moments, I had a great time. Steinway reps came, Cherry Lane Publishing came (more on that with #2), the President and VP of the record label came, family, friends and fans from my early hotel gig days. William H. (Bill) Macy, my friend and acting teacher, came and brought flowers to the stage. My husband brought flowers to the stage. I had three standing ovations/encores. I sold it out and it was so much fun I did it again with fellow musicians Tingstad and Rumbel a few years later, and then again for the Epilepsy Foundation of NJ.

It seems people are really impressed when they find out you've played at Carnegie Hall. What's weird is that they would be even *more* impressed if someone had paid me loads and loads of money to do the concert and nothing *but* the concert. I am not sure I understand that. Isn't it more impressive to know I designed and printed the tickets myself, personally took care of every box office order, catered the after-party, and arranged for my own media interviews? No. The answer is no. It turned out no one wanted to know about my doing stuff. They mostly wanted me to be the lady in the pretty dress who floated on stage and played piano. *That* is impressive. All the other stuff just disappoints people, but I tell you, I don't know anyone who has "made it" without at some point doing all this behind-the-scenes stuff. Lots of stuff.

Number two on my list was to get a publishing deal. I don't

know why I had this so stuck in my head. I had imagined that once a big company came along and put out my sheet music, it would sell like hotcakes and I'd be "legit" in the composer world. Well, I got what I wished for and it was a complete disaster. The publisher made a beautiful book from my solo piano recording, *Songs of the Spirit,* but had no idea how to market the book. It just kind of sat there in their stock. I was tied to several more books by contract and pretty soon realized that although it *looked* really cool to have a publisher and a fancy book contract, the reality was that I would do better if I had self-published my sheet music. Again, that wasn't the glamorous way to go, but it was the truth. So with the help of a good attorney I got out of the dumb deal and instead of being paid cash, I took my payment in books so I could sell them myself at shows, on Amazon and my Web site. Much better. I began publishing the rest of my sheet music catalog and have to say I've enjoyed the process. The whole publishing-deal-turned-indie-deal provided me with another chance to learn how to do more stuff. I learned about ISBN codes and how to get them assigned, book layout and design. I worked directly with transcribers and printing houses. I guess you can say I checked off #2 on the list (getting a publishing deal) and learned a little something more about doing stuff.

Third on my list was playing overseas. I kind of/sort of achieved this with an impromptu concert at the Waterford Crystal Gallery in Waterford, Ireland, in 1997. I hadn't planned on playing a concert there but the piano was so darn irresistible that after the tour of the factory I couldn't help myself and then a crowd gathered. The Waterford management presented me with a beautiful hand-blown vase that had just come off the factory line as a gift. You can play in a foreign country too. There are pianos everywhere. Find one and play it.

Eventually I got to do several "real" tours overseas in South Korea (planned concerts by promoters, not impromptu ones like the one I did in Ireland) and they were great fun, so now my number three is partially checked off. I liked playing overseas so much that I moved this item to *another list*, which specifies specific countries like Spain and China.

Fourth on this list was a 20-city US tour. This one had me stumped for a little while. I wanted to get out on the road and play and see what it was like to be a touring musician. What if I made all this headway, and it turned out I hated touring the way it turned out I hated auditioning for acting jobs? I needed to know. I thought I would like it, but I wasn't sure. It wasn't the playing I was worried about; it was the travel and logistics. I wasn't sure how to create a 20-city tour for myself, but was determined to find out. I made calls. I pounded the pavement. It turned out to be pretty difficult to convince people to sponsor my solo piano show and get a tour lined up. Some presenters wanted to know if my show was jazz. I said no. Some asked if it was classical. I told them no. So now the classical and the jazz series were closed to me. I was asked if my music could be described as modern. I said no, not really. I described my music as "acoustic-instrumental-American-neoclassical-newage-melodic piano". No one "got it", and no one had heard of my music, so why would they hire me and take a box office risk? "But I talk to the audience during my show," I told them. "I tell stories! It's fun! I've sold a few hundred thousand CDs!" Nada. Hmmm.

Then it dawned on me. Why spend all this time frustrated and waiting for a yes from some stranger when I could just *do stuff* and put it all together myself?

I researched smaller-sized halls with pianos and looked into renting them. I created a budget. How hard could this be? You need a box office number. I already had an 800 number so I could check that one off. You need to know how to write a press release. Check. You need to make posters, send out flyers, call radio stations, buy ads in local papers, create and print concert programs. Check, check, check, check, check. You need to find piano technicians in each city, and a good lighting/sound person. You need to price the tickets properly so that the cost of each show is covered if you only sell 50% of the house. You need to find retail stores that would be willing to sell your music and/or serve as a ticket outlet. You need a volunteer or two who are willing to usher and help at the CD table in exchange for a free ticket to the show. The list of doing stuff grew nice and long and then I set to work on flights, hotel rooms, set lists and a practice schedule. Before I knew it I had a 20-city tour in cities I actually wanted to play in and it was great fun. Again, fans of my recordings really didn't want to hear about my doing all this stuff. They just liked that I was finally on tour. People seemed impressed that I had twenty concerts lined up that month, but the truth is, the concerts were the easy part. They were my bliss.

What was nice about doing all this stuff, is that it led to other stuff. No one cared or even asked if I had rented halls or if promoters had booked them. I was out there as a touring artist (and yes, loving it), and before long I was being asked to just "show up and play" for a fee. Still, it is nice to know how to do this stuff just in case people stop asking.

As for number five on the list, it's just a good idea to take your pets to the vet for checkups. Mine are due now, so that one is still on the list. I am making the appointment today.

Carnegie Hall debut, March 15, 1997

PART IV
PRIVATE PARTY

HAPPY BIRTHDAY, MR. JENNINGS

Peter Jennings's 50th birthday party was just going to be a small gathering of friends. The ABC *Nightly News* anchor had friends who wanted to surprise him. That's what Mr. Gabriel said, and he should know; he was the host. Mr. Gabriel met me at my steady gig to discuss the surprise party in detail. We chatted briefly during my set break in the lobby of the Grand Hyatt Hotel in midtown Manhattan. Mr. Gabriel hired me to play on his now familiar 9' Steinway during cocktails and dinner. He was also planning on hiring an award-winning a cappella group from Europe, a 20-piece marching band, a Madonna impersonator, and an opera star to flesh out the evening for the small gathering. Itzhak Perlman, who lived in the same apartment building as Mr. Gabriel, was planning on stopping by to play "Happy Birthday" on his fiddle at cake time. And oh yes, would I please just accompany the soprano opera star if I didn't mind. She was not yet sure which aria she was going to sing; that would depend upon what kind of "voice she would be in" after making the overseas flight from Germany just for the party — but no worries, it wouldn't be anything I couldn't handle.

Nothing I couldn't handle? Was he kidding? The nightmare of my life was unfolding before me. I developed a fear of being handed new music to play on the spot after having illegible handwritten arrangements thrust before me at weddings, bar mitzvahs and anniversary parties over the course of a decade. So when I heard Mr. Gabriel mention the part about accompanying the opera star I panicked. What if the piece was some tricky aria I had never heard of or played before? I needed a little time alone with the music to feel solid. Any happiness and excitement that had been building inside me for being part of this extraordinary and exclusive affair came to a screeching halt at the mention of the word "accompany".

"Call Jay," Goldsby advised me. "He's a great accompanist."

Jay was the one who had performed the gig at the Grand Hyatt for seven years before I arrived on the scene. He was fired for reasons unknown to me. I had auditioned for the steady gig and won the job without even knowing whom I was replacing. After a few years any awkwardness about having the cocktail waitress he once knew from another hotel gig being chosen to replace him in the lobby of marble, glass and brass was long gone. I had proven myself right for the gig and Jay had another steady of his own. Jay now subbed for me on occasion and we occasionally crossed paths on the piano hotel circuit in our comings and goings.

After sight-reading as best I could through the dusty book on the top shelf of my bookcase, *Arias of the Great Operas*, I rang Jay.

"No problem, Robin. I'll do it." A great relief spread through me instantly.

"Thank goodness, Jay. I really appreciate it. I'll need you to be at the party from 9-10pm; that is when the diva plans on singing. Mr. Gabriel says her performance will be about three minutes. Will a hundred bucks cover it?"

"A hundred bucks? Are you kidding?" he asked. "No, no!"

"Too much? I mean it is an hour of your time and you do have to put on the tux."

"No, not too much. Too *little*! Three hundred."

"Three hundred? C'mon Jay. That comes to a hundred bucks a minute. You live within walking distance of his apartment!"

"Well, it is my evening. I can't exactly take another gig, can I? And you need me, right? I think that's fair; after all, I don't know what she's going to ask me to play either and I could be put on the spot."

"But I'm getting paid $500 for the entire night. You want $300 for one song?"

"Take it or leave it."

"$250, Jay. That's more than fair."

"See you there."

I hung up feeling both annoyed and relieved. I wish I felt more confident about my accompanying skills.

The apartment was even grander than I had remembered. The Steinway D glistened in the specialty spotlights aimed to light its inner workings. The instrument's lid was raised all the way, at "full stick", against a wall of floor-to-ceiling windows overlooking Central Park. The other walls — adorned with original Picassos, a Rembrandt and several equestrian oil paintings — shimmered in candlelight. Tall vases of white lilies overflowed their crystal containers on every surface in the room. The rich crimson velvet draperies that framed the windows were tied back with velvet and silk rope sashes woven in gold and silver. They framed the windows so the view itself looked like a painting. I took a moment to join the catering staff in the kitchen, knowing this would be my only chance to see the food offerings for the evening. I stopped dead in my tracks when I spotted the cake.

I had never seen anything like it. The cake was a work of art that contained a 60-piece orchestra, complete with 60 edible players, music stands and instruments. The detail on each figure was incredible, down to legible miniature pages of music on the conductor's stand. It would be a shame to eat such a cake, I thought to myself, and I was glad to not have to be one of the guests guilty of destroying it.

The bell rang its school-bell chime signifying the first guest was about to arrive by elevator. The greeter moved into position, to the side of the elevator doors. I glided on to the piano bench and drifted into pianoland while the bell's rings increased in number until the room was bustling with happy guests in tuxedos, cocktail dresses and updos. Mr. Gabriel's beautiful blond seven-year-old daughter, Emma, was at my side within minutes of my set.

"Robin! You're back! I always tell Papa to pick you! I am so glad he listened. You are my favorite ever!"

"Thank you, Emma. I like being here. I like playing your beautiful piano…and you know, I appreciate having a job to do."

"Want to hear me play?"

"Okay. You sure it's alright?"

"Oh yes, Papa won't mind."

I moved off the bench and stood against the wall-to-wall windows. It was dark now and my reflection stared back at me as the little girl adjusted herself on the piano bench. I watched Emma put her black patent shoe to the sustain pedal as she launched into a wobbly "Twinkle Twinkle Little Star". When she finished I applauded.

"That's excellent, Emma. How long have you been taking lessons?"

"A year now."

"Well, you certainly have a beautiful piano to practice on," I said, still a little disappointed that she hadn't progressed much since my last visit six months ago. I continued my set of original romantic ballads as Emma sat on my right, chatting about school and her upcoming trip to Japan.

"Wow, Japan! That's far from here. Sounds exciting, Emma. Is the whole family going?"

"Well, Papa is conducting there and I always wanted to visit Japan, like *forever*!"

"He's conducting business in Japan?" I asked with cautioned curiosity. I always wondered what Mr. Gabriel did for a living and how he had acquired such wealth. Nosy, I know, but I couldn't help myself. The 12-room apartment was huge and decorated to the hilt.

"No, silly! He's conducting Mahler's Ninth! See? Look!"

I don't know why I hadn't noticed it before. I followed Emma's pointing finger to the wall behind me. On it hung a long framed poster advertising Mahler's Ninth Symphony performed by the New York Philharmonic. The poster was one of those long subway posters used to advertise concerts, Broadway shows and special attractions.

In big bold letters it read, "Conducted by Byron Gabriel."

I felt myself gasp but steadied myself as I was still playing. Emma ran off with a "see ya!" and left me with my thoughts.

Oh my God, I thought. He's a conductor? That would explain the cake...the friendship with Itzak Perlman, the soirees that always involved music, music, music...but why in the world would he hire me if he had access to any, and I mean *any* piano player in the city? It boggled my mind. Suddenly embarrassment and self-consciousness crept in where it wasn't before. I worked to shake it; it only made my fingers unsteady. My self-inflicted shake of confidence was put on hold when shouts of "SURPRISE!" from the guests practically bolted me off of the bench. They welcomed an unsuspecting Peter Jennings into the room. Debonair in a long dark winter coat, his face changed quickly from shock to appreciation, embracing each guest in the room. Kisses. Laughter.

I enjoyed watching all this, but what came next was even better. At precisely 7:30pm, the guests quieted as Madonna (not really Madonna, but someone who looked like Madonna) entered the room in a long silver shimmering body-hugging gown. The costuming and makeup was reminiscent of her role in *Dick Tracy*; the resemblance absolutely remarkable. Madonna shimmied up to the microphone in the center of the room and sang Sondheim's "Sooner or Later" from *Dick Tracy*, and when she sang the lyric, "I always get my man" at the song's end, she sat on Peter Jennings' lap. Applause, cheers, laughter. I removed myself from the piano bench and tucked myself off to the side of the crowd. Only the marching band that performed next interrupted the jubilance. Entering from a spare bedroom, they emerged in matching black and gold marching band uniforms playing a Sousa march. They weaved their way around furniture, guests and sculptures while keeping a perfect beat. The room filled with sound. It was electric. I felt my body vibrating with the bass drum. Jaws dropped. Guests craned their heads to see the end of the line, the tuba player, dipped and swayed as he played his way into the elevator. And before anyone could react, a wall of perfect sound washed over us in the form of a cappella voices singing. So perfect were their harmonies, so tight and beautiful were their intervals, I felt myself start to swoon where I stood. My knees sank into the ottoman in front of me. This is when I felt arms around my waist. They were Jay's. He was there. I hadn't seen him come in.

"Wow, this is some shindig," he whispered in my ear. I swiveled around on one knee.

"Can you believe these harmonies? They are making me dizzy!"

"Wonderful. Nice piano, I noticed. Did you meet the diva yet? Do you know what she'll be singing?"

"Nope. She's sequestered away in a back room somewhere. I have no idea what she has chosen. "Danny Boy" for all I know.

Wouldn't that be funny?"

The all-boy a cappella group took tentative bows, their faces flushed by the enthusiastic applause. Mr. Gabriel took center stage for a toast to the birthday boy.

"Oh my God," I muttered to myself. It dawned on me that the diva was going to sing Happy Birthday as her "aria". After a toast and roast to Peter Jennings, Peter's favorite singer was introduced. She walked over to the piano where Jay and I stood. I reached out to her to shake her hand and she met it with a smile and warmth in her eyes. As we shook hands, I said, "Ms. Milo, this is Jay. He'll be accompanying you this evening for your selection."

"Oh wonderful," she said as she moved to the curve of the piano and faced outward toward the expectant crowd. Jay positioned on the bench, gently leaned in and asked, "And what will you be singing this evening?"

"Oh. Didn't they tell you? 'Danny Boy', B-flat."

Jay looked at me for a moment before beginning his improvised introduction. There on his face was a smirk he didn't even try to hide. I could have done the gig on my own. He knew it. I knew it. "Danny Boy", for Pete's sake. There was a certain satisfaction in Jay's demeanor and in that moment I just hated him. There he sat with that na-na-nana-na look on his face that only I could decipher. I experienced a brief impulse to sit down next to him and duet my way into accompanying the diva or shoving him off the bench completely, but thought better of it. I might as well enjoy the show and let the piano man do what I was paying him to do. I helped myself to the lone glass of champagne still left on the waiter's tray and applauded enthusiastically for the diva after her big finish. Tears were in Peter's eyes. The guests were escorted to the dining room for cake. Jay found me to say goodbye, his coat draped over his arm.

"Thanks Robin. That was fun."

"Thanks Jay. It was…fun."

"Next time trust your instincts. C'mon…what did you think she would sing? She was bound to pick something that everyone could recognize."

"I suppose you're right. Still, glad you could come; it was worth the peace of mind and the good night sleep I got last night."

"See ya."

"See ya."

The elevator doors opened and Jay stepped in as Itzhak Perlman began his dazzling once-in-a-lifetime rendition of "Happy Birthday". I watched Peter blow out the candles, but couldn't bear to witness the cutting of the cake.

PIANO SERENADE

I kept a stack of Harlan Ellis's business cards with me at all times. At first he worked at Jerry Kravat Entertainment on Lexington Avenue, and when he moved over to Hank Lane Entertainment, I moved too. So did Goldyhead. If someone approached me at any of my gigs about playing piano for their private event, I'd hand over my agent's card. But there were occasions, when I was referred by a friend of a friend, a relative, or another source for a private party, in which case I engaged myself.

I played one such private party for a total of twelve minutes.

The party was to take place in the Presidential Suite of a fancy Manhattan hotel for a group of corporate executives. At least that was what I was told, that this was a company party. Mr. Brewer, who had hired me by phone, had heard me play at someone's wedding and got my number from the bride. He wanted me to play a mix of standards and my own original neo-classical pieces at the company party. He said my music would provide the perfect ambiance for his private party, which was going to be an elegant, upscale event. I donned a black cocktail dress, swept my curly hair up in a twist, fastened my pearls around my neck and set off to the Presidential Suite at the Hilton in midtown. I had a fake book in my bag *just in case*. Mr. Brewer answered the door personally when I knocked. He was dressed in a dark black silk suit. He shook my hand.

"Ah Robin! I'm so glad you're here," he exclaimed. "I can't tell you how much I've been looking forward to this evening." It was 6:45pm and the party was to start at 7.

"Hi," I said. "I'm sorry, but did I get the time wrong? Mr. Brewer, you did say 7pm?"

"Oh, call me Tom. You are a tad early, but no worries. This is perfect. Champagne?"

"No thanks, um, Tom. Can I use the ladies room?"

"Of course. This way."

The Presidential Suite restroom was extravagantly appointed, complete with marble floors, brass fixtures and thick spa towels. I touched up my makeup, reapplying lipstick and powder, and tucked a few stray curls into place. I wanted to look my best. This party could lead to other executive parties. The money was great and the pianos were great. I loved the sophistication of playing in this suite; diplomats and dignitaries had stayed there. U.S. Presidents had stayed there. I took a deep breath and one last look at my reflection before heading back to the suite. There was no one there, and it was 6:55pm. People in New York do like to be fashionably late, so I put my bag under the piano against the wall and began playing "Moonlight in Vermont". Mr. Brewer popped a bottle of champagne and poured himself a glass. He then sat down on the loveseat facing the piano.

"Cheers," he said. "I hope you don't mind I'm spoiling myself a little bit!"

"Not at all," I said, but my instincts were telling me something was amiss. At around 7:05pm I started getting this strange feeling that no one was going to show up. Maybe this was a private party. As in *private party*. Could it be there was just the one guy? And champagne. A few bottles. And me in my little black cocktail dress. I eyed the room as I played. There was a hospitality table with fruit and cheese, but certainly not enough for the thirty people Mr. Brewer said would be there. I mustered up a little courage.

"So, where is everyone?" I asked. "Another party, perhaps?"

I tried to sound as nonchalant as possible. I noticed the door from which I had entered was now locked and bolted.

"Well, to tell you the truth, it's just going to be us."

Shit.

"Oh, I thought you said this was for your company."

"Well, yes, it's on the company's tab, all this. But I'm feeling a little selfish, so I didn't end up inviting anyone else."

Oh no.

Panic swept over me. Was this man just eccentric or was he a real threat? I wasn't going to wait to find out. I had to go, but first I had to finish the song. Or did I? I did. I finished the song, and, in an ironic joke to myself it was the theme from the *Goodbye Girl*, and then I swept up my bag and headed for the door.

"Whoa, whoa, wait!" Tom cried out. "Hey! I ordered dinner," he confessed as he stood up and followed me. "I rented the piano! I can pay you more money. Five hundred more. Just play and stay for dinner," he pleaded. I turned and faced him, my heavy music book of most-requested-songs-at-parties in my bag, I was ready to bash him on the head with it if I needed to.

"Goodbye, Mr. Brewer. I don't play these kind of private parties, sorry." I ran down the hall to the elevator. As the doors opened I heard Tom exclaim, "Jesus Christ, what a bitch," and his door slam. I didn't ask for or receive any payment. I just felt stupid, stupid, stupid and naïve, naïve, naïve. All dressed up and nowhere to go.

The Valkovs were a wealthy Russian family living in southern Florida. Their five-year-old daughter had started piano lessons, and according to the father, was extremely gifted at the piano already. The little girl had told her parents that Robin Spielberg was her very favorite pianist of all time and that for her birthday she would like a private concert arranged. I knew ahead of time that I would be playing piano for the Valkov family, and for them alone. My husband, who was handling all my concert scheduling by this time (thank goodness!), had me booked in Florida for several concerts. He remembered fielding the call from Mr. Valkov a few months earlier, so he was able to schedule this private date at the tail end of the tour. I looked forward to it. Mr. Valkov had sent me several emails about his daughter and I couldn't wait to meet the young prodigy.

The afternoon was simply delightful. The Valkovs lived in a beautiful mansion equipped with its own music room and 9' Steinway. Five-year-old Lily, dressed in her Sunday best, answered the doorbell. "Ms. Spielberg, I can't tell you how delighted I am to meet you in person," she said. And then she *curtsied*. A uniformed maid appeared. She took my purse and sweater with a nod of her head, and Lily escorted me to the music room.

"Are your parents home, Lily?" I asked.

"Yes. Mama and Papa are upstairs. You can begin though. This is my present, and I would like it now, thank you very much."

What a precocious thing. I had only read about creatures like Lily in books. The Steinway was open with its lid full stick. The room was round, its front wall completely windowed. It was a sunny Florida day and the view overlooked a manmade pond complete with swans swimming.

"I would like you to start with music from *Heal of the Hand* please," said Lily, and with that she jumped up on the light gray damask sofa, placed a cushion on her lap, dug her elbows into it, her head resting on her hands, and poised herself to listen. I obliged.

Lily cheered, hooted and hollered after every song and gave divine commentary after each piece. "I like how you expressed yourself in that version," she said after I played "After the Rain".

"I like the recording too," but she went on, "this one was very suited to how it feels here now, in the present, with the sun shining and all."

Was this child for real?

"Can you play 'Maneki Neko' next?"

"Of course, Lily. We have a whole other hour."

"Oh, but *wait! Wait*," she cried as she jumped off the sofa. I have to get something from my room."

Lily left and I was alone in the music room for a few minutes. I tinkered at the piano. It was such a divine instrument. When Lily returned she was dressed as a ballerina complete with a pink tutu and white leotard.

"I want to dance while you play," she said. And then she did.

It was hard to take my eyes off of Lily. She was such a delight. Her dance was beautiful and went so well with the song. She had obviously been taking ballet lessons and had developed a technique already. Her body was light and dainty and she jumped about doing arabesques and piques around the piano. When she finished there was light applause.

"Oh, hello, Mama and Papa! I didn't see you come in!" said Lily.

"Lily," said her father, "can Mama and I join you for a while and listen?"

Were they really asking their five-year-old for *permission*?

"I suppose," she considered. "I've had Robin all to myself all this time. You can sit down. But first, Robin, would you like some tea? Our maid will get it."

"Um, no. That's okay. I'm fine with my water for now, but thank you." The maid had set out a pitcher of lemon water on a small table next to the piano and I had already poured myself two glasses. Lily plopped herself down in the middle of her parents on the sofa. They were a foot away from the bench.

"Robin," said Lily's father, "it has meant so much to us that you agreed to come here and play. It is all Lily has talked about for months."

"She is a delight," I said. I played the next hour and then Lily played me some of the songs she had been learning. She was quite good. I don't think Lily's mother said a word the entire time during my visit; perhaps she didn't speak English. She was dressed impeccably in a skirted suit that looked Chanel. It was she who retrieved a cash-stuffed white envelope from a drawer upon my departure and placed it in my hands.

"*Do* come again," pleaded Lily at the front door. "We *so* loved having you!"

"Lily, the pleasure was mine," I replied, copying her movie-line phrasing, and indeed it was. It was.

I thought a lot about Lily and the piano parlor soiree we just had on my ride to the airport. I thought about how I would have been in my element in the nineteenth century when piano parties were commonplace. I imagined going from home to home by carriage, performing for wealthy individual patrons of the arts. Parents with values like Lily's were not the norm now, but imagine if they were, and what that would mean for artists and for children? The idea of having a professional musician come to the home to educate, perform, entertain — how inspiring and alluring that would be for a child. It sure was for Lily, and the cost was less than going to a rock concert or professional football game. I rolled over the idea in my mind all the way to the Orlando Airport: How could I resurrect the soiree?

At Belcourt Castle in Newport, Rhode Island, Harle Tinney made it her business to resurrect the idea of a piano parlor soiree, and she had the perfect space. I performed in the French gothic ballroom of the mansion she owned with her husband, Donald, on a dozen of occasions. With 12th century stained glass from Spain lining one wall of the room and suits of armor on the other, the room transported everyone who stepped inside into another time and place. Playing on Paderewski's piano (the first artist to endorse the Steinway piano), the atmosphere, décor, candlelight, and acoustics blended perfectly to create a soiree that brought the audience into an intimate world of music and dreams. It filled the senses. These annual concerts of mine ceased shortly after Donald passed away, but my daughter still remembers that "concert place with the red carpeted staircase and men wearing silver metal uniforms watching the concert." So inspired was I by this setting that I composed the piece "Piano Parlour Soiree" based on the concerts that took place there. Each time I play the piece I think of Belcourt Castle, its unique history, owners and the concerts that transpired there.

Over the years I have serenaded a host of people from all walks of life at the piano both on purpose and accidentally. I have played concerts throughout the US, at the Waterford Crystal Factory in Ireland, in concert halls in Korea, at a rehearsal studio in Germany, at a juvenile delinquent center in Montana. I have played for the board of directors of Jaguar and Steinway. I played at New York City's Steinway Hall and Carnegie Hall's Weill Hall across the street. I have played in art galleries, hospitals, hotel lobbies, piano bars, and restaurants. I have played for dance recitals, weddings, memorial services, funerals, bat mitzvahs, birthday parties, anniversary parties, Christmas parties, Chanukah parties and for Easter Sunday brunch. I have played for New York Mayors Dinkins, Koch and Giuliani. I have played for Prince Rainier. I have played for residents of nursing homes, benefit concerts for a number of medical causes, and the corporate officers of Chrysler Motors on the top of the Chrysler Building in NYC. I have played at The New York Gift Show and the Car Show at the Javits Convention Center in Manhattan. I played at the Boston Gift Show and at Faneuil Hall. I have performed for psychologists, philanthropists, music therapists and educators. Through my recordings I have played for people making love, "on hold" on the telephone line, getting a massage, having their teeth cleaned, taking a yoga class, learning Reiki, indulging in a manicure, getting a chiropractic adjustment and wooing one another over a romantic dinner. Women in labor have brought their children into the world to my music, and patients have listened to it during their chemotherapy treatments. And yes, I've been told, that people have been buried to it too. I have played for my cats. And my husband. And myself. And maybe I've played for you. It's been my pleasure, and still is.

Performing a special holiday concert for the factory workers of Steinway & Sons on the factory floor (Astoria, NY)

A REASON TO BELIEVE

There is a fantasy that lives in every young music artist. It is the desire to be rescued from a life of turmoil, struggle and hard work. Surely someone, some day will come along and make all the artist's deepest dreams come true. If the right person would only come along, he thinks, and hear the music, he would recognize undeniable talent and undoubtedly say, "You are so gifted, so deserving, so special. Someone like you should never have to wait tables to pay the bills or play in dark smoky bars where your talent goes unappreciated. I will make *it* happen for you. You just work on your art. I will help you achieve your dreams."

This fantasy, no doubt, involves the music artist receiving a good deal of money, no questions asked, for living expenses, paying collaborators, recording sessions, and marketing expenses without having to repay a dime. This money would be a gift well deserved. It might take a while for the financier, agent, benefactor, philanthropist, or Good Samaritan to come along, but once he or she did, surely the artist's unique offerings would be recognized. And then, *Easy Street.*

Artists aren't stupid. Artists know that success in the business of music requires a hard work ethic, a little luck, a lot of patience and a strong devotion to their craft. The idea of someone coming along to "make it happen" is a ridiculous notion. But that doesn't mean that the heart of an artist doesn't wish for it anyway. Artists see the possibility every time a well-off friend, relative or acquaintance congratulates or admires "the work".

I was not immune to this fantasy.

One day, while playing one of my steady engagements, a middle-aged man enjoying cocktails and conversation with two twenty-something businessmen stopped talking and began listening — to my piano music. The younger men wore smart suits, shiny shoes and sported spiffy haircuts. Their hair was slicked back just right so their blond highlights were accented in the candlelight. They had expensive leather briefcases open and paper proposals splayed over the mahogany cocktail table. Their martini glasses were in front of them, ready for the next toast. But the man they were with, the obvious alpha male at the table, was the unusual one. He had his eyes closed and he swayed his head in time to the piano music. He was adrift; he was floating on the sea of music I was creating that no one else seemed to notice.

One of the younger gentlemen approached me at the piano as I played "Vincent", the Don McClean song often remembered as "Starry Starry Night". He leaned over the piano, his face inches away from mine, and said, "You see that man over there?" He gestured with his head toward the middle-aged man of honor. "He's is a very wealthy man. We're helping to make him even *richer*." He put a fifty-dollar bill on the piano desk. "He asked *me* to ask *you* to join us for a drink on your break."

Still playing, I replied with my standard memorized answer.

"That is so kind of you and I would love to join you, really, but management does not approve of my drinking with guests."

"Oh, well, then we'll have to come over here then."

He returned to his table, said a few words to the elder, and as Mr. Big Wig approached me at the bench, his wards gathered all their things and transferred them to the table next to me, the only seating in the room that was just inches from the piano bench and the only table unoccupied. No one liked sitting there. It was too close to the piano, too loud.

Mr. Big Wig introduced himself as Len. He wasn't drunk, but his speech pattern was a bit sloppy by nature and had the slurred quality of someone who had one too many. Unlike his guests, his auburn hair, splashed with gray at the temples, was disheveled and unstyled. It stood up on end in some places and was wire-y and curly in others. His tie was loose around his neck and his jacket open. His pants hung a little too low. His extra weight was concentrated in his stomach, evidence of many nights like this one, filled with fancy dinners and drinks with associates.

"I'm Len and you are gorgeous," he pronounced. "What music you play! What is your name? Who are you? Where did you come from? You play like an angel." His cocktail swirled in his hand as he waited for a reply.

As I began "Over the Rainbow" I told him my name and thanked him for the compliment.

"I'm glad you like my playing."

"Are you sure you cannot join us for a drink? C'mon. Just one. Right over here honey, next to me." He gestured at his table; his young comrades now situated at the table next to me smiled and nodded.

"No, sorry. I'm a working girl," I replied with a professional smile. "I've got to stay right here on this bench until my next break — thirty minutes from now...and that break takes place in the employee lounge."

I said this even though there wasn't an employee lounge. The words just came out of my mouth as a self-defense. I normally took my breaks in the swanky hotel lobby with the Hungarian harpist from the next room. She drank Russian vodka from an Evian water bottle on her break and her conversations were always entertaining, but that's another story.

"Well here's another twenty bucks. Play me something."

"What song would you like?" I asked for his request with confidence because I had Mr. Fakey with me. Mr. Fakey was my giant spiral-bound "fake book" that I purchased from Carl Fischer Music near NYU downtown. It had a zillion songs in it. When my repertoire of 750 or so pieces fell short when it came to requests, I took out Mr. Fakey and looked up the song. Goldyhead lived in Germany now; I could no longer call her on my breaks. There was a directory of hummable bars in the back of the book. If a guest forgot the name of a song, he or she could hum it and I could still look it up.

"Oh, I request that you play whatever pleases you most," said my new fan. What a heavenly answer. I segued from "Over the Rainbow" into an original piece I was working on called "Circle of Life". Len listened with eyes closed, both elbows on the piano, drink still in hand swirling by his ear now, gently swaying to my song. He looked pretty ridiculous. His slick Wall Street friends looked on in awe of their god. They looked ridiculous too. When I finished the song, Len told me that I was indeed an angel. He placed his business card on the piano desk.

"Call me if you ever need anything. And I mean *anything*."

I played piano at the Hilton's piano bar, The Retreat on Monday, Tuesday and Wednesday evenings. The hotel was located in the wealthy New Jersey suburb of Short Hills and was situated across the street from the famous Mall at Short Hills. Not the Short Hills Mall, mind you; The Mall *at* Short Hills. Before work I would sometimes window shop the upscale shops and check out the sales at Bloomingdale's, Saks Fifth Avenue, and Neiman Marcus. If I had enough tips to splurge on a sale rack item, I did. Thanks to Len, that is what I did the following Monday. I purchased a new black piano skirt I had been eyeing on the Bloomingdale's sale rack; it was the perfect piano skirt. It had an A-line shape, which made it comfortable for pedaling, and when paired with a silk blouse and fabulous belt I felt dressed for the room.

I entered the piano bar that night in my new black silk skirt and found Len and his cohorts already seated next to the piano, drink glasses empty. Len wasted no time. Before I could even raise the piano lid, he stood up and announced,

"Sweetheart, I've been giving it a great deal of thought. I couldn't get my mind off of you and your beautiful music all week. It has stayed with me. I've been dreaming about it. I think that you could be *big*, really big."

"Why thank you, Len, I appreciate your vote of confidence," I said. "You've already made my night and I haven't even started my first set." I sat down and began to improvise while he continued his praise.

"Why don't we meet for drinks *after* your work is done here tonight, and talk about how I can help. Do you have a business plan for your music?"

"Of course," I lied without even thinking. I kind-of-sort-of had a business plan, if you could count a list of goals on a piece of paper in my top desk drawer a business plan.

"Good, good. You bring me your business plan. I will review it. Then we will meet."

You know that little alarm you have in your head? The one that goes off when something makes you a little wary, a little nervous? Mine started to buzz a little bit — just like it did when Len asked me to take my music break at his table the week before — and so

I said, "Well Len, you know, my husband Larry, he's been working with me on the business part of my music. We should really all meet...together."

I figured if this turned him off, then that meant he was full of hot air and only wanted a date, but Len didn't flinch.

"Great idea! I would love to meet him. Let's all meet. Bring me your business plan and we'll see where I can fit in."

I floated through my sets that night. My hands were playing, but my mind was spinning. I imagined an influx of investment money pouring into my bank account and into my work and what that could mean. My lifelong dream of orchestrating my work could be fulfilled. Or maybe that publicist I couldn't afford to hire — the $20,000 per month publicist who said she had connections to the *Oprah Winfrey Show* — maybe I could hire her and perform on *Oprah*! Maybe Len could underwrite a tour or introduce me to other clients that perhaps could endorse me. Maybe he had connections to an airline executive who would sponsor all my travel. Maybe he knew a clothing designer; I would need a killer set of concert wear for touring. I could finally have enough money to produce a large quantity of CDs, a requirement for approaching the big box stores and QVC. No more "short runs" of inventory. I could, perhaps, stop worrying about the mortgage for a change and have the freedom to work on music projects freely without thought of the finances. Wow: it was true. You never knew whom you would meet! You never knew who could be listening! I had spoken these words of wisdom myself to several other players with steady gigs who sometimes felt stuck, bored, lost, and I had meant them. But now I had experienced their truth for myself! A wealthy financier was intrigued, fascinated, beguiled, enlightened, touched, moved by my music. And he was going to help me. *Save* me.

I told Larry about Len that evening. I knew he would be skeptical; it wasn't the first time I was hit on at work, but when I told him that Len wanted to meet him as well, and only after reading our business plan, he caught my excitement.

"We have to approach this correctly, Robin," he said. "We really do have to have a proper business plan in place or we won't be taken seriously."

The next day we called several entrepreneur friends asking for advice on writing a business plan. It was a whole lot more involved than I had thought. Needless to say, we were not in a position to hire a professional and not experienced enough to write our own, but with a little research, friends to give us feedback and brainstorming sessions each day, we cranked one out in two weeks.

Writing a plan for what we called The Scintilla Project was an eye-opening exercise. Our company would be a one-stop for artists: a record label, a CD distributor, an artist management agency, and would offer promotional services. Indie artists would no longer need an agent, manager, publicist, and record label — they could operate independently and retain all publishing rights to their work (something most traditional record companies made artists sacrifice upon signing). Our company would allow the artists to retain all rights to their work, and would earn income based on commissions for booking, distribution and sales. I would be one of the artists working with The Scintilla Project, but also a co-founder and principal along with Larry. Launching it would take capital and that is where Len came in.

When it came time to arrange a meeting with Len, Larry began to get a little nervous.

"This guy slurs his speech, Robin," he said after talking with Len on the phone. "Is he drunk?"

"No, no. I think that's just the way he talks," I said. "He's legit. I mean he buys $150 shots of whiskey for his colleagues each week for goodness sake! They told me he does all kinds of deals all the time and really has helped a lot of people. He has a philanthropic streak. He really believes in my music! I am so excited!"

"Well, let's meet him here in Montclair then. I'm more comfortable with that. But not in the house."

Larry's caution annoyed me. I took it to mean he didn't trust my judgment. I had pictured cooking a nice meal for Len and Larry and discussing our project in the comfort of the music room.

"If not at the house, then where?" I asked, trying not to show my frustration.

"The photography studio. It's in town and easy to find."

My husband owned his own business, Deja View Photography, which specialized in commercial advertising photography. Shortly after we met, he had outgrown his former space, which doubled as his living space, and together we shopped for a proper studio space. The Cooper Building in Upper Montclair was the perfect spot. Across from Starbucks, the post office and the Cheese Shoppe (which sold the best sandwiches and salads on the face of the earth along with, yes, cheese), the building was a former livery and town landmark. The lease came with two parking spots, a feature hard to come by in most leases, as parking was at a premium in Upper Montclair. I sometimes "ran film" for Larry, meaning that while the clients lunched, I would bring the test taken that morning to the processing lab, a few miles away in Little Falls. After lunch, the clients would look over the test film and either make changes to the set-up or continue on film with the one in place. I helped Larry pick out the photography studio's floor surface, the waiting area furniture, and the commercial kitchen appliances necessary for food shoots. The space was nice and roomy — roomy enough to hold 300 boxes of smarties candy necklaces in the corner without anyone really noticing. My job was to go through all those necklaces and find the most perfect one for the macro shot. Ah, the days before Photoshop! (I wore and eventually ate many of the rejects.)

I dusted the IKEA coffee table of the waiting area, rearranged the magazines, fluffed the sofa pillows and waited for Len to arrive.

Len drove his BMW into the lot and rang the Deja View bell at exactly 1pm. After showing him around the photography studio, we sat in the client waiting area I had just made perfect for the visit. Three copies of our business plan had been bound and copied at Alphagraphics and were stacked on the coffee table.

Len looked different in daylight. I noticed a few stains on his blue suit; his tie was untied around his neck, dangling, wrinkled and droopy, and when he sat down and crossed his legs I noticed his socks didn't match. He was more disheveled than I had remembered. Larry noticed this too; I could tell by the glance that went from Len's socks and over to me. I simply nodded in acknowledgement and gave a slight shrug.

After a little small talk where Len answered Larry's questions about his investment company, his philanthropic interests and current dealings, all of which I found impressive, Len started to talk about his philosophy.

"I don't want and I don't allow any negativity around me, *at all*," he declared in an out-of-adjustment booming voice. "I only surround myself with *positive people!* Are you positive people?" He didn't wait for an answer. He stood up and began pacing the lounge area.

"I don't want to hear about problems, or hear the word 'no'.

I *do* things. Together we will *do* things."

"Len," I started, "do you want to see our business plan? We can go over that if you like."

"No no, I don't want to read a *plan*! Plans are *boring*! I want to *talk* about what it is you *need*. What I can *do* for *you*." His pacing kept up; his head to the floor. Larry and I exchanged looks of bafflement. Where did this person come from? This was not the same Len I met at the Hilton. Something was off.

"*You Robin*, should be an important musical...music...musical *person* in people's lives. How are we going to do that? What do you *need* to get your music to people?"

"Actually, that's all here in our business plan. Maybe we should have a look."

Len picked up one of the spiral bound presentations from the coffee table and began flipping through it while pacing. He fixed upon a random page.

"What does this mean? Here," he questioned as he pointed to a paragraph in the middle of page four. "It says you will need a marketing professional *and* a publicity coordinator. You don't need these people! We need to call Oprah, get you on the show."

"Well Len," I began gently, "to be honest, I know it doesn't work that way. You can't just call Oprah. She won't take your call. Her show's producers are pitched constantly and to have a shot at the show you need to know someone who has the ear of the producer... someone who can at least give your pitch some consideration. That's where a publicist comes in because..."

"Wait!!! Wait!!! Did I just hear you say you *can't* call Oprah? Did you say the word '*can't*'? Did I actually hear this? Larry? Did she tell me *can't*? *I told you people!!!* I do not want any negativity! You are giving me negative vibes, negative vibes!"

Len then marched right out of the studio. Larry and I sat on the sofa with our mouths agape, not knowing what to think.

"He left his jacket," I said. "I guess he'll be back."

"Robin, this guy is nuts. You do see that, right?" Larry said.

I'm not sure why, but I immediately began defending Len.

"Not nuts, not nuts. I think he's just *eccentric*," I explained. "Maybe he's nervous. He wasn't like this at the hotel. He wasn't. He is a bit...strange, I'll give you that. But he came all the way out here. He's a wealthy man, Larry, an important player...I see him all the time at the piano room with different Wall Street guys each time. I see him spend money on fine liquor like no tomorrow. Who cares if he is a little wacked? If he believes in what I do and genuinely wants to help by funding our start-up..."

"I don't know," said Larry. "Seems like you just attract these types like a magnet." That was true; I had a file of stalker-type fan letters that the police told me to keep "just in case" something should develop.

Within two minutes Len came back into the studio. His face was now calm and his eyes bright; it seemed like he had apparently walked off all those 'negative vibes' in the parking lot.

"We need sushi!" he said. "Do you like sushi?"

On the sofa, side-by-side, Larry and I nodded in unison.

"I know a great place just below the George Washington Bridge. Let me take you there for an early dinner. We'll have some sushi, talk about your plan, your business plan."

Things were looking up.

Larry and I followed Len's BMW in the studio's leased Nissan Pathfinder. During the ride we went over the fine points of The Scintilla Project. We had the numbers, goals and mission statement memorized. We had to now find ways to approach Len that would not upset him, set him off. It would be a shame, we thought, to miss an opportunity all because we took the wrong approach. We needed to cater a bit to Len's quirkiness in order to be heard. We decided to substitute the word 'problem' with 'challenge'. We would swap out the word 'obstacle' with 'opportunity'. Our anxieties were alleviated somewhat when we entered the restaurant, Len holding the door open for us.

"Ren!!! Ren! You are here!" exclaimed the head sushi chef. "Look who come in! It's Ren!"

The hostess seated us and before the tea was poured, the kitchen staff and restaurant owner immediately surrounded our table.

"Everyone, I want you to meet my good good friends, Robin and Larry." Len was back to himself now. He seemed to be the same man I had met at the Hilton. What had happened at the studio, I wondered.

"Hello, hello!" Lots of smiles and nods.

Len continued, "Robin and Larry are good friends. Robin is a brilliant musician. She creates music that is angelic. She's like an angel playing the piano. A gift. We're going to work together and she's going to be very very famous!"

"Ahh, famous musician. Good news, Ren," said the sushi chef. "Ren, you want menus for your friends?" He looked at us, "You've come before?"

"I love sushi," said Larry, "but we haven't been here before."

"Ah, we are best. You will like us."

"Len," I said, "where can we start? What do you need from us as far as a return on your investment? What do you hope to gain from participation? I'm sorry I'm not experienced in how this all works, but I figure here we are, and we should put our intentions right here on the table, don't you think?"

"You're a genius! An angel! She's so *bold*, Larry. Don't you love her? She is so bold! She wants to discuss the project. Now! Over this beautiful dinner. No, sweetheart. We won't talk about this now. We'll wait for the last tea cup to discuss this."

And so it went on. One, two, almost three hours passed before our plates were cleared and we sat, teacups in hand. We had talked about politics, war in the Middle East, weather, pollution, technological advancements, but not about the reason we were all there sharing a meal. Len asked our waiter for a check, dismissed our attempts to contribute to the meal with a wave of his hand, and declared,

"I need some air. Let's talk someplace else. I know! I know! There's someone I want the two of you to meet! A very important person. He's just a short way from here. Why didn't I think of this before?"

Len whipped out his cell phone and pressed a speed dial number. Moments later, he screeched into the phone.

"We're coming over. Now. What do you mean *who*? Me. And the angel I told you about!"

He hung up.

"There. It's done. Let's go."

As we headed to the parking lot, Larry said, "This is getting a bit crazy, don't you think? It's almost ten o'clock."

"I agree," I answered. "If we don't get into a conversation about The Scintilla Project with Len tonight, let's just forget the whole thing." I tried to hide my disappointment and slipped my hand into his. "Dinner was good, right?" Before Larry could respond, Len was at my side.

"Angel, you ride with me. It's five minutes from here. Let Larry follow. I have a few questions...just for you." He turned to Larry.

"Larry, is that okay?" Len asked with a wink and a smile. "Can I have her for just five minutes?"

"Uh, no...Len, why don't we just follow you since you know the way, and we can all talk together when we get to your friend's house."

Len turned to me. "Robin! I think your husband is jealous! You mean I can't talk to her alone for *five minutes* while we're driving? It's a short drive and I just want to brief her on who we're meeting so we can have the best approach here. Larry, listen, I'm making a social call, but this man I'm taking you to has a lot of influence, you'll see. Let me borrow your wife for just *five minutes*."

I gave Larry a pleading look. Please, I begged through my eyes, don't blow this opportunity over a five-minute car ride.

Larry looked at Len, and assessed his pathetic posture, his has-been appearance and weighed the risks. How much further into the evening did we have to go for Robin to realize this guy was a complete kook — that is what he was probably thinking. I couldn't wait to prove him wrong.

"Okay, sure, I'll follow. What's the address in case we get separated?"

"Oh you won't need that," Len dismissed, "but it's the apartment complex in Fort Lee right off exit 12; you can't miss it. We'll meet in the lot."

Riding with Len in his BMW, I felt a little uneasy, but I wanted desperately to prove to Larry that my judgment was sound and my initial impressions of Len were not clouded by my wishing, my dreaming. I tried hard to ignore that little alarm buzzer in my head that began to make noises and increased my adrenaline output.

As we drove out of the restaurant parking lot, Len turned to me. "Sweetheart," he said. "What are you *doing* married to him?"

The question sounded like an accusation and I didn't like the tone of Len's voice. I didn't like the question either. It took me off guard.

I could only respond with "What?"

"We don't need him! We...you and I can work on your dream together. We can be partners. Take your music to a whole new level. Let me be part of this, Robin. I need *you*. I need this to work. I want to be your *partner*." Studio Len was back. Hilton Len was gone.

"Len, I'm sorry, but I think you misunderstand something here. Larry and I are *married*. And we work together — as partners; you know that."

Len took his hands off the wheel for a moment and rubbed his eyes hard. When they were back on the wheel they gripped tightly and his teeth clenched.

"Tell you what, Len," I said. You're getting upset and I don't want you to be upset. Why don't you slow down, stop the car on the shoulder — Larry will pick me up and we can call it a night."

"*No!* Let's just *lose him!*" he shouted. And with that, Len put the pedal to the metal. The BMW began zigging and zagging in between cars on the crowded New Jersey highway.

"Len!" I said, trying not to sound too scared. "Larry won't be able to follow us...you're going too fast."

"If you won't lose him, then I will!" said Len, his eyes now wild, his head lurching forward over the wheel. His eyes darted between the rear view mirror and the road ahead as he swerved between cars and trucks, coming alarmingly close to several vehicles while maneuvering lanes. It was then I realized what was happening. I was being *kidnapped*. This is what kidnapping was: taking someone somewhere without their knowledge or consent of where they were going. But not really. Didn't I agree to get into this car with Len? Didn't I agree to meet some person I didn't even know? Didn't I see Len at work at the Hilton at

Short Hills with lots of different investors entertaining his guests and being toasted and honored all these months? Didn't Len drive all the way out to Upper Montclair to meet us to talk about my music? Didn't he just buy my husband and me an amazing dinner so we could get to know one another better? What was going on? All these questions swirled in my mind as I saw Larry in the passenger side mirror trying desperately to keep up with Len's crazy driving. The Pathfinder was two cars behind us, then three, then four and then out of sight.

"A-ha! I think I did it! He's not going to find us now! We escaped! We made it! Just you and me now, my angel."

I felt my cell phone in my pocket and was comforted that it had a full charge. Now it began to ring. It was Larry.

"*Don't answer that!!!! Don't!!!!* I'm driving. I don't want any distractions! I can't have people talking to *other* people while I'm driving!"

"Okay, Len," I said. "It's probably just my mom. I'll call her back later." I figured Larry had the plate number and description of the car well enough and would call the police. Now I felt not fear, but incredible shame and embarrassment that I was literally being taken for a ride. Len was clearly insane; he had some kind of mental disorder that made him brilliant, funny, warm and talented one minute, and unreasonable, illogical and crazy the next. Len pulled the car across four lanes of traffic to make an unbelievable exit somewhere in Fort Lee, New Jersey.

"Where are we going, Len?" I asked rather nonchalantly. I figured showing any fear or questioning any of his moves was not going to be in my best interest.

"*I told you!!!!!* There is someone you need to meet!"

"Oh, that's right. What's his name?"

"*You will see!!!!!*"

Out in the parking lot of an enormous apartment building below the George Washington Bridge I considered my options. Going upstairs to meet this "friend" seemed like the best one. The "friend" was probably sane and could extract me from this ridiculous situation, or at the very least, provide me with a bathroom from which I could call Larry and direct him to the kidnapping location. In the elevator, Len turned to me and said, "I don't want you to worry. I know what I'm doing. We'll get you reunited with you know who soon enough."

I nodded.

"Robin, I just need a few minutes to *show you*."

With his hand at the small of my back, Len led me into the apartment building lobby, devoid of any security personnel, and pushed me into the waiting elevator. He pressed the button for floor seven. His breathing was hard and he paced in the small elevator like a caged animal. When the doors opened he walked ahead to the apartment right next to the elevator, took out a mangled group of keys from his pocket and opened the apartment door. Was this *his* apartment?

"Hello!!! I'm here!!! Where are you? Come on out! I have someone for you to meet!!!" he shouted into the air.

I heard a door open from down the hall, and out came a disheveled old man, an older version of Len, his shuffled walk aided by a walker that dragged along the dirty-carpeted floor.

"Pops! Guess what! Here she is! I told you I'd bring her to meet you!!! Here is my angel."

The old man, who I by now concluded was Len's very old but seemingly sane father, shifted his weight to one side and held out a shaking hand to touch mine.

"Well?" asked Len of his father. "Don't you have something for my bride?" Len eyed the room and spotted something. "Oh, there it is!"

Len approached an old wooden cracked display cabinet filled with dusty artifacts from a past life. Vases, tarnished silver plates and other pieces that were once proudly displayed as show pieces sat forgotten until this moment. Len slid the dusty, smudged glass door of the cabinet and found the object of his desire. He held it up for me to see.

"This," he said, "is from my father. A gift to you! What do you think?"

I couldn't tell exactly what the piece was. It was round, made of wood, with several holes in it. I must have looked perplexed because Len grew very frustrated.

"You can't tell what it is!!!" he shouted. "It's an ancient African art piece, used only by warriors during special tribal ceremonies! It's a wedding gift to you from my father! Say thank you!"

I looked at Len's dad, who was now rocking in an old green padded rocking chair. He looked sad. He said nothing.

"Sir, do you mean to give this to me?" I managed.

"Of course he does," said Len. "That's why he invited us over! Silly angel." With the wooden object in my hands Len hugged me in a bear-tight hug; the art piece dug into my ribs.

"Oh, and I have more for you!" Len disappeared into a back room. My chance to escape was here, but I didn't take it. I just waited, feeling quite safe and quite sympathetic for Len and his father.

"I'm sorry about this," I told Len's father. "I was meeting Len with my husband to discuss a business matter and he convinced us that we should come here. I'm so sorry to have disturbed you; you were obviously asleep."

Len's dad stood to tighten the belt on his flannel robe, picked up the newspaper on the side table, shook it, folded it in half, sat back down in the rocker and began reading it. Len returned to the room with a bunch of strange objects: a yellow shot glass, a wooden spoon, and a silver candlestick.

"More gifts for you, my sweet! More gifts for you!"

"Oh Len, these are lovely," I said, "but I can't accept these. These are things that belong to your father."

"Is it because they're not wrapped?" Len asked, looking a bit sad.

"No, not at all...it just seems a little rude to take things that obviously belong to someone else."

At that moment I noticed Larry in the doorway like a superhero. I don't know how long he had been standing there, but the look on his face told me that he had assessed the situation and had a handle on things. He knew what to do, what to say.

"You know, Len," he said, "I think we have to go. It's getting so late and we're all so tired. Time for sleep."

"Ah yes, yes, sleep," Len said. "You can stay here if you'd like! Both of you!"

"No," said Larry. "I think we're going to go home. To our own house. Thanks for the lovely dinner." Len walked over to Larry, reached out and shook Larry's hand. "We'll talk soon!" Len retreated to the gold-plastic-covered sofa, took his shoes off, and began flipping through the TV Guide listings at his side.

Larry and I exited to the parking lot without a word between us. Once in the car I couldn't help myself but to ask how he had found me.

"Just like he said, first apartment complex off the exit. His last name was on the buzzer next to apartment number 714. Are you okay?"

"Yes, I'm okay. That was so weird."

"What are you holding?"

I realized while I ditched the shot glass, candlestick and wooden spoon, I still had the supposed "ancient African tribal artifact" with me. It was on my lap.

"I have no idea. It's just a reminder of what just happened, I guess. I love you, Larry."

"I love you too, and partly because you're so open and trusting...I'm not going to say 'I told you so', but well, you know."

"Yes, I know."

"Hard work, Robin. Hard work and focus. Just like your piano teacher Alan Wolfe said, it's all about practice, patience and persistence. No magic."

I went to bed that night feeling a little wiser, but also a little defeated. At 3:30am the phone rang. It was Len.

"Robin! Meet me at the post office in Montclair."

"What? Len...do you know what time it is?"

"I can't sleep. I can only think of you. When I do sleep, I dream only of you. I need you to meet me. I need to be with you."

I hung up.

At 4am the phone rang again, and this time it woke Larry.

I answered it in my spare bedroom-turned office and heard the same, now familiar voice. Studio Len.

"Robin! I'm sending a town car to your house. I just need the address. It'll pick you up and take you to a spa in upstate New York so you can breathe, relax. I bought you a spa package and several massages. Once you're all relaxed you'll be able to think clearer and see that you need me and that we were meant to be together."

"Len," I said gently. "I don't think you should call here anymore. I don't think we'll be doing any business together or socializing anymore. Please don't call here again, okay?"

"What??? What are you saying? *Are you breaking up with me?* I cannot have it. I will not have it! I will find you! I am coming to Montclair!" And with that he hung up.

I relayed the conversation to Larry with a soft edge even though I was shaken up when I slipped back into bed. I felt badly for bringing him into this drama and I wanted to handle it myself. "He said he wants to treat me to a spa vacation and that he wants to send a town car for me."

"How nice," said Larry just before rolling over and falling back asleep.

The next day at the post office I was picking up my mail at the P.O. box when Pete, one of the postal workers spotted me. "Hey Robin...there was someone in here this morning looking for you. Said he was a friend of yours. Wanted your address."

"Oh no, Pete. You didn't give it to him, did you?"

"Of course not. I told him I didn't know who you were. 'We don't have a famous piano player living in this town to my knowledge,' I told him. Ha!"

"Thanks, Pete. You didn't have to go that far," I joked.

I crossed the street to Larry's studio and rang the buzzer.

"Larry," I said, "I'm so sorry...but I think you're going to have to keep your studio door locked until this Len thing is resolved. He apparently asked Pete at the post office for our address."

"I'm calling the police."

Although I thought involving the police was a bit overboard I let Larry take charge. After all, the calls had to stop, and I didn't want to worry about seeing Len again at my piano gig.

The police were at the studio within minutes and I allowed Larry to relay his experience of Len. So much for handling this on my own; I was a flop. Familiar with mental disorders of all types, the police promised to be gentle when they visited Len.

Whatever they said to him worked, because I never heard from or saw Len again. And as for that ancient African tribal artifact: upon further examination, we concluded it to be an ashtray that someone (maybe Len?) had made in a high school shop class and stained with a mahogany-colored wood stain. I kept it for a while to remind myself that being gullible is not one of my best character traits, but then donated it to Good Will after it didn't sell at a garage sale.

PART V
NAKED ON THE BENCH

GETTING DRESSED

On the morning I was scheduled to have lunch with the president of a record label in Manhattan, I stared into my closet. I didn't know what to wear. It was a big day. I wanted to look great. I dismissed the scores of nostalgia dresses I had bought in East Village thrift shops, the corporate lunch suits I donned for the "power breakfast" gig at the Grand Hyatt, the little black dresses I relied upon for cocktail-hour gigs in piano bars, the skirts with crinoline I often chose for pre-Broadway hour. None of these seemed quite right.

I was performing at the Grand Hyatt that morning, the hotel that sits above Grand Central Station and plays host to east Midtown's executives for breakfast and lunch meetings. The hotel lobby also served as an oasis of sorts, complete with a massive marble fountain that attempted to soothe commuters longing to escape the toil and trouble of the city. I had to be dressed for the gig, but I didn't want to be mistaken for a midtown executive. As my eye scanned through the blacks, I spotted a hint of brown. A-ha! The dress I bought with Lisa when she was being fitted for her wedding gown had spoken! The fabric of this dress was brown stretch velvet. It had a simple ballet neckline, a slim waist, and then a generous A-line skirt, which made this dress a classic. The fabric was modern and unique. This was the dress.

At the bus stop I thought about my meeting with anticipation. I was already signed to the label so I wasn't nervous, just excited. Mr. Waterman was coming down from Rhode Island for our first "strategic planning meeting" for the marketing of my recordings. It was a whole new beginning for me. I daydreamed on the bus

191

into Manhattan in my beautiful dress while my friend Lenore chattered away about her latest boyfriend woes. Lenore is one of those women who are incredibly intelligent and physically fit. She bicycled with the guys, coached a swim team, was enrolled in law school, and was always training for a triathlon, a meet, a race. Our rides on the bus were the only time we talked intimately about our lives; once in the Port Authority Bus Terminal we went our separate ways, her downtown, and me crosstown.

We were closing our conversation on the escalator at the Port Authority Bus Terminal when I felt what I thought was a child tugging on my dress. When I looked down, I saw that my beautiful dress was caught in the escalator itself. It was the sharp edges of the escalator stairs doing the tugging. "Look, Lenore, the escalator likes my dress." But the look on Lenore's face told me she didn't think this was funny.

"Oh my God," she screamed.

Lenore leaped up the few steps to where I was and together we worked to pull the dress free. Nothing doing. As we moved along closer to the Port Authority lobby, the dress was getting pulled further and further into the escalator stairs. This was one long escalator, but even I could tell we didn't have much time before this was going to become serious.

"Lenore, please…do something!"

Lenore raced to the bottom of the escalator and hit the big red button on the bottom of the escalator marked "Emergency Stop".

Have you ever wondered what could possibly be so urgent that you would have to stop an escalator from operating at 1 mile per hour? Well, this. The escalator came to an abrupt halt. People started yelling. Angry commuters pushed past me with their briefcases and brushed me with their *Wall Street Journals*. I was exactly halfway down this escalator ride, completely trapped by my dress and the sharp-toothed mechanics of the steel staircase. I was unable to move. Lenore came back up to where I stood.

"Robin, I'm going to get the police. Stay here."

"Police? Aren't we over-reacting?" But she was gone. "Well, of course I'll stay here," I said to myself, and then screamed out, "Hurry!"

Seventy percent of the commuters were unaware of my predicament, or if they were, they simply didn't care. The other thirty percent laughed, pointed, and stared. One group of construction workers had a real fun time with me. As they traveled down on the escalator next to mine, they shouted, "Hey lady! Wanna come with us? Oh yeah, you *can't!*" and "Hey lady! Did you know your dress is stuck in the escalator?"

When the police arrived they laughed too, but they did seem genuinely concerned for my safety. "Excuse me, officer? Can you find someone to put this thing in reverse so I can get free?" I asked.

"Sorry," said the officer in charge. "It seems the maintenance guys are on a union break."

Lenore apologized that she had to get to class. I told her to go, not to worry.

"Bye," she said. "Have a nice...day. See you tomorrow."

Half-way through the Port Authority lobby, she looked over her shoulder with apologetic eyes before racing through the lobby doors to 42nd Street.

"Look, lady, you can't just stand there on a stopped escalator blocking all the commuter traffic," complained the short and burly police officer. "Can you take the dress off? It looks like you can. It looks like it's made of that stretchy fabric...what's it called?"

"Lycra."

"Yes! That's it. Lycra!," said the second officer. "A miracle fabric if I say so myself. My wife…"

"Yes. No. I am mean, yes I can, it is made of this stretchy stuff, but no, I am not taking it off!"

"Okay, okay. Fine. Have it your way. I'll get some scissors."

"There's a Hallmark store on level one," said one officer.

"No! No scissors!" I cried out, but he was gone.

Repeated attempts at tugging the dress did not work, and so when the scissors arrived, I took them and did the honors myself. It turned out the bottom of the dress was not stuck, it was a section about six inches above the bottom, and so my cut resulted in a hole the size of an orange on the right side of my dress, right below the knee. I gave the scissors back to the officer with a shrug and a half-hearted smile.

"You know, you got awfully lucky, miss," he said. "This could have been a real tragedy."

"Yes, yes, you're right. Thanks for your help." I hailed a cab to the Hyatt to make it in time for the 7:30am butt-on-the-bench time.

Sitting on the piano bench, no one could see the tear in my dress, but standing and walking were another story. All I remember about my meeting with the president of North Star Music was how I worked to conceal the hole in my dress. Did he ever see it?

My sunny yellow suit was really fun. I loved it. Short skirt, slim jacket. I wore it with black high heels. On a spring day, this outfit was the perfect breakfast gig suit. Looking back, I probably looked like a bumblebee. Working a double shift (that was breakfast from 7:30am-10:30am and then lunch from 11:30am-2:30pm) was common for me this time of year. Earl Rose normally played the breakfast gig, but as he was" bi-coastal" as he liked to call it, this was the time of year he spent in California working on soap opera music scores. At 10:30am I went for a leisurely stroll to stretch my legs and enjoy the sunshine between the two shifts. It was a beautiful day on Lexington Avenue. There was a small market a few blocks down that sold fresh fruit, muffins and lilacs. That's where I was headed when I tripped. Head over feet I fell right over one of those steel metal delivery doors. I hadn't even noticed the door was up and open what with the glare of the sun. Pain in my arms and legs registered immediately as a stranger tried to help me to my feet.

"Let me call 911," he said.

"No, why? I'm fine, really."

"But your legs."

I looked down and noticed a bulge at my right knee and a bleeding scrape on my left. Pantyhose torn and bloody, I smiled and thanked the stranger, got up, and went on my way. Every nerve cell in my body shrieked and told me to stop and get some ice and sit down, but the stares of the crowd that had gathered encouraged that other part of me that told me to just keep walking and pretend nothing had happened. So that's what I did. I listened to that part of me. I bought my muffin and a banana, and headed back to the Hyatt, buying a new pair of pantyhose at the Duane Reade drugstore on the way back.

In the Hyatt ladies room I tended to my wounds as best I could, but putting on new pantyhose was simply too painful, so I went back to the bench barelegged. As I began to play the pain disappeared and I disappeared into the music, into pianoland.

And then, "Hey! Aren't you the lady who just fell on Lexington

Avenue?" A middle-aged woman sipping coffee had been listening to me for a few minutes before making the positive identification. She approached the piano as I continued to play.

"No," I lied. "What lady?"

"Huh, you look just like the lady who took quite a fall on Lexington Avenue. It was something all right. She was just walking along not watching where she was going and boom! Hit an erected metal delivery door and went right over it!"

"Wow," I said, playing "Try to Remember" from *The Fantasticks.*

"Wait a minute, wait a minute. *You are her!* Look at your knees! They're still bleeding!"

"I don't know what you're talking about," I said as I wrapped up my *Fantasticks* medley and moved on to "Haven't Got Time for the Pain" by Carly Simon. My accuser shook her head and walked back to the lobby to finish her coffee. When my set was finished I could hardly stand.

Finding the right outfit for the steady gigs proved challenging, and it took me a little over a year to get it just right. The male pianists wore tuxedos on weekends and smart dark suits during the week, but it was trickier for women. In my first few months of playing steadies I asked Robin Meloy Goldsby how she managed to always find the perfect thing to wear. She gave me some tips. On one of her leads, I headed to the Betsey Johnson boutique in Manhattan. There among the sleek and avant-garde clothing were some real unique ensembles that stood out. One outfit seemed just perfect for Sunday brunch. Think Mother's Day gig. Think Easter. Think Sunday matinee. The long skirt was white cotton with lace eyelet trim. Paired with a red crinoline skirt liner, the skirt became slightly Southern Belle. The top was a colorful floral Lycra stretch-cotton fabric on a white background, with an open neck and peplum bottom. Small lace ruffles at the sleeves matched the lace at the bottom of the skirt. I loved this outfit. While the top was form fitting, the bright floral pattern prevented it from being overtly sexy. Instead, it was sweet. Young. I just loved it. I could picture how the skirt would fall on the bench as I played. So romantic.

As I crossed the street to the Hyatt in my new outfit the next day a truck driver pulled on his horn. It stopped me dead in the middle of the street.

"HEY! BO-PEEP!" he yelled out through his window, "WHERE'S THE SHEEP?" He and his riding buddy were hysterical laughing, and so were several people in their blue business suits who were jaywalking across 42nd Street.

But if they could only see me play *piano* in it, I thought.

One of my concert gowns was just a bit too long and laziness prevented me from taking it to the tailor. It wasn't a problem really, until of course, it was a problem. During one New Year's Eve performance for First Night Montclair, I managed to snag the bottom of the dress under the heel of my shoe. Every time I pumped the sustain pedal, a bit more of the dress would pull underneath. Rather than stop in mid-performance or admit to what was happening, I just kept going. By the end of the song I was standing, leaning over the keyboard itself, practically sucked inside of the inner workings of the piano. The show must go on.

The week before Larry and I were planning on doing the photo shoot for the album cover of *With A Song in My Heart,* I once again came to an all-too-familiar conclusion: I did not have anything to wear. The CD contained popular songs of nostalgia and romance. After picking my daughter up from the YMCA's swim class, I dropped by a fancy dress shop in Upper Montclair. This store ran ads in our local newspaper showing their elegant, fashionable and sometimes one-of-a-kind dresses. I had passed Alex's many times, but as the shop had a reputation for being very expensive, I had never gone in. Well, I figured it couldn't hurt to look and maybe get some ideas. I was close to canceling the shoot altogether. Plan B was a stock image of a Steinway.

I walked into Alex's and began to scan the racks of gorgeous dresses. I noticed a photograph of Olympia Dukakis holding her Oscar hanging on the register wall. I smiled to myself. Olympia lived at 222 Upper Mountain and I lived at 22. I sometimes received her mail by accident and loved driving over to her house to deliver it. When I was younger she was one of my idols because she ran a theater company in Montclair called The Whole Theater Company. It was in this theater that I saw Greek and Shakespearean theater for the first time performed by professional actors. She shopped here and we lived on the same street. Good sign.

I suppose I didn't realize how I looked when I walked into Alex's with my baby. With no makeup, hair pulled back into a scrunchy, jeans and tee shirt — I suppose I didn't look like Alex's clientele. Having a dripping wet baby in tow fresh from her swim lesson at the Y didn't help things. The sales ladies took one look at me and quickly put their attention back on the racks they were organizing. Except for one.

Linda had a bright smile and bright eyes, and reddish curly hair like mine. Her physique seemed a lot like mine too, and when our eyes met, she asked if she could help me. I told her I was planning on shooting an album cover in a few days and needed a dress that would photograph well. Turned out Linda used to work in Hollywood as a stylist so she understood exactly what I needed without me having to explain too much. Together we found a red dress, right off the rack, that didn't need any adjustments and didn't break the bank. I was amazed. Linda set me up with a lot of my concert attire over the years. She dressed me for Carnegie Hall, my debut in Korea, and outfitted my entire 2005 tour. Sally, the manager of Alex's, was especially kind in allowing me sale prices on a few items that had not yet gone on sale, and special fittings with designers during non-trunk show hours. While I lived in New Jersey, Linda, Sally and Pauline helped me find the most amazing concert wear.

I still adore the dress that apparently was purchased by Meryl Streep's sister-in-law and fitted to her for the Academy Awards. I suppose she ended up not going to the Oscars that year, as she never picked up the dress when it was finished. It remained in the shop's attic for seven years, and Sally didn't know what to do with it. It was officially purchased and couldn't be re-sold, and was too beautiful and expensive to throw out. One day while in the fitting room of Alex's, Sally came into my dressing room and point blank asked me if I thought I was the same size as Meryl Streep's sister-in-law. Before I could even ask her what on earth she was talking about, she vanished. She returned with the now-famous $3500 dress. It was a knockout. It was black velvet, fitted mermaid style, with silver and rhinestone beading around the heart-shaped bust line. A little velvet jacket came with the dress. I tried it on; it fit beautifully.

"Fifty bucks and it's yours," said Sally. I threw my arms around her in response. I wore this dress for my New Year's Eve concert that year and for the album cover of my Christmas CD, *The Christmas Collection*. A photo of me in the dress soon adorned the wall behind the cash register of Alex's, right next to the photo of Olympia Dukakis accepting her Oscar. We no longer lived at 222 and 22, but there we were, side by side on Alex's Wall of Fame.

My closet contained beautiful ball gowns, tee shirts and sweatpants, jeans. I never bothered to buy anything in between that would work for presenter dinners, radio interviews, CD-signings. Linda set me up with a couple of outfits that were "un-mom-like" as she put it. I felt like a million bucks. I splurged on a pair of jeans that fit so beautifully, they seemed custom-made.

"Who do you think you are, Robin Spielberg?" I thought to myself when I wore these. "These are darn expensive jeans. $180! Who are you to buy these?" But heck, they were comfortable and very flattering and I looked professional and chic at the same time. I paired them with a black peasant top with sheer cap sleeves and a lace-up bodice, black patent heels. This is what I wore to my radio interview prior to my show in Camden, Maine.

Larry was driving and Valerie was in her baby seat. She was an absolute doll the entire nine-hour car ride. We stopped for diaper changes and meals. Every time I peeked at her from my front seat she was either asleep or looking at one of her little books. We pulled up to the radio station twenty minutes before the interview was set to air live. I unbuckled the baby from her car seat. She said, "Uh-oh" and threw up, projectile style all over me.

"Oh no, Larry. She's carsick. Help!" The throwing up continued until there was no more left. Poor baby. Poor me! Larry unpacked the wipes from the diaper bag and we began our work of getting clean curbside. Larry worked on cleaning Valerie, while I started wiping my pants clean.

"Here, let me have her," I said. "We'll go into the restroom inside and clean up better in there."

Just as Larry handed our daughter to me, the unmistakable and overwhelming smell of baby poo wafted through the air. And then I felt it. Seeping from her diaper, her clothes and inching up the back of her shirt was the lava of loose hot pungent diarrhea of the most fowl kind. We were out of wipes. Oh my God.

"Larry, you go in and tell them we're here, then find out where the restroom is and come back outside and let me know how I can get to it without running into anyone! And throw this away," I said, handing him a plastic bag now filled with dirty wipes.

"Good idea," he said. Larry to the rescue.

Valerie, stunned and uncomfortable, began to cry. I bounced her as I paced on the sidewalk, my left hand completely covered in poo. I made the mistake of patting her head. Now her hair had poo in it too. Larry emerged from the building a minute later and said, "Okay, here's the plan: walk down the corridor, turn left, then another left, and there it is. I'll chat up the host."

"Got it."

The radio station's bathroom was completely white except for the floor, which was a gleaming ceramic of black and white tile. The paper towel dispenser above the sink was empty. I grabbed the one roll of toilet paper from the single stall with my free hand. I undressed Valerie and sat her in the sink. The room stunk to the high heavens in short order. I bathed her in the tiny white sink as best I could until the water drained clear. The hand soap dispenser was out of soap. Just my luck. I wet wads of toilet paper and dried her with it as best I could until the paper ran out. Valerie stood naked and wet on the bathroom floor. Now what? I looked in the mirror. I was a horror. I wet my pants and blouse with cold water. "Better to be wet than to go in covered in shit and puke," I said to my reflection. I waited. What to do now? I didn't want to walk around the station with a naked baby. I had thrown all the soiled clothes in the trash. They weren't salvageable. A knock on the door.

Larry?

"Hey Robin, open the door. It's me. You're on in a few minutes." I unlatched the lock and let him into our hideaway, quickly closing the door behind us and locking it.

"Oh sheesh. Wow. What is going on in here?" he said. I followed his eyes. Valerie had just had another bout of diarrhea, which was now dripping, down her leg to the floor.

"You're on in five minutes. They need you in there."

"Shit!" I said.

"Yes, shit! It's all about shit all right."

We started to laugh. This was insane.

"Okay, we'll get through this, Robin. I'm going to run back to the car and get a blanket for our naked child. Clearly we just take her around naked wherever we go; we don't clothe our baby."

"Yes, clearly."

I rinsed dear Valerie once again in the sink and wrapped her in her car seat blanket when Larry returned. Her disposition was so good; she knew things were not quite right, but she didn't cry. She seemed to be enjoying all the attention. I gave my hair a few strokes in the mirror with my hands and applied lipstick. In the hallway I handed the baby to Larry and told him, "Diaper her in the car and listen to the radio feed from the car, not the waiting area. I've done my best in there. I'll meet you outside when it's all over. Wish me luck."

"Good luck. You stink, you know. You are one stinky pianist," he said as he carried our smiling happy clean baby outside to the car.

"Yes," I muttered to myself. "I stink, but I *look* okay."

The bathroom looked fairly clean, but it smelled otherwise. I had not used soap on the floor or sink. Yuck. I hope it was regularly maintained. I walked into the broadcast room just in time.

"Ah, here she is, welcome to the show, Robin Spielberg!" boomed the radio host. He was a large man with a big belly and no butt. Bright red suspenders held up his pants. There was hardly room for the two of us in the room, never mind the engineer who sat on a stool in the corner, headphones over his ears, hand on the controls.

"We're so glad to have you live with us!" the host exalted to the radio listeners. "For those of you just joining us, we just played music from Robin Spielberg's *In the Arms of the Wind.* Robin is a pianist and composer with several best-selling albums on the North Star Music label. She's *live* at the Camden Opera House tonight. Robin, tell us about the show!"

During this introduction the engineer donned my head with headphones so I could hear the interviewer and my own responses. We stood side by side, sharing a mic, and I couldn't see his face. He was taller. I concentrated on his voice, his questions. I remember talking about the music, the concert details, the stories behind the songs, but I was thinking about Larry and Valerie in the car and wondering if they were okay. Then I began to smell myself. It was subtle at first, but the control room was small. Tiny in fact. It didn't take long for the stench emanating from my clothing to permeate the air. The combination of my sweaty body odor, Valerie's throw up and diarrhea on my designer $180 pants and hot mama chic blouse intermingled with the perfume I sprayed on my clothes. This futile attempt to cover up what had happened a few minutes earlier was overwhelming. I wanted to get some fresh air.

"Who do you think you are, Robin Spielberg?" I thought to myself, "thinking you could be some little hot chic mama with a baby on the road...thinking you're hot stuff to have a radio interview? You are nothing but the poop and throw up you are wearing. You stink. Literally." What a disaster. The odor registered with the radio host shortly after these punishing thoughts throbbed in my head. He pulled a handkerchief from his pocket and coughed and semi-gagged quietly into it away from the microphone before asking his next question. Surely this unbelievable stench could not be coming from the nicely dressed piano lady standing next to him. I would deny it all the way to hell.

"So what's it like traveling with your family?" he asked. The engineer coughed, and then with his head down, he pinched his nose.

"Great! It's great!" I said. "I love having them with me. It has its challenges, but in the scheme of things, those challenges are minor. I mean, some days it is just amazing, and others, well, we all have days that kind of stink, right?"

And I meant every word I said.

In my favorite dress ever rejected by an Academy Awards attendee
Photo: Larry Kosson for The Christmas Collection CD cover shoot

FROM ONE TO FIFTEEN

The first producer I worked with was truly amazing. I found him by going through the CD bins at Tower Records and Sam Goody in the "New Age music" section. I spent a lot of my paycheck from playing hotel piano gigs on music from those bins, and coincidentally his named appeared in the credits of many of the acoustic recordings I favored. A few phone calls to some recording studios resulted in my getting his number from the Rolodex of a studio in California. I dialed up my dream man in a moment of courage and told him I wanted to make a solo piano recording of the music I had composed over the last six years.

This producer/engineer had worked with some famous instrumentalists — some of whom I had heard over the stereo system in Star Magic. When we spoke, he confirmed my suspicion: he created their "sound". It was the "sound" of their recordings that garnished them good reviews and success in the music business, not necessarily the work itself. I didn't know this. I didn't know anything about creating a "sound", but I was hopeful that this man could lead the way. He seemed interested in engineering and producing my project, but there was a glitch. The producer laughed at my naiveté when I told him I was prepared to record my debut album, *Heal of the Hand*, in an afternoon.

"Can't be done," he said when I called him from the managing director's office of the Atlantic Theater Company. I was practically living in the company office in those days, my "I am a working musician only to support my nonexistent acting career" days. I could hear the smirk in his voice. "Why not?" I bravely responded.

He began to teach me. "You don't understand. Recording is

different than performing a concert. The microphone is placed closely to the piano and the recording must stand up to repeated listens. It'll take many many takes of each song to capture the music as you want it to be heard. Then I'll work to edit the best moments together. You could easily have a hundred edits or more on this record." And then he named a few very famous musicians who had, apparently, hundreds of edits on their own records.

Really?

"Why don't I send you my demo and you can see what I mean," I offered. He was certainly the expert and me green, yet I couldn't imagine what he told me to be true. I was ready. I was prepared. I was going to record my own compositions. What could be hard about that? Okay so I'll play them more than once each, I thought. That will still leave me plenty of time to get the job done in an afternoon. It was fifty minutes of piano music for Pete's sake.

After visiting half a dozen recording studios in Manhattan I selected Sear Sound for its rich and sometimes temperamental Steinway circa 1926. Walter Sear met me at the elevator door that opened to his studio.

"Spielberg," he said, in a tone suggesting we had met before, "are you related to other Spielberg musicians?"

"Why yes," I said, caught a little off-guard. No one *ever* had mentioned knowing my relatives, the musicians, only that other famous Spielberg. The *ET* one.

"As a matter of fact…my great-uncle Herman Spielberg played for Toscanini's NBC Symphony Orchestra, and my grandfather subbed there…and also played for the Metropolitan Opera House. You couldn't have possibly known that."

"I played with that orchestra," he said with a big grin. "I was a young tuba player with Toscanini. Nice to meet you."

Somehow this connection to my grandfather and great-uncle comforted me immensely and put me at ease. I had never met anyone before who knew them outside of our family and I longed for information, observations, and anecdotes, anything that could give me insight into what their experience must have been. Walter didn't give much, but what he gave I treasured.

"Oh yes, it's true," he said. "Toscanini was quite a taskmaster. Everything just so. Your grandfather must have been very good to have had played with him, and especially your uncle. Oh my, yes."

I wondered what Walter would think of my music; if he would even be there to hear it.

But my question was answered before I could even finish that thought. He introduced me to Roberta, the studio manager, and his house engineers who were busy readying microphones around the piano. They looked up at me and waved in acknowledgement and then went back to their setup routine. Walter retreated to his office and closed the door.

I opened the door to the engineer booth and saw my producer/engineer sitting at the console adjusting knobs and levers.

"Well, hello, Robin! Here you are. Ed is just finishing touching up the piano. Why don't you go check out the instrument before he leaves?"

Ed Wedberg, Steinway technician, was just packing up his tools, or his bag of tricks, as I would come to call them. He told me he placed some red felt inside the piano and that the piano was "feeling well" today, but I might experience some sympathetic ringing. If that were to happen I was to beep him and he'd come right over. Steinway Hall was just a few blocks away from his apartment.

"I'll be seeing you when you record on New York Steinways," he informed me. I take care of a lot of those. What are we recording today? Chopin? Mozart? I want to make sure I've set everything just right for the material."

"Um, no," I said. "I'm actually a composer of new piano music and I'll be recording some of it today."

"Oh. I see. Well, good luck."

I thanked him and he was off.

The stool next to the piano was a worn black artifact rich with history. Countless musicians had sat on it. Countless greats had set their coffee mugs on it. Today it was mine. I placed my bottle of apple juice and my box of fig newtons on the stool. I unpacked my new piano journal, a small bound notebook with a decorative cover, and put it on the piano bench, right next to me so it touched my body. I would know it was there. On page one was a list of songs to play for the recording and their tempo markings. The other two hundred pages were blank.

After engineer assistants Fred and Tom finished setting up microphones, my hired engineer/producer spoke to me through speaker monitors from behind the glass. Through the glass window between us I could make out the top of his head as he sat at the large mixing console. I felt very alone.

Tom dimmed the studio lights, which gave a warm glow to the wooden floors in the room. I looked around me. On the wall behind me hung a beautiful ornate-looking velvet rope and its golden tassel tie glimmered. When I got up from the piano bench to have a closer look at it, I saw there was a small plaque hung next to the tassel describing it as a remnant from the Metropolitan Opera House before it was rebuilt. I reminded myself to remember to tell Walter Sear that my grandfather was the flute in *The Magic*

Flute; and had also played the amazing flute solo in *Lucia di Lammermoor*, but as I was concentrating on remembering operas my grandfather might have played in, the Voice of Oz spoke. At least that is who he reminded me of, The Wizard in *The Wizard of Oz*. There I was in the studio, lights dim, golden light reflecting off of the wooden floor, and a faceless voice boomed from the studio monitors.

"Time to play for me," bellowed Oz from the studio speakers. "Let's hear how this first song goes." I played *Back to You,* a piece inspired by the nature of on-again, off-again romantic relationships.

"Okay, play the loudest you will play in this piece."

I complied.

"Okay, play the softest you will play this piece."

I complied.

Silence.

Waiting.

Oz then bounded into the room and began moving microphones. When he seemed satisfied he returned to the engineering room and made the same requests again. I played loudly. I played softly. After a few rounds of this, my nerves dissipated. I was getting bored.

After an hour of adjusting microphones, I recorded *Back to You* and it was just fine. Fine indeed. Oz asked if I wanted to play it again just in case.

"Okay, let's do one more."

In the quiet dim light of that room, and in the intimate setting of just me and the Steinway, I remember thinking that there was no place in the world that I would rather have been, and that I was doing exactly what I was meant to be doing in that moment. All the events in my life, the people I had met and lessons I had learned had all conspired for me to be here in this place on a chilly February morning in 1993.

The recording of the rest of the album went just like that. I played each piece a few times and moved on. I nibbled on fig newtons and drank my apple juice. I recorded my impressions in my journal so I would remember which takes I liked. I wrote a poem. I entered "the zone" and became the piano. It did everything I asked it to do, and more. Then it kind of played itself so I could daydream.

Oz could do anything. I was just the artist, the composer, and the one making the record. I had borrowed $10,000 from a real estate attorney turned fan to pay engineering and studio fees. I put the manufacturing and marketing bills on my Visa card. But it was the famous and magical Oz who was creating my unique "piano sound" and I felt very special and very grateful to have him there. He was going to take my music to a new level. He listened to each take and knew what they were about. He told me that all the fine playing in the world wouldn't necessarily translate to a good recording. The microphone technique and room sound was of upmost importance. Maybe the most important.

"You know it really is a shame," he said while adjusting a microphone for the third song.

"What?"

"That the whole solo piano thing is over…that whole George Winston thing."

I was taken aback by the remark.

"I'm not trying to be George Winston," I said, rather offended. "I've always composed music for the piano. I mean, that's just what I do."

"Yes, but that whole solo guitar, solo piano thing is way over."

"Oh c'mon," I countered. "You can't mean that. Good music is never way over. If it's good, people will want to listen to it."

He took that in. And then he looked me right in the eyes and said, "Well let's make a good record then."

"Yes," I said. "Let's."

We finished the task around 4pm. I shook hands with everyone in the room, and then left for the Port Authority Bus Terminal. Oz said he would call me in a few days after he had listened to everything.

Riding on the #33 bus to Montclair, NJ, I couldn't help feel accomplished yet let down at the same moment. Hadn't I just made my first record? Yes. And was I indeed taking a commuter bus home to my empty apartment? Yes. Shouldn't there be a party or something?

On a beautiful late February day, sunny but cold, I rang the buzzer to Oz's sublet apartment in the Village. My master was ready for me to pick up and take to the manufacturing plant.

Oz's voice came through the intercom kind of crackly. I could make out that he would be right down. I sat on the cold front step of his building and waited. And waited. I thought up all kinds of reasons why I wasn't invited upstairs to retrieve my master recording. Maybe the apartment was messy. Maybe he had a girlfriend up there. Maybe he was in his pajamas. I was freezing. I waited some more.

"Hi Robin," Oz said as he appeared at the front door about twenty-five minutes later. "Here's your master, here's a backup copy, here's the invoice, good luck." He handed it all to me in a big padded envelope.

No praise. No pat on the back. That was it? But we had become friends. No. Not friends. I had bared my soul with my music, it was true, but that was my job. And it was Oz's job to listen and do the work to record my music. Standing in the cold on the corner with the master in my hands, and the invoice in my pocket, I felt so disappointed and so alone. The high from the recording studio gone, I was just a girl holding some magnetic tape on a freezing cold day blocks away from the subway station. What did I expect? To be told I was amazing, that it was a sheer pleasure to work with me, that I was a professional, that I was worthy, that I would succeed? To be asked out to dinner to celebrate my first record? All of the above.

Richard Waterman loved my record. We sat in his Cranston, Rhode Island, office at North Star Records and he wanted to know if I would like to make another six recordings or so for his label. I was so happy I could have burst.

"You know, Paul told me I was probably wasting my time in sending you a copy since he said piano music doesn't really sell."

"Well, I'm glad you did send it, Robin. Good music always sells. The most important thing is that it is good."

Out in the parking lot, as I backed out of my parking space I felt a tap on the window.

Oh no, he's changing his mind, I thought.

"Robin, just one more thing. You know, North Star does a good deal of business with Christmas CDs. Do you think you could make one for us this year?"

"Sure," I said. I mean, I am Jewish so I'll probably have a good fresh take on Christmas music!" He laughed. "As a matter of fact," I added, "I was working with a cellist and a guitarist recently and the only common ground we had was Christmas music. I mean, the cellist has a huge classical repertoire, the guitarist knows jazz, and I'm a Broadway show/pop person…but we all know "Jingle Bells"…hey, I think I even have a rehearsal tape in the car. Here." I handed Richard the tape.

Luckily Richard was able to hear past the boom box recording, the hiss and buzz, the stops and starts of our jam. He loved what he heard, and offered to sequester our new trio for six weeks so we could concentrate on making new arrangements of traditional Christmas music without distraction. Those six weeks were magical, frustrating, exciting, exasperating, creative, inspiring, beautiful, hurtful, argumentative, joyful, and finally, triumphant. We emerged with fresh arrangements with original interludes that gave the music we all knew new life. We knew we had something special.

I insisted Richard allow me to call the famous Oz in to the session. This, I knew, would ensure the success of our recording. After all, *Heal of the Hand* was the best-selling album the label had had in over ten years and it contributed to getting the company out of its Chapter 11 debt (something I did not know about when I signed, but was privy to at a special lunch party during a toast to the CD). That microphone technique must have been very very good, because *Musician Magazine* and some of the tougher critics in the biz gave my debut CD rave reviews.

We agreed to record the session in Rhode Island in Jack Gauthier's studio; a studio the label often contracted for recordings. I stayed at my sister's house in Framingham, MA. The cellist lived in Massachusetts so he and the guitarist, Chris, stayed together and commuted to Rhode Island for the sessions. On the morning of session one (there were to be two days devoted to this record; a real luxury in my book), my sister called me into her kitchen.

"Bad news. Your session is going to be delayed. Your engineer was in some sort of accident on the way over."

"What? No! Is he okay?"

"He's okay. He called Richard at North Star who's meeting him on the highway and giving him a ride. Just wait another hour before you head over."

When I arrived at the studio and saw Oz I had to hold myself back from throwing my arms around him and thanking God he was alive.

"What happened?"

"It's fine. I was in a rental car and I skidded on the road a bit. The tire blew out. No one hurt. It's fine. Let's make a record."

Jack, our host and owner of Lakewest Studios, was quickly demoted from capable studio engineer/producer to cable wrangler, air temperature controller, and coffee fetcher. Oz ordered him around like a busboy and although I felt badly about this I knew that Oz would work his magic and allow our instruments to synergize in the mix. My stomach turned just a little when the second day of the recording session concluded and Oz told me, my fellow musicians and the record company president himself, to leave the premises so he could work on mixing the tracks...alone.

"Hmmm," said Richard. "I suppose he knows what he's doing and he doesn't need our help. Although as president of the label I have never been asked to leave the mixing room before."

"Yes, I know he does," I said. "Well, shouldn't take too long to mix this, right?"

"Don't know. Nice day. Good to be outside again."

Byron, the cellist, and Chris, the guitarist headed off somewhere for a bite to eat. I remained behind with Richard. We sat in plastic chairs outside the Rhode Island recording studio. Spring jacket weather. Hour after hour went by. My stomach grumbled.

I had a few fig newtons in my purse. I shared them with Richard. After seven hours we pretty much knew one another's life stories, aspirations, hopes, dreams and disappointments. Richard told me Oz's car accident the day before was a whole lot worse than Oz had made it out to be. Richard said when he arrived on the scene and saw the rental car completely totaled, he was surprised its driver walked away unscathed. Richard sipped a beer. I drank an ice tea I had made in the studio kitchen.

"Wow, I'm glad you didn't tell me that yesterday," I said. I felt my eyes tearing up. Perhaps Richard thought I was in love, but the truth was I wasn't in love with Oz. It was worse: I was in awe with Oz. Again I had handed over my complete trust and empowered him in every way an artist can empower someone. I held him responsible for whether or not the record would be any good.

The record was good. Very good. It sold better than anything North Star had in years. We were in my Montclair, NJ apartment preparing for a concert tour when we got the call that The Nature Company chain ordered 30,000 copies of *Spirit of the Holidays*. Byron, Chris and I thought we should celebrate somehow.

"Is 30,000 copies good?" asked Byron.

"I don't know. What's normal?" I asked.

"No clue," said Chris.

"Let's ask Oz!" I offered.

I dialed him up. I knew his number by heart. "Hi, it's Robin. I'm here with Chris and Byron and, well, we were wondering, is 30,000 copies good?"

"It's not good, it's great! There are indie records that sell 5,000 or 10,000 and that's considered a success. You should all be very happy. If this were sound scanned you guys would chart on the Billboard chart with those kind of numbers — on the New Age

Chart."

"Great. Thanks." I hung up and we opened the champagne.

We drank the champagne on the floor of my living room. We were light and free. We re-lived the recording session moment by moment. My favorite moment of the session is still memorable. It was when I finished recording "Hark! The Herald Angels Sing" in one take, my solo piece, and Oz said it was perfect in every way a take could be perfect and it was time to move on to the next piece on the list. I never heard this kind of praise from Oz again, but spent about five more projects and eleven more years trying to get it.

Although we shared a lot over the next few years, my relationship with Oz was always a little odd. We'd have months of talking to one another and then nothing. Our conversations were personal; he'd tell me of his girlfriend woes, I'd talk about grieving my father's death. Sometimes they were light; we argued over which New Jersey high school really invented Ultimate Frisbee, his or mine. Then months would pass and we'd only forward an e-mail joke on occasion. Then I'd find myself feeling lonely and bored while driving alone on long stretches while on tour and call him to help keep me awake until I got to the next gig. We'd talk for hours.

We spent days talking about the "dangerous women" he dated and the company they kept, the pitfalls of working late in a studio while trying to date people who were not in the business. There was the folk singer. Then there was the hot model wannabe singer. Her motives seemed transparent to me, but he worked endless hours on her demos until their "artistic differences" and her manic highs and lows eventually ended it all. Oz would call me, and I would drop what I was doing, take the portable phone into a quiet room and close the door. It felt good to be needed by Oz in some way, even if it was to just listen about girlfriend woes.

Usually our conversations would turn to music at some point and I would hear about all the amazing people Oz was working with. Through all this namedropping I couldn't help but wonder what Oz thought of me as a musician and as a talent. I never knew where I stood in this regard and somehow that kept me hanging on to Oz. He fed all my insecurities perfectly. On days I was down, feeling unworthy, not good enough, I found myself dialing his number. He would inevitably remind me that my insecurities were all founded. This person was working with that person. This person was the real deal. That person was on her way up. The business is so hard.

What would I do without Oz, I wondered? After five very successful recordings he was there to remind me that I was still signed to a "stupid" label and the people running it didn't really know anything about the music business. According to him, most of the musicians I chose to work with were "bozos". I kind of went along thinking maybe I didn't know much about anything and who did I think I was anyway, to trust my own instincts when famous Oz had worked with *everyone* who was *anyone*? I needed him to set me straight.

You would think I would understand that I was deluded about the nature of our friendship when he didn't show up at my Carnegie Hall debut or when he planned a trip to Italy to coincide with my wedding date. But I didn't. Instead I managed to hold it all in my mind this way: Oz was too important and too busy to bother himself with the "applause" events; he was all about the music and the rest was trivial. I was silly to feel hurt or let down; who was I to expect his support anyway? He was beyond that sort of thing and I should be too. I was lucky he called me when his girlfriend broke up with him.

A documentary filmmaker I knew in New Jersey agreed to help me with a promotional video shoot. Larry and I worked to line up a number of professionals who would support me on camera. The president of Steinway & Sons and its Concert & Artists liaison were both on board and gave beautiful interviews describing why I was a good choice for the Steinway Artist Roster. Richard Waterman, President of North Star Music, also gave a glowing interview, his voice-over accompanying footage of me walking to the stage of a New England concert hall. Oz agreed to meet the camera crew at Nola Recording studio where I had made my first demo. After the sound check and describing how we met, Oz somehow managed to steer the interview to a new project he was working on with a singer/songwriter. He praised her voice, her talents, and the nuances of her writing. He declared she'd be a big star one day. I watched dumbfounded from the control room. Didn't he know why he was here, being interviewed? After an hour of hearing of Oz's accomplishments and predictions about the future of the music industry, we called it a wrap. Larry and I reviewed the material and couldn't find one quote that could work for the Robin Spielberg promotional video.

300,000 CDs sold and several years later, I still found myself calling OZ whenever I planned to record original music, but by the new millennium I had a few CD projects that were recorded elsewhere. They all sounded fine, but in the back of my mind I felt a twinge of guilt.

"I should have paid the extra money and hired Oz," I e-mailed my friend Robin Goldsby.

"But why? Your lullaby CD sounds so good! And so does *With A Song in My Heart*," she replied. "You can do this without him… you know enough now to know what sounds good. Heck, you produced my records—you can surely produce your own."

In fall of 2007 I was ready to record my fifteenth CD, *A New Kind of Love*. This recording was my first of all new solo material since the 2000 release of *Dreaming of Summer*. I was in a quandary; I couldn't afford Oz's going rate. I found myself dialing his number anyway. I reasoned that I had taken loans before and had never recorded a CD of all new original material without him. I made up my mind that if I were to record an album of originals without him, it would be because he rejected the project outright, or gave me permission to go elsewhere.

"Why hello!" he said when he heard my voice on the phone. "Talk to me."

"I'm touring through the East Coast and was wondering what you thought about Will's recording studio in Vermont? Should I go check it out?"

This was my way of opening that door just a crack. Maybe he'd say, "Great! I'd love to meet you there for this…it'll be fun." But he didn't say that. He didn't seem to care. He said, "By all means. I know the studio well and helped Will outfit it with microphones and gear. Their house engineer is perfectly capable."

While on tour in November 2007 I checked out the studio in the Vermont woods, the one made famous by Windham Hill Records founder Will Ackerman. It was wonderful to finally meet Will and he was incredibly generous with his time even though he had a session that very morning. Will and I connected the dots of all the people we both knew, but I didn't connect much with the house Steinway. Will was most understanding of this when I called him to tell him the news.

"Will, I want to love it, I do," I said. "It's just that the studio piano…it just doesn't…speak to me…does that make any sense at all? Do you think I'm being a little crazy?"

Will more than understood. He relayed a story to me about the time his favorite guitar was damaged in an accident and he had to go without it for several months while it was being repaired. "I literally wept when I got that guitar back," he said. "The others I was using were okay, but that was my guitar, my sound, it was part of me. Yes, I understand your need to feel a connection to the instrument."

He wished me luck with my project, and as we said our goodbyes, I felt a little more than foolish that I was turning down the chance to make a record in a world-renowned studio. Several piano records had been recorded there...dozens actually. In this relationship it was definitely me, not the piano, who was being difficult, but I also knew it would be a difficult session for me unless I loved everything about the studio piano: its key dip, its resonance, its action, its timbre, its feel, its response.

I rang Gerry Putnam of Cedarhouse Sound. We had worked together a decade before on *In the Arms of the Wind* for the overdubs.

I remember Oz telling me, "They won't know how to create your sound in New Hampshire. There will be an inconsistency to your original work. You can't just go to some hick studio and expect to get the same results. Let me at least record the piano tracks in New York." And so that is exactly what I had done.

I recorded my tracks for *In the Arms of the Wind* at Sear Sound on my favorite New York City Steinway. Ed tuned. I had brought the tracks with me to New Hampshire so Gerry at Cedarhouse could record all the overdubs with New England area musicians. I have to say, it was a real pleasure to sit behind the glass for a week and not worry about my piano tracks. The New Hampshire studio was nestled in the woods and Gerry and I got on right away.

I was a producer on *In the Arms of the Wind*; Richard from North Star stopped in once or twice, liked what he heard, and left us to our creativity.

With New York studio prices sky high and the Vermont studio not quite right for me, I recalled how nice it was to work with Gerry at Cedarhouse. He didn't record my piano tracks, but that wasn't because he wasn't capable — that was because Oz had convinced me to be scared of changing "the formula". Gerry mailed some piano CDs he had worked on so I could hear how his piano recorded. I liked what I heard and booked the session for *A New Kind of Love*.

Those two days in January at Cedarhouse Sound were the most easy, leisurely days in the studio I had ever spent. The piano was a dream, Gerry was easygoing and most accommodating; the session flew by. My friend John Gfroerer, a documentary filmmaker who lives in New Hampshire, stopped in to tape some of the session. There was a beautiful snow that second day and that added to the mystical, magical quality of the afternoon. I recorded the title track, an eight-minute piece, all in one take. It felt like 1993 again when I was naïve and knew everything I needed to know; I was one with my compositions and knew exactly how I would play them.

I learned so much from Oz and I wanted so much for him to be proud of me. He taught me how to listen, truly listen to a piano, to tell the difference between microphones, the importance of consistency in playing, preparedness, the value of giving up a technically perfect take for a more "musical" one that might have a technical error. I sent him one of the first copies of *A New Kind of Love*. He never acknowledged receiving it, but then again, maybe he was just too busy to give it a listen.

A few reviewers and more than a few radio programmers mention the "G" word in the same breath as the album. When a publicist Larry and I both respected and admired told us that the CD was indeed Grammy-worthy in her opinion, we started to get excited. Our task was to reach out to the music professionals we knew to give them the opportunity to listen to the CD. When we went through our databases we realized we knew a lot more people in this business than we had thought. Oz was on Larry's list of calls to make.

"Of course you have my support," he said. Oz knew how all this worked. You couldn't just sit back and hope to be "picked" by members of the recording academy. If you wanted a Grammy nomination you needed to pursue one.

I let my imagination soar. I was full of hope, wish and desire. How I longed for some peer recognition. I allowed myself to daydream about what I would wear to the Grammy ceremony before dozing off at night. It was a stretch, but certainly not impossible. I had been to the Grammy Awards once, the year the awards were held at Madison Square Garden. I enjoyed the pre-telecast part of the show so much, where awards were handed out for not only my category (best New Age album), but to singers, songwriters and producers in folk, jazz, classical and even polka. The awards lasted for hours, but only a small segment was televised live around the world. Larry had sat next to Gwen Stefani without knowing who she was, and struck up a conversation about music and clothes. She was wearing a lovely Asian-inspired silk robe. Later in the evening she was on stage singing with her band No Doubt. We were giddy with excitement.

Larry was excited about the 2009 Grammy's too, but for a different reason. As my booking agent, having a Grammy nomination would be a good sales tool. Enya was the only female soloist to ever win in the New Age category so just having a nomination would be a nice accomplishment — something he could tell presenters about.

Cora, my newly hired publicist, wrote a lovely piece about my CD, which we emailed to music professionals along with a link to listen to the music for free. I spent evenings scouring my email history looking for names to add to the list and stumbled upon the last joke Oz had sent me. It contained cc's of about thirty people in the business, some of whom I recognized by their email addresses, some of which I didn't. I wrote a short cover note to accompany Cora's letter and hit "send". She got it right away and sent out individual letters to each person on the list. She cc'd Oz of course.

Oz called me almost immediately. He was furious. He didn't want his name associated with this undertaking. He accused me of spamming his friends.

"But you said you'd support the CD to NARAS members," I said. I had never heard him so furious. I fought back tears. "I don't understand…how were you planning on giving the CD your support if you weren't going to recommend anyone you know listen to it?"

Larry heard the commotion and picked up the extension in his office. I found my way to our bedroom and threw myself down, letting the tears come. How could I have been so stupid? I shouldn't have sent out that email without talking to Oz specifically about it first. Stupid, stupid, stupid.

Larry came upstairs and sat at the foot of the bed.

"He's really mad, Robin."

"Was I wrong?"

"Well, he thinks you were. I think we misunderstood what he meant by 'support'. I don't think he had any intention of helping you in any way and lending any credibility to your record. I don't think it would have been any different had he engineered it himself."

"What should I do?"

"He wants you to apologize to each and every person you sent the email to."

I worked up the courage to call Oz back. I apologized profusely.

"You must have been in a manic state," he said.

"No. I am not 'manic' and I never was. I think I misunderstood what you said your role would be. I've worked with a few of the people on your list and we've been sharing music jokes back and forth, so what was so wrong about sharing a music link? All I did was send a link offering a free listen. If they're offended they'll delete it. I'm getting emails like this daily from people who want me to listen to their work — looking for either a quote from me or advice or just the consideration of someone's work. I don't understand why you're so upset. Explain this to me. Please."

"First of all, your publicist is an *idiot*," he said. "Did you read her letter? She talks of your piano 'artistry'. Laughable."

"Wait a minute. That's just mean. This doesn't even sound like you. What are you saying?"

"I'm saying write an email, send it to everyone, cc me. Fix it." Click.

Another hour of crying went on before I could call Cora to tell her what had happened. Her response surprised me.

"Robin," she said, "this person is not your friend. This person is a bully. You have absolutely nothing to apologize for. The letter came from me, your publicist, not you. If anyone is to blame, it's me. I should have made certain that it was okay with the producer first to send out this particular email. But he doesn't own these people. You have contact with them too. Your name isn't even in the signature of the letter. It's mine. I get loads of emails every day that are minor annoyances and if that's the case I simply delete them. This was a very pleasant, warm invitation to listen to some beautiful music. It doesn't even ask for a vote, just a listen. There is absolutely nothing to apologize for. I am so sorry you are so upset that this happened. It should be a happy time. You made a beautiful recording. And, you *did* apologize. Not in writing, but you did and it sounded like a heartfelt apology."

I knew she was right, but the tears came again nonetheless. Oz left me at least one message after that saying he was waiting for a recanting email. It seemed ludicrous to send one. What would it say? "My publicist requested you listen to some pretty piano music, but we really don't want you to listen to it. My former engineer and friend didn't really mean to support the record you see; that was just something he said on the phone to humor me."

Larry and I watched the Grammy nomination show live. He sat with his laptop on his lap, refreshing the screen every few minutes as the announcements for the little-known categories like mine were not being made on national television. Forty-five minutes into the program he gasped. And without turning to me, he said, "It didn't happen. I am so sorry it didn't happen." The phone rang. It was Cora. She asked Larry if I was okay. I was. I was a little stunned, but okay, trying to absorb the meaning of the moment.

"Well, that was an interesting exercise," I said. "What a journey, right?" I managed a laugh.

"Oh Robin. I'm so sorry. I got your hopes up. I was so certain it would happen," she said. "The positive response to your music was absolutely overwhelming."

"You know, Cora, I have to say I really enjoyed daydreaming about it, thinking about it and working on it. But it's over now and now it is back to my real life."

In 2005 when *Memories of Utopia* was not nominated for a Grammy I bought myself a leather jacket. I called it my "I was not nominated for a Grammy jacket". What would I buy now?

A jazz artist in his '70s won the Grammy for best New Age album that year.

I never heard from Oz again.

COWBOYS OF THE SKY

Thanks to the work of Agentman husband, in 2004 I land a tour that will take me through much of Montana. I am so excited! Not only will I get to put a new pin in the big USA map that is mounted to foam core in my office, I will see a part of the country I have always longed to see. It sounds exotic to me, Montana. I envision driving from gig to gig in a sporty rental car, my maps on the passenger seat beside me, listening to cowboy music. I picture the blue sky, the scenic landscape, and the men in cowboy hats. The tour is for twenty-two engagements in twenty-eight days. Nice and busy. Perfect.

After analyzing the schedule, I realize that driving to all of these towns will be a challenge if not impossible. Big Sky Airlines offers commuter flights across and around the state, so I arrange for a few flights, make my rental car reservations and pack every wrinkle-free piece of clothing I own into my Samsonite. It will be the longest I have ever been away from my husband and daughter, but I am so delighted to be going. I get to support my family *and* renew my spirit at the same time. I leave our music businesses and home life in the capable hands of Agentman husband.

After a long day of travel via car, tram, bus, and airplanes, I arrive in Fort Benton on a beautiful November day. The temperature is 72 degrees. Montana is everything I imagined it would be. Fort Benton is a town right out of a western movie; the Grand Union, which has stood on Main Street at the mouth of the Missouri River has served as a hotel/restaurant since the beginning of time, and while it is perfectly restored, I can easily imagine gatherings there a hundred years ago. It must have been the place to be all right. Its solid brick windowless facade facing Main Street makes a commanding statement. Main Street is wide. There is a footpath next to the hotel that leads into a beautiful park. I read on the plaque at its entrance that the Lewis & Clark Trail begins here. A few blocks away stands an impressive statue of the explorers. A bridge, that seems like it has been here since Lewis & Clark themselves visited, crosses a river and leads travelers into the wilderness.

Most of the leaves have already fallen, but on this Indian summer day, the view is still beautiful, tranquil and colorful. I stroll across the wide wooden bridge. It creaks and groans with every step I take. In the center of the pass is a bench and I sit there, in the middle of two worlds, and stare out into the river for the longest time. It feels everything I have ever done in my life has led to this moment, this bridge. I will be in this beautiful state for almost a month, and I am free of mundane obligations. No family laundry, no cooking dinner, no vacuuming, no office work, no bill paying, no making beds. All I have to do is the one thing I love to do most in the whole word, which is play the piano.

I check into the Grand Union and treat myself to its posh dining room. The chef here is renowned and I am impressed with the beautiful selection of food, and especially the chocolate dessert I choose from the menu. I thank the chef personally for the meal; it is divine.

My show is being produced by a group of ladies who are warm, hospitable and very kind. The audience is lovely, and afterward I return to the Grand Union for a bite to eat and a good night's rest before the next day's travel.

Only the restaurant is closed. I go back outside. The town is closed. Nothing open. All dark. I don't remember seeing a grocery store. I'm starving. I skipped lunch in my excitement for the sound check. I pull a half-eaten fig newton from my coat pocket. It is stale, but I eat it anyway. Lesson One: small towns in Montana, which are really most towns in Montana, roll up the sidewalks early.

At 5am my alarm rings, reminding me I have a school performance at 10:30am in a town a little over three hours away. The wind and the cold take me by surprise. Wasn't it just 72 degrees the day before? I am not dressed for this, but it is winter today, about 15 degrees, and so I hurry to my car, my skirt flapping about in the wind. The rental car is not the sporty thing I imagined driving. It's a Ford Taurus. I'm lugging one huge Samsonite, one big box of CDs, and a travel bag filled with songbooks that wouldn't fit into the Samsonite without going over the airline's regulation weight. My car is sandwiched between two other cars, and it is a little tight maneuvering my luggage, so I have to lift my suitcases high overhead to get to the trunk. It's a little comical, and I feel embarrassed. I know that is silly because I am alone out here at 5am in the dark, but I can't help but have the feeling someone is watching me as I lift each heavy piece over my head, my skirt flapping over my waist.

As I put my key into the car door I sense movement behind me and jump. I turn around and see nothing. I fumble with the keys at the driver's side, and there it is again: movement from behind me. I throw my purse into the passenger seat, and pop the trunk. Okay, no bodies in there. I manage to get all three pieces of luggage to the back of the car and as I am about to lift them one by one into the trunk, I hear a giggle. Then a shriek. I turn around, but there is no one and I am so spooked by the voices in the wind, I hurry even faster. Just as I slam the trunk I hear a moan. And then

I see them. There are at least four people sleeping in the car next to mine. Seems I've woken them up. Various limbs are tossing and turning under old blue floral blankets and pillows. One sleepy head faces the back of the car and I walk around the back of the vehicle to have a closer look. It is the face of an audience member from the show the night before. No doubt. What is this middle-aged woman doing in the freezing cold sleeping in this car? Who are these people? I know I shouldn't, but I can't help but take a closer look. I am peering into the car now, my hands wrapped around my face, my nose pressed to the glass of the backseat window. The audience member I recognize is still in the clothes she wore to the show; a black sequined sweater and wraparound skirt that is no longer wrapped around. Her makeup and earrings still on, she looks like she just decided to take a nap in the backseat of an SUV, but the pillows and blankets give her away. This was her intentional resting place for the night. The others are under blankets and too hard to make out. A giggle. I am out of here.

As I drive out of town I pull out my cell phone to call Agentman husband and tell him about the gig and the sleeping car people but there is no service. I turn on the radio. There are only a few stations available and I listen to country radio. I don't know any of the songs. The commercials are for ammunition and gun shops interspersed with announcements of cattle for sale. It's funny. It's not funny. The music provides the perfect soundtrack for this lonely drive through fields and fields of nothingness.

The sky is big all right. Big Sky holds to its promise. I have never seen a sky so big. No trees or mountains or buildings to obstruct the vastness of the open sky. The cows on the little hill look like they are floating in the sky. I pull over to take pictures of them. They are huge, these cows. I don't think I have ever seen cows this big...and look; they are floating in the sky. Against the sky. If I frame the photo so you don't see their feet they will look like flying cows. Now *that's* good. I am alone on the road, so why not pull over and take a picture? As I am about to take my first photo, a pickup truck appears next to me. A very good-looking cowboy right out of Central Casting asks me if I need help. I say no, no thanks, I am fine. He then asks, "What cha taken pictures of out there?" I tell him the cows. The cows in the sky. He shakes his head in confusion and disbelief and rides off.

I am hungry and I figure I will stop for a bite to eat on the way to the school, but I don't see any signs of civilization until I get to the small town on my schedule. With about fifteen minutes to spare, I stop at a little food store, in search for a yogurt or a banana. I find neither.

I settle for a pastry that is marked "day old", but tastes like it is three days old, and a small bottle of apple juice. I then stop for some gasoline. Mr. Taurus is thirsty too. As I am paying inside, the clerk at the register asks me where I am from. He looks like he, too, was hired by Central Casting. He is wearing a flannel checked shirt, a cowboy hat that looks like its been surgically attached to his head. An unlit cigarette dangles from the corner of his sixty-something-year-old mouth.

"I came here from New Jersey," I say.

"Wow!" he says. "That's a ways off!"

It is exactly the kind of reaction I was hoping for. Someone who appreciated my effort to come all this way.

"Well, what brings you out this way?"

"The school. I'm a musician and will be performing this morning for the students and teaching a class about music."

"Music, huh?"

"Yes."

"Music. Now what do you think we need that for?"

I don't have an answer. At least not one I can give in a short amount of time. I shrug, I smile. I accept my change, and leave the gas station totally deflated. Maybe the guy has a point. What do they need me for? What am I doing here anyway? I get back into the Taurus as the wind picks up my skirt again. I turn down the road to the school. The entire school is scheduled to come to my "informance" program in the gymnasium. The janitor has placed an upright piano in the middle of the gym and hands me a microphone. About twenty students file in and sit on the bleachers in front of me. I smile at them, and they at me, and I wait. And wait. The principal approaches me and asks me to please start. Oh. Apparently this *is* the entire student body. There are a few children in each grade here and so the ages span 5 to 17. I should have known. The hallways are decorated with photographs of students from each graduating class since the school opened in the 1920s... and they all fit.

Every picture of every student who has ever walked these halls is here on a wall along some corridor in this building and there is room to *spare*. Coming from a graduating class of 700 this is really different, and I can hardly wrap my head around the idea of only having a classmate or two when I am introduced as "the young music lady from New Jersey" and it is time to begin.

This is a great group of kids. They are attentive and intelligent; their questions are smart. They participate. They are appreciative. Hands shoot up when I ask when the piano was invented and when I call for volunteers to compose a song with me. Some of the most well thought out inquiries relating to music, composition, the piano and my workshop itself come from the students I meet in

Montana. My workshop culminates in the song we co-write as a group, and I leave with e-mail addresses and hugs and thank yous. Some promise to write me, including an exchange student from Korea who tells me my music is popular in Seoul. I've gotten back a bit of what Mr. Gas Station Man managed to take away, and I drive to the next town.

I find a roadside diner. I am so happy. I am starving. I am dreaming of some fruit with yogurt on top, or maybe a turkey sandwich and a salad. Or maybe salad and a hot bowl of soup. As I enter the diner I notice a group of about twelve men on one side of the dining room. They are in baseball hats. There is another group of about ten men on the other side of the dining room. They are in cowboy hats. No one is sitting in the middle of the restaurant. All stop talking and eating when I come in. They look up. They stare. Then at once, I hear "Ma'am" while hats are tipped in respect.

The ranchers and the cowboys are eating, talking, and laughing on opposite sides of the restaurant. Still feeling the weight of their stares, I decide not to take sides. When I was in *Oklahoma* in the seventh grade, there was a song called "The Farmers and the Cowboys Should Be Friends". Well, apparently they are not. I sit in the middle of the dining room.

I look to see if there is any fresh fruit or yogurt on the menu, but no. No salad either. Eggs seem to be the safest bet. I order mine scrambled, eat rather quickly and leave. Before the door closes I hear a roar of laughter emanating from both sides of the diner.

The rest of my concerts and school programs in Montana go well, although everywhere I go I am reminded just how *different* I am from the people here and how I don't fit in. I like to imagine I am a citizen of the universe, able to live anywhere, but my trip to Montana makes me truly doubt that. I am late getting ready for a show along the hi-line of the state due to a dressing room lock out. Turns out the weather report predicted a storm was coming and the presenter had to move her herd of sheep to a safe location before coming to the concert hall to meet me. Sure. That happens. The excuse is so new and so out of my realm of understanding that I just nod and smile, unable to sympathize, empathize, understand. I hurry into the small office she opens to me as she describes the trials and tribulations of moving an entire herd by yourself when the weather is turning, as I dress into my ball gown.

In Montana, my search for a banana and a yogurt is a constant. I don't find them, but I do find an underground city in Havre. Aptly named "The Havre Underground", the remains of a saloon, brothel, pharmacy and general store constructed during the prohibition are accessible from a tunnel downtown. For a few bucks you can tour the Underground with a guide. The brochure stirs my curiosity and so I sign up. The tour is kind of cool, kind of spooky, and kind of surreal. Iron twin beds with old yellowing sheets are in the brothel, separated by decrepit curtains. Dusty cobalt blue and chocolate brown glass medicine bottles line the pharmacy counters. The general store display includes food packages from the era, wooden basket displays of candy and old soda-pop bottles. The whole place looks like a movie set, ready for John Wayne. After the tour, I go into the western wear store next door. I wonder how many people do the same thing after the tour. With the Wild West on my mind I imagine buying a cowboy hat, an embroidered denim shirt and maybe even cowboy boots. There is a purple and red pair that is just outrageous. I browse and dream, dream and browse, but practicality wins and I wind up buying a very ugly, but warm, black polartec hat.

I call Valerie and Agentman husband from people's homes

and payphones. My cell phone still has no service. No chatting to friends from home, "Hey, it's Robin! I'm in Montana just driving through the plains!" No, this is an alone trip, but I am not lonely. I meet great people everywhere I go. There is a sense of spirit and authenticity here that I don't experience in my everyday New Jersey life. People here manage to be openhearted while still maintaining their privacy. I drive most of the time in silence, accompanied by my own soundtrack buzzing in my head.

Most of my six rides on Big Sky Airlines are taken up with thoughts of how to stave off nausea. The airline has the nickname, "Big Scare Airlines", and I have learned why in just the first of my six scheduled segments. The planes are small, the rides are bouncy and pitchy, and the safety features minimal. No restrooms on board, no service, no flight attendant. On Big Sky, it's just you and a few other passengers riding over the unpopulated wilderness of Montana. I try not to think about what would happen if a plane like this went down; if anyone would even bother looking for it. Dramamine fails me for the first time on Big Sky. Everyone else on the flights are fine, just fine, but I always emerge from the aircraft green and gray, and sometimes with a little airsickness bag full and sealed neatly and ready for disposal in the first ladies room I find.

After my fifth segment on Big Sky I am to be greeted by the local concert presenter, who is bringing my next rental car to the airport for me. Prior to the trip, I called her to arrange a meeting place at the airport but she was noncommittal. She kept telling me that I wouldn't be able to miss her. I figured she must have green hair, or an outrageous sense of clothing style for her to have made such a statement. My strategy is to hit the ladies room to wash up and put on fresh makeup before heading over to baggage claim, but as soon as we touch ground I see that's not going to work.

Thing is, the airport is not really an airport at all, but a shack of sorts, with a driveway/runway next to it. I emerge from the aircraft: green, sweaty, feeling (and probably looking) like hell. I manage to smile anyway, but that doesn't fool either of us. The first words out of presenter-lady's mouth are, "Good Lord, are you okay?"

"Sure, sure. On terra firma now! I'm great."

"Okay then, here's your car for this part of the trip, and directions to the hotel. I'll see you tomorrow!" And then, "Are you sure you can drive? You don't look at all well, dear."

"No, I'm just tired. This is how I look when I'm tired. See you tomorrow."

I knew it was a stupid thing to say as soon as the words left my mouth. This is how I look when I'm tired? Yeah. That's it. I turn green and sweat like a racehorse whenever I feel sleepy. That's me.

Once in the car I roll down all the windows, take a few deep breaths. I am at the homestretch now. Just two more shows, two more schools to visit, and my life will return back to normal. I'm glad, but I'm sad. There was much about the trip I loved. But I am homesick. And airsick too. Yep.

It is snowing, and the family I am staying with is as bright and cheery about it as a Hallmark greeting card. The concert in the small town of Sydney goes well, and as I drift off to sleep that night, I think about how lucky I am. I played piano for twenty-two audiences in schools, hospitals and concert halls throughout Montana. I met great people; I saw a beautiful part of the country. Yeah, I was lonely sometimes. Yeah, I threw up on Big Sky Airlines a few times. But hey, isn't this great? Just great?

Jill drives me to the airport. My flight leaves at 6:45am, but she says it is so close, that it's fine to leave the house at 6am. This makes me nervous, as I am accustomed to being at least an hour early for a flight, but I listen. It is minus four degrees and I don't have clothes for the weather. I wear the super-duper ugly polartec hat. It is black and covers my entire head. I look like a burglar.

The van swerves a little this way and that as we travel along the deserted streets of Jill's Sydney neighborhood. I would call this skidding, but it is less like skidding and more like a drive around an imaginary obstacle course. Each swerve feels completely unexpected but there is no tension in Jill as she traverses the unplowed streets. "They never plow around here," she says apologetically. It is so annoying!" Annoying, yes.

Crazy, actually. We arrive at the airport. It is completely dark. I can't see anything. Not an airplane, not a building. We are just driving down what seems like a long narrow driveway. I don't see any sign that this is an airport. Jill stops in front of a small stone shed and puts the car in park.

"Here we are!"

"This is the airport?"

"Yes," she says. "Don't worry, they're just not open yet. It's only 6:15."

"But my plane leaves at 6:45...shouldn't they be *open*?"

"You betcha. They will be open real soon."

We listen to the radio. We talk about the cold. We talk about the winter. 6:20, 6:25. I step out of the car and walk carefully along the icy path to the door of the building. It is locked all right.

"Hang on! I'll take your picture!"

Snap.

Back at the car, Jill says not to worry.

Then we spot headlights.

"Yep, you see? Here he comes."

I don't know who "he" is so I keep my mouth shut and wait. The headlights draw closer and closer and then they disappear. The car has made a turn into the Great Beyond.

"Huh," says Jill. "I wonder why he went over there!" Something tells me I should be alarmed, but then again this is Jill. She is confident, cheery, bright, and reliable.

A few minutes later we see another light. The man driving the car has stepped out of his vehicle, and using the car headlights as his guide, opens the hangar he has parked next to. He then proceeds to hook the small *Big Sky* aircraft to his car and tugs it out into the runway field.

6:35am

The building's lights come on.

"Okay! Airport open!" Jill says.

I thank her again for her hospitality. Staying in her beautiful Victorian home has provided me with the best sleep I had on the tour.

"Come back real soon," she says as she swerves out of the lot. I enter the stone building. It is tiny; about the size of a doctor's waiting room. There at the ticket counter is the man who just tugged the airplane out of the hangar. He is also the ticket agent and pilot. There are three other people in the waiting area, all here to board this flight. I hand over my ticket; it is the old-fashioned paper kind, the only kind this airline issues. In the waiting room is a physician's scale, and a woman in uniform asks me to step on. My weight is recorded. When she sees my inquisitive expression, she reassures me, "To balance the plane, that's all."

There are four passengers on this flight. One is Santa. He is dressed in full Santa regalia. From what I've overheard, he is on his way to Minneapolis to do a stint in a shopping mall there. It's an annual gig for him and everyone here, passengers and airport personnel included, seem to know him.

Passenger number two is an older woman. She is knitting. She seems to me to be too old for this sort of bouncy adventure, but her disposition is so casual and relaxed, I assume she is accustomed to travel on Big Sky. The third passenger is a girl, possibly a college student. She is wearing flannel pajama bottoms, a tee shirt, an unbuttoned gray fuzzy sweater, a Santa hat, and a pair of furry bunny slippers. No coat. She is too cool for this trip. Way.

I am passenger number four. I am wearing my Montana-bought very ugly polartec black cap, mittens, two sweaters, a coat, long underwear, pants, and a scarf that wraps around my neck and face. My teeth are chattering.

The airport chief/ticket-taker/pilot now opens the door to the great outside and tears our tickets. We climb aboard the tiny plane. Everyone has to duck in order to get into his or her seat. There are only a few rows. I am in front. The wind takes me by surprise. It is not just gusty out here; the wind is steady and strong. When the pilots take their seats I lean over. "What are the winds today?"

"Oh, 65 at times. It's windy alright."

"You betcha," says his partner.

"Wow," I say as I lean forward so they can hear me through their earmuffs. "You know, my last flight was diverted to Bozeman because of high winds."

"Really? Well, what airline were you on?"

"Northwest."

"Oh, they're real pansies over at Northwest," says Pilot #1 as he slaps his partner on the back. They laugh.

"Well, no, no, I don't think so," I stammer. "You see, they said it was some sort of FAA regulation or something...not to be able to fly these small planes in winds that high."

"Sit back, sweetheart, and enjoy the ride," says Pilot #1. "We are not pansies. We are the Cowboys of the Sky."

I sit back. I try to relax, but my teeth are still chattering. "Oh the heat will come on once we're airborne. Can't get that going now, sorry," says Pilot # 2.

I daydream. The pilots are checking their clipboards, checking their controls. Then, "GOSH DARN IT! NOT AGAIN!"

My heart races in alarm.

Pilot #1 turns to us. "Seems like last night's guy left the generator clear on the other side of the airport and I can't start the plane without it. Anyone have a pickup truck parked here?"

Without a pause, the other three passengers are taking out their cell phones. Calls are made to friends and family members asking if they can come over to the airport with their hitch to move the generator over to the plane. This is like no big deal. It is as if the pilot asked anyone if they had a tissue or a piece of gum. This is absurd. Why do you need a generator to start the plane, I wonder. Can't the plane just start by itself...with a key or something? A few minutes pass, no one has a taker.

"Okay then," says Pilot #1. "Here's what we do. We all get out and we push the generator over. There are a few groans, but gloves are donned, scarves wrapped and my fellow passengers disembark. Pilot #2 taps me on the shoulder as I unbuckle my seatbelt.

"*Not you,*" he says. "Not you."

I do not argue, but I do wonder, why not me? I am the only passenger appropriately dressed for the weather. I watch through the tiny window as the five come toward the plane with the box-shaped generator.

"Woo-hoo!" says the old lady. "We did it."

"Now *that* was refreshing," says Santa.

The girl in the bunny slippers just takes her seat and reopens the tabloid magazine she had been reading. I look at her for a shiver, for a sign of the cold. There is none. She looks perfectly comfortable.

"Yes sir," says Pilot # 2. "Like I told you! We are the Cowboys of the Sky!"

As the plane takes off I say my silent goodbyes to Montana. We soar into the sky and are flying high now, flying in no particular direction. We are being carried by the wind and I don't care.

I think of the landscape of Montana, of Lewis & Clark, of the Korean exchange student I might meet in Seoul one day, of cows floating in the sky, of the Victorian house in Sydney, of Havre's Underground, and what it would be like to have to move your herd when the weather turns, and I nod off to sleep.

Performing in a Montana school gymnasium for the entire student body K-12

RULES OF THE GAME

In February of 2007 my glamorous career took me to Florida. Florida was not a bad place to be in the middle of winter, and I was very grateful to Agentman husband for putting the dates together. I kissed my sleeping daughter goodbye at 4:00am on an eight-degree Sunday morning; Larry helped me to the car with my luggage and I was off.

The first four engagements on the Florida tour were scheduled for the private Century Village retirement communities. Beyond each CV gate existed a whole separate world of shopping villages, medical centers, libraries, post offices, synagogues, performing arts centers, restaurants, fitness centers, and thousands of apartments grouped together in clusters. Who knew? It was wonderful and weird at the same time, or weirdly wonderful I thought as I gained entrance past the first security gate in Boca Raton. The guard had carefully examined my driver's license, asked to see my performance contract, asked where I was coming from, and, after squinting between me and the photo on my ID several times, called another office to make sure I was deserving of entry. By the time the gate lifted, I felt as though I had won something.

Each community within Century Villages had its own "clubhouse" with — you guessed it —shuffleboard courts. But the clubhouse also housed a large gym with the latest in exercise equipment, as well as card rooms and meeting rooms. Each clubhouse also housed a surprisingly large, state-of-the-art performing arts center that could accommodate thousands of people. There was entertainment scheduled nightly in some CV communities. It was one of the perks of living there; a shuttle bus picked up residents nightly from their homes for the evening's 8pm show. It was not uncommon for concertgoers to be unaware of what or who was playing until curtain time, and they didn't care. Maybe that was part of the fun of living there. A surprise every night.

The performance contract for the Century Village engagements was like no other I had ever seen. It was a simple contract, consisting of one page, but there were lots of exclamation marks throughout as well as bold, underlined, capitalized words. One of the first "rules" of the engagement instructed the performer to **NOT** speak **Yiddish** on stage because this might make the patrons angry.

"Do not assume our residents understand Yiddish," the contract stated. The contract continued with a warning that if you spoke Yiddish, the audience would **LEAVE!!!** While I paused at this section of the agreement, I realized I didn't have anything to say to the audience in Yiddish; so I concluded that clause, while weird, was perfectly okay with me.

Another paragraph of the contract instructed the performer not to take **FAKE BOWS** under any circumstance. I spent a few minutes trying to understand what a "fake bow" was. Why would anyone "fake" taking a bow? Why wouldn't the performer just take a regular bow at the end of the show?

The contract continued, "If you insist on taking a fake bow, the audience will **LEAVE!!!**" I made a note to myself to ask the stage manager about that one.

Another request that I found unusual was for the show to run ninety minutes straight without an intermission. In addition, no CD sales or merchandise sales of any kind were permitted. I found this demand most unfortunate for me from an economic standpoint. Perhaps if there were to be an intermission the audience would...LEAVE?

I estimated the woman assigned to greet me at the first clubhouse to be about 4'2", and seventy-five years old. She wasn't particularly friendly or talkative and any attempts I made at conversation were met with a simple "Uh huh." Perhaps at one time she made idle conversation with the performers but that time had come and gone. She met her assignment with the minimal requirements: she unlocked my dressing room door and pointed to where the restroom was and where I could hang my concert gown. Then she told me to wait.

When Steve, the stage manager, arrived a few minutes later, he showed me to the stage and I began practicing on the venue's grand piano. What a relief it was to finally play after all the driving, wrong turns, waiting and worrying. The hall had about 1200 seats and the sound of the piano echoed. I realized that in a few hours these very seats would be full of listeners. Silly rules, funny contracts — what did it matter? The main point was that soon I would be playing for a full house and for two hours I would feel connected and full of purpose. So what if I couldn't speak *Yiddish* on stage or *pretend* to take a bow?

Backstage, the walls were papered with 8 x 10 glossies of performers who had all performed there as part of their own Century Villages tours. There were a lot of names I didn't recognize; a lot of people fell short by a long shot of being famous, but, like me, made a living performing live. Then there were the ones I did recognize: The Shirelles, Marvin Hamlisch, Beatlemania. Then there was the photo of the buxom blonde who claimed in her autograph that she was one of Bob Hope's favorite singers. It said so. "I'm so proud to be one of Bob Hope's favorite singers! Love love love, Kathryn Harlowe."

Due to the median age of the demographic, I was asked to play my "Moonlight and LoveSongs" program, which featured music from yesteryear; film songs, Broadway songs, standards. I donned my peachy pink gown, entered into my makeup ritual, read a chapter of a novel I had brought with me, worked on the needlepoint project I had in my purse and at five minutes before curtain was told by the production manager to stand in the wings at stage right as Mark, the Master of Ceremonies, made his way to the stage from stage left.

You see, like all the Century Village theaters, this theater came with its very own Master of Ceremonies. The M.C. and the production manager ran each show. Each M.C. had his own dressing room/office, reported to the theater at 6pm, spoke with the production manager about the evening's act, changed into a tuxedo, and, finally, introduced that evening's performer. All four M.C.'s I met on this tour told me that they had done voice-over work for a living, acted on stage, and claimed that moving to Florida was the best decision he had ever made. All the M.C. men had booming voices, good stage presence, and offered me coffee. (I don't drink coffee, but it was nice to be offered.) As Mark made his way to the center of the stage, I noticed he held a Shure vocal microphone in his left hand, and a few large index cards in his right. I took a deep slow breath to relax as he began to introduce me, another ritual that tends to help me focus.

"Robin Spielberg is an internationally acclaimed pianist and composer with over a dozen CDs to her credit," he announced. "She has performed throughout the United States and will be thrilling us this evening with a mix of original and popular songs. But first, before I bring Robin to the stage, I have a few announcements."

The audience, which was still settling in, now came to a complete and utter hush.

"There will be a free blood pressure screening session in the main lobby of the clubhouse on Tuesday at 1pm." Mark flipped to the next index card.

"Due to popular demand, line dancing lessons will continue on Wednesdays from 2-4pm in the main lobby. That is 2-4pm." Next card.

"Under no circumstance will balls and racks be loaned to guests of The Villages. Residents must use *their own* ID cards when loaning billiards items to their guests." Another card.

My head began to spin.

"The Scout Club is extending their blood program through next Thursday. For just $1.50 premium, you will be entitled to up to *three units* of blood for any hospitalization you may have during this calendar year. Of course we hope you won't *have* any hospitalizations this year, but if you *do*, it is quite a deal! Imagine, you are unexpectedly hospitalized and need blood! *Not to worry!* You paid your premium, and it is there for you — blood, just when you need it." Enthusiastic applause.

"And now, please shut off your cell phones as we welcome Robin Spielberg." Mild applause, a smattering.

It was by far the strangest introduction of all time, but off I went into the pool of light that was waiting for me. I reported to the piano, said hello to the audience, and began my journey into Pianoland, my home. As I played "Hi Lili Hi Lo" the audience began to sing along. It was the sweetest sound imaginable.

Prior to the concert I did ask Steve the production manager to define a "fake bow". He said, "A fake bow is when a performer leaves the stage, but comes back for another bow. That's fake!"

"Well," I said, with amusement on my face and in my voice, "I have to disagree with that definition. That's not *fake*…that's just how you make an entrance for an encore."

"*No encores at Century Villages!*" he snapped, almost as a warning. "I mean, *some* people do it, but the audience is most likely to *leave*. It makes them upset."

It was then that I realized that this audience was really like no other. While they had choices each day, their lives were very scheduled. When they were told a concert was going to last 90 minutes, well then, it was going to be 90 minutes. Everyone wanted to get a good seat on the shuttle bus after the show after all.

I complied with all the rules.

My performance resulted in appreciative applause and a partial standing ovation, which I am still convinced would have been a total standing ovation, *if*, I had been permitted to take a **FAKE BOW.**

After the performance Mark knocked on my dressing room door to tell me there were some audience members who wanted to meet me. This was a surprise, as I knew the shuttle busses were waiting. Mark advised me to come back out in my concert dress, but I preferred to change back into my civilian clothes first.

"They probably won't be there when you come back out then," he said. "They'll probably leave."

My instincts told me otherwise. Once in my jeans and sweater I greeted a group of about ten women who had gathered by the lip of the stage. They were a sweet group and they kindly told me they loved my original songs more than the standards I played and asked why I didn't have "tapes" for sale. I explained the rules, which they declared were "*stupid, stupid, stupid*", practically in unison as they shook their heads.

"I love gardening too," said one woman with short red curly hair. "I read you like gardening. And cats! I like them too! And we both have red hair." She was quite enthused to meet me and requested an autograph and photo. I complied.

"I bet you will be well known years from now...after you are gone, dead," said the gray-haired woman at her side with a giggle. I think this was a compliment.

"I loved your story about your grandmother," said the woman with the blue purse and chemo scarf covering her head. "When will you be back?"

Before I could tell them about the CV policy of never having a repeat booking, another woman chimed in, "It is obvious you love playing the piano and you do it so well. You are a lucky woman."

I had to agree.

Telling stories in pianoland

RIDES WITH STRANGERS

Shortly into the car ride from the Minneapolis airport Doris told me that she had two vaginas. Not one, but two. We had just met for the first time an hour earlier at baggage carousel number four. Now we were driving to the venue, talking the small talk that you talk when you first meet someone — how was your flight, what is the weather like at home etc. — and in the first silence that came along, she blurted out this news. Maybe it was supposed to explain her point of reference for everything that would follow that weekend. She could state any opinion about anything at all and I would think, "Well, of *course* you think that. You have two vaginas." We drove through cornfields and long long stretches of highway while she chatted away about a variety of topics, but it was hard for me to shake that particular piece of information.

When you travel around the country as a musician, sleep in strangers' homes, ride in their cars, have dinner with sponsors and presenters and arts council board members you have never met and will probably never see again, something very odd yet freeing happens. A sense of intimacy develops. True, it is false. False intimacy, that is, but that is better than being alone and lonely. And so, everyone silently agrees in this crazy business to just pretend to know one another a whole lot better than they actually do. Because performing artists breeze into town as quickly as they breeze out, there is no getting-to-know-you period. There are only a few days or hours to become the best of friends. I am guilty myself of sharing the ridiculously personal with the absolute stranger. I like to think of it as free therapy. Obviously I am not the only one.

Carl in Ohio told me all about his marital woes only five

minutes after we met. I guess he figured I was an artist and the "sensitive type", but most attractive to him was that I was held captive in his Ford pickup and had no choice but to listen. For three hours we traveled from airport to venue in the middle of Ohio through a terrible ice storm. The weather had slowed traffic down to a crawl. And so I clicked my tongue and shook my head when he told me he wasn't getting the respect and attention he needed at home. I sighed with disapproval when he told me of being passed over for the promotion at the concert hall he worked in. I nodded in sympathy when he told me his teenage daughter was not interested in going to college even though the venue he was affiliated with allowed for 100% tuition reimbursement for his kids.

"That's terrible," I said. "It's too bad she can't see what a great opportunity that is," I continued. "Maybe one day she will. Let's hope."

"Yes, let's hope," he said. "I'm glad somebody understands."

Yes, somebody. And for a moment, I really thought I did understand.

Betty was having a terrible fight with the board of directors of the arts council where she served as head of booking. After my sound check she showed me to the dressing room where I hung up my concert gown before going with her to meet several members of the board for dinner before the show. As I unpacked my dressing room bag Betty complained, "Hardly anyone on the board wanted me to bring you in, you know. I had to really really convince them! No one had heard of you, and then when I played them the music from your press kit, no one could figure out what kind of music it was. Was it classical? Pop? Certainly not jazz. It was amazing I managed to get you booked at all."

"Oh, thank you, Betty. It sounds like it was hard to convince them but I'm glad you did. You know, I get that a lot — about people not being able to categorize my music. I just call it 'new music for piano', but neoclassical fits just fine too. I don't know."

"Oh, I didn't convince *everyone*. There are a few who are pretty darn mad that you're the season opener. But, well, you're here. Let's just say I won that battle."

I spent most of that dinner trying to figure out which board member hated me most.

Doris's vaginas were an entirely different matter. Instead of belonging in the TMI category, I would say it belonged in the *way* too much information category. We might have been talking about our kids. How worried mothers get. How I often wondered and fretted about what sort of future my own child would have. Her teens were struggling with this and that, and then wham! Out of nowhere, "You know, I've had my share of struggles. I mean, I have two vaginas!"

"Excuse me, what did you say?"

"Yes, two. I had some pain, you know, down there and no one could figure out why. Well, upon further...*investigation*, it was discovered that a few inches into my vaginal canal there was another opening that was actually another vagina."

"That's pretty unique, Doris. Did you have to do anything about it?"

"No."

"Oh. Good then. That's good."

"Do you mind if we stop at the Costco on the way over to the tennis match?"

"What tennis match?"

"Oh, my son is in a tennis match at his high school.

I promised him I'd go. And the Costco is on the way. He's all out of Hot Pockets and he really loves them for his lunch at school."

I wanted a nap. I wanted a shower. I was hungry. But Costco and tennis match it was.

The Costco was huge. There were food samples being given out by servers in white jackets and chef hats. We indulged as we continued our chat.

"Are all the Costcos in Minnesota as big as this one?" I asked.

"Not sure. Oooh, look! They have those candles I like."

"Didn't you need to get Hot Pockets?"

"What are those? Oh yes, yes I do. Thanks for reminding me."

Sitting on the green-painted wooden grandstands of the high school tennis courts, I questioned my life's purpose once again. Here I was in a Minnesota suburb watching a high school tennis match with complete strangers. I had no connection to this place, to these people, to this match. It was as if a spaceship had dropped me off and I landed here. Doris talked to me during the match about antiques, woodworking and her husband's endless amount of unfinished projects that were in the garage.

"I'll show you. After the match." And so she did.

Doris's house and garage were filled with beautiful grandfather clocks, tables and cabinets from all different eras, all in disrepair. Some were sanded down waiting to be stained. Others had parts missing and needed new wood ones cut and attached. Some just needed a coat of varnish to be perfect, but nothing was finished. The house looked like an antique dealership. I visited each piece with Doris and her husband as if it was a new friend that needed to be introduced.

"This clock belonged to a man in town who sold it to a dealer in Ohio who couldn't unload it. Well, he was stupid! The finish was not original and the clock wasn't keeping time. I came across it and brought it back here to restore. It's been here four years but I think by next year this time she'll be back to how she was when she was first built in 1902!" Doris rolled her eyes as she escorted me once again to her car for a ride to my hotel.

Conversations with strangers I knew I would never see again have occasionally gone to that deep meaningful place. Questions posed to me by complete strangers have opened doors to better understanding of my own life's purpose and journey.

"Why do you think you want to perform? How does it feel to you?"

"When did you first know this is what you were going to do for the rest of your life?"

"Do you miss acting? New York?"

"Do you think you'll travel for the rest of your life for the love of the piano work or do you think at some point you'll have had enough?"

"Who do you think encouraged you the most musically? When people talk about the Robin Spielberg *sound*, what do you think they mean?"

"Describe your songwriting process. Describe your relationship to the piano. How do your husband and daughter feel about the time you spend with your music? What would you do if you couldn't play the piano anymore?"

Are these not the questions that need to be asked and answered in my life and isn't it only strangers who would dare to ask them?

On occasion I am surprised by my own answers, and sometimes learn something along the way about a complete stranger I never thought I'd learn. Truly fascinating things. For example, a woman can actually have two vaginas for most of her lifetime and never even know it.

Signing CDs after a concert in Seoul, Korea 2006

I AM A GREAT PENIS

It was autumn of 1996. I was performing a concert in Newburyport, Massachusetts, and at the end of the show, I took my bow and exited stage right.

I could hear the applause of the audience swell with each step I took. I had the sinking feeling I might have to go out and take another bow. I waited a few moments to see if the applause would die down, but it did not. I don't think I had ever experienced that kind of enthusiasm before. I decided not to take another bow; that seemed pretentious, but the stage manager stopped me on my way to the dressing room and asked me to please get back on stage and play an encore.

Uh-oh. An encore? I hadn't planned one. What would I play? I re-entered the stage and was met with thunderous applause. It was embarrassing. It was wonderful. I took another bow, and sat back down on the bench. The audience quieted and they sat down too. They expected something fabulous. What to do? I had ended the show with "Ireland", one of my grandest pieces. And then, perhaps out of habit from my Grand Hyatt days, I began "doodling" at the piano while trying to figure out what to play. The "doodle" was the opening bars to Pachelbel's "Canon in D". You know it. It's a familiar piece. You've probably heard it a zillion times. In fact, it is one of the most over-recorded, overused, overplayed pieces of music in the history of the world. Why I started playing this, I will never know, but it must have been angels whispering in my ear that night because it was the smartest thing I could ever have done.

Even smarter was that I didn't know how to play the song in its entirety. When I got to the point of forgetting how it went, I did

265

what came naturally: I improvised. It was scary but thrilling to be doing this in front of an audience this large. I forgot where I was. This was not the Hyatt. This was a concert hall. I remember having no idea how to get out of the circular pattern of the piece and come to a conclusion...until I did. I was relieved. The audience was surprisingly enthralled.

From then on, whenever there was a call for an encore, I played the "Canon in D", improvising it as I went along. It became my signature encore. I never played it the same way twice; rather, I relied on my improvisational skills that it would somehow just work out, and it usually did.

"I suggest you record the piece, or stop playing it as an encore," Larry said when we got to the hotel one night after a show. "You don't know what it's like to be the bearer of the bad news at the CD table. It's really not fun to see so many of your fans unhappy. I'm not used to it! Everyone wanted that one stupid song." And so, when the *Dreaming of Summer* recording session wrapped, I told the engineer, "just one more" and I began playing take after take of the "Canon", each one a little different. I still had never properly learned the song; so I made it up as I went.

I selected my favorite take of the day and, still a little embarrassed for recording the piece to begin with after so many had done so before me and had done it well, I didn't call it by name on the CD tray card. That was probably the dumbest thing I have ever done. Instead, I listed the piece as "Bonus Track" for listeners to discover. Fans of the encore piece were told at the concert that this CD had their favorite song of the evening. Everyone was happy.

One day a long e-mail came in from a young woman living in Seoul. She asked me if I had ever seen the television program that had used my version of the "Canon in D" as part of its sound track.

When I replied that I hadn't, she explained that there was a very popular Korean drama that was loved for its beautiful story as well as its musical score. My version of the "Canon" was played during the most romantic moments of the drama.

I was flattered and flabbergasted at the same time. It was certainly wonderful that my music was selected for such a popular TV show. It was certainly awful that it was used without my permission and without recompense. When my new Korean friend told me I could buy the DVD set online, I didn't hesitate. I plunked down $80 on my credit card and bought *A Winter Sonata* known in Korea as *Gyeoeul Yeonga*. I figured having "the evidence" in hand was the first step toward compensation.

The DVD set arrived within a week. I popped in the disc, selected "English Subtitles" in the set-up menu and began to watch. My plan was to fast-forward through the series while searching for my music track, and to takes notes that I would then report to ASCAP, but within five minutes of watching *A Winter's Sonata*, I was hooked. The cinematography, the storyline, the beautiful actors…they were all so appealing. A thrill I can hardly describe overtook me when just a few minutes into the first episode, the main characters boarded a bus, looked at one another with affection, and the music cue that accompanied the moment was unmistakably *me* playing "An Improvisation on the Canon in D" from *Dreaming of Summer*.

I decided then and there that I had nothing to be upset about. First, I did not compose the famous "Canon in D". Pachelbel did. Four hundred years ago. Second, the music that was used was really a short "music cue"; there was never more than a few bars included; it could have been anyone playing, really. But it wasn't; it was me.

I watched all the episodes of *A Winter's Sonata*, often with a box of tissues on my lap. "Canon in D" came on every few episodes during the drama's most poignant moments.

I was sorry when the story ended but my husband was glad to have me back. The drama piqued my interest in modern Korean culture. It amazed me that not only did folks in Korea recognize the music cue; they recognized it as *my* playing. This took a sophistication I didn't come across often at home.

Several months later a Korean record label contacted me. The label was interested in my music for Korean distribution. I was thrilled. *Dreaming of Summer* would be heard half a world away! It was not lost on me that this happened to be the CD that contained the "Canon" as its "bonus track". Mr. Kim called one day to go over the logistics.

"Miss Spielberg!" he said. "Is it really you?"

"Yes," I replied. "It's me. Robin. Nice to hear from you, Mr. Kim."

"Miss Spielberg! I have few things to discuss in matter of record. So can we do it?"

"Go ahead…I'm listening," I said.

"K. Now, we as prestige record company of utmost importance and reputation in Korea would like to make changes to current record. This okay with you?"

"What kind of changes do you have in mind?" I asked.

"*Dreaming of Summer* not good title," he said. "In Korea we do not dream of summer. You see, it too hot. That not make any sense. So title of record: I have determined it's no good."

"Oh, I see," I said, feeling a bit humored by Mr. Kim's dilemma. My brain was also busying itself trying to find an alternate solution but Mr. Kim beat me to the punch.

"We think other title of song on record good title: *Remembering*

You. That is second song on album and very sentimental, very sweet in nature. Good cry piece for remembering someone."

"You know, Mr. Kim," I started, "I think that is a great substitute. That will work fine."

"Miss Spielberg!" he shouted. "Another matter!"

"Yes, Mr. Kim?"

"Also the cover of the CD no good."

"Really? Why?"

"Your picture on it!" he said, as if this were an obvious problem.

This objection hit a little closer to home. Larry and I worked hard on the artistic direction of the CD packaging. *The Dreaming of Summer* cover was featured on the cover of *Discmakers Magazine*, a premiere resource for indie CD duplication, as a fine example of an indie CD cover. Plus, I thought, what is wrong with having the artist's photo on the cover? I have to admit I liked the way I looked on the cover.

I was silent as these thoughts whirled in my head. Mr. Kim continued, "Photo of American girl not going to sell in Korea."

"Oh. Well, if you explain it that way," I acquiesced, "I see your point. What do you suggest the cover should be?"

"Oh, we can put flying eagle! Or we put pretty tree in winter scene."

"I imagine that would work well," I said, thinking that he was looking to create a Windham Hill-esque cover of a dormant tree in the winter snow.

"Thank you for your understanding of these matters, Miss Spielberg. And now there is one more matter of importance to tell you. This is concern of order of songs. Sequence not good for Korean market."

"I'm not sure I follow, Mr. Kim," I said with courage. "The

sequence of the songs is something I have thought of carefully. I worked to create a certain journey for the listener; there is an arc to the album set."

"But, but, but, Miss Spielberg! You must understand, your big hit at *end*. Big hit cannot be at end of record!" Mr. Kim declared, his voice having now risen in both pitch and insistence.

"Mr. Kim, what big hit would that be — do you mean *The Canon*?"

"*Canon!*" he exclaimed. "Yes! *Canon in D*! Big famous piece!"

"But Mr. Kim, I didn't even write that song. I just arranged it. And so many people have already recorded it," I said, in defense of my original sequencing.

"Let me put it to you this way, Miss Spielberg. You…you are a big penis. A great penis. You bigger than Michael Jackson. You need big hit not at end of record, but close to beginning! This will make nice record if we can accomplish these three things," he finished.

"Okay then. You go ahead and make these changes. And please do send me a few copies of the new release when they're ready." When I hung up the phone I was exhausted.

Within months I received the Korean CD and a wire transfer to my bank account. I brought *Remembering You* with me to my pedicure appointment in Montclair, New Jersey, at the Korean nail spa. There, the employees gathered around me to read the Korean liner notes.

"Oh, I see you like cats!" said Jenny. "You have song about it!"

"Ah, very romantic vision of music," said Mr. Sun, the owner. "We like this."

"So the Korean liner notes make sense?" I asked. "The grammar seems okay — it is easy to understand? I know sometimes things get lost in translation."

"Oh, this looks like nice music. We will listen to it in shop. You famous pianist! We didn't know! Oh…so this is why you never do polish on hands! Only feet!" said Jenny.

"Yes," I said. "This is why."

A few months later I shared the news with Jenny and Mr. Sun that I had signed to an artist agency in South Korea. My first concerts and television appearances were being planned for the following fall. Oh the *Canon in D* had served me well.

I spent long weekends learning the music from *Winter Sonata* with a cellist and guitarist who shared the bill with me in Seoul. We met at the Atlanta airport for our flight to Seoul and together we experienced spicy kimchi, the Korean subway system, visits to Buddhist temples, ancient palaces, and of course the Seoul Arts Center itself. To say it was exciting to perform for such a large audience would be an understatement. It was amazing and exhilarating to have all the elements so perfectly in place. The hall was beautiful and acoustically sound. The piano was phenomenal. The lighting and aesthetics of the stage were perfect in every way, and the audience itself most responsive and enthusiastic.

The concert was taped for Airiang Television, a broadcast company that services all of Asia. The autograph line following the performance was long, and the concertgoers approached the table with broad smiles on their faces. Many held up their cell phones above their heads. This gesture seemed akin to rock concert audiences holding up lighters to salute the rock band; we didn't know quite what to make of it. The camera phone had not taken off yet in the U.S.

Two years later I was invited to return to Korea; this time as a solo artist. The trip revolved around my newest CD release in Korea, also for some reason called *Remembering You*. The twenty-song compilation was released the day of my first concert in Seoul. I was especially excited to visit the port city of Busan on the far eastern side of the country.

Hae-Kyun, my agent, and her assistant, Rosa, met me at the airport. Their smiling faces gave away their excitement at my arrival and we embraced like old friends. It felt great to return to Korea. After the long airplane journey and ride to my hotel, Hae-Kyun said,

"You have choice of having dinner tonight with myself and Mr. Kim from Telecom Company, or rest tonight and dinner tomorrow."

"Perhaps dinner tomorrow would be better," I said. "I do feel tired from the travel."

"Oh no! What you say?" yelled Hae-Kyun with a frown and an admonishing furrowed brow. "Mr. Kim waiting for us in parking lot! He in car! We have reservation! We go tonight! Late!"

I had forgotten that many of the questions posed to me in Korea were not really questions at all, but rhetorical possibilities. I was expected to politely go with whichever one Hae-Kyun was leaning toward. I was tired and a little out of practice.

"Great idea!" I said. "Just give me five minutes to freshen up."

My room was a comfortable suite and as I brushed my teeth and changed clothes I tuned into the World Series, which was airing on the military channel. It was still yesterday at home and here I was going out to dinner in the U.S. version of tomorrow. The World Series was yesterday's news.

Hae-Kyun must have done some research, for she had concluded after my last visit, that not all Americans like Korean kimchi. Hae-Kyun and her boyfriend (another Mr. Kim) took me to a lovely Italian restaurant in Seoul. We were each handed large menus. The tables were made of dark thick wood and the surroundings and ambience could have passed for a restaurant in any city in the USA. The waitress had to refill my water glass several times before we were ready to order.

"So, what is it you will have?" asked Hae-Kyun.

Before I could answer, she said, "It is our opinion that you should order this combination." She pointed to a meat dish that came with vegetables and hot red sauce. I am not a fan of spicy sauces, so this dish was not on my short list of possibilities.

"Actually, I was thinking the ravioli looked good," I said politely. I was still scanning the menu for other options.

"That not good. I never had that," said Hae-Kyun. "You must eat what would be good for best physical optimal condition for concert. You order this?" She once again pointed to the meat selection.

When the waitress returned, Hae-Kyun reached out and collected the menus on the table. She ordered first, and then Mr. Kim. The waitress never once looked at me before leaving.

"I order for you," Hae-Kyun said rather matter-of-factly.

"And now," she continued, "Mr. Kim will show you new cell phone that not in America yet. This phone brand new. He works in big position for KT, which is big telecom company in Korea. This company is a sponsor of your concert, so look at what he shows you."

Mr. Kim slowly and proudly took out the cell phone device from his breast pocket and placed it on the wooden table. At first glance it didn't look out of the ordinary, although its sleek metal design was a bit on the futuristic side. Holding the object, he demonstrated, "Here is keypad for dialing. Very usual," he said, peering over his glasses at me for a sign of understanding. I gave it.

"And of course you can listen to music, use wireless, plug into computer. But this — this is most good..." Mr. Kim took the already slim cell phone and slid it apart and then unfolded another hinged section that revealed a computer keypad.

"This also computer for Internet, e-mail, fax communications. Also, you can watch television on the screen. You like this?" A broad smile crossed his lips and then he began to laugh. "It's so good, yes?"

"Oh yes," I said, duly impressed. "This is, as we would say in America, very *cool*, Mr. Kim!" I was really amazed at the invention and turned it over in my hands, so surprised by its light weight.

"You will get this in U.S. soon. Maybe even next year."

Mr. Kim smiled in delight at my enthusiasm and interest.

The last time I had visited Korea I remember someone looking at my iPod with curiosity. It turned out the interest was really in seeing an MP3 player that clumsy and big. It turned out my brand new iPod, a first generation version that was cutting edge in the U.S., was archaic compared to the devices in the Electronics Mart in Seoul, a building that housed hundreds and hundreds of booths of the latest gadgets, gizmos and computers. It was there I saw MP3 players in every color and shape, some so beautifully designed they could be worn as jewelry.

I scraped as much spicy sauce as I could off my entrée and chatted with Hae-Kyun and Mr. Kim about the week's itinerary. Hae-Kyun, a petite woman with fine and delicate features, devoured her meal leaving nothing behind.

"You not finish!" she exclaimed, when she saw my plate was not clean. "You must finish for best optimal physical condition for concerts!" Mr. Kim nodded in agreement.

"Oh, it's been a long two days of travel. I've eaten enough. I'm fine," I said.

Hae-Kyun's response was to shake her head in disapproval, but I had grown used to this from the last visit. As my agent for Asia she saw her role as part manager, part booking agent, and full-time nanny.

Because I had traveled alone to Korea this visit, Hae-Kyun's assistant, Rosa, was assigned to me, to be my guardian, translator and companion for my time spent outside concert halls. Rosa was in her mid-twenties. She had long black silky hair, wore wire-rimmed glasses and modern clothes. She picked me up at my hotel and took me on a stroll through Seoul that gave me a walking tour of downtown. It was a clear, crisp and sunny October day. We enjoyed a sushi lunch and took in an outdoor folk-dance performance played out in traditional costumes. Rosa's translation skills came in handy when I found a souvenir I wanted to purchase. I had learned a few key phrases for this trip from the Pinsleur Korean tapes, but outside of saying hello, goodbye, thank you, thank you very much, nice weather we're having, have you had lunch yet? How do I get to...? I was lost. It had taken me two full months just to nail those phrases down, and Hae-Kyun seemed both impressed and amused at the airport when I rattled them off while waiting for my luggage to appear on the conveyer belt.

"You blending better in Korea now!" she said. "Audience will appreciate this effort."

I had grown comfortable enough to walk the streets in certain sections of town, and ventured out the next morning prior to my rehearsal to seek out the vendor I refer to as The Glove Man. The Glove Man, as I recalled, was usually situated with his cart near The Sock Man. He displayed his wares on a large wheelbarrow but could always be found in the Namdaemun Market, located in a part of Seoul, which was frequented by foreigners like myself.

These streets were lined with tailors and seamstresses with tape measures around their necks standing outside their shops. They solicited passersby to have custom shirts, suits and dresses made. I had heard the prices in Seoul for custom-made clothing were incredibly reasonable and that anything could be made in a matter of days. I was told that a good seamstress could just look at a photo in a magazine of a dress and copy it no problem, but that this would take one week and several fittings. I was leaving for Busan in a few days' time, so no custom made concert gowns made of Thai silk for me, but a girl can dream. I wandered into several silk shops just to gaze at the beautiful fabrics, before stumbling upon The Glove Man in a narrow alleyway talking to his friend The Sock Man. I bought several pairs of leather gloves to bring back home, and cycling socks for Agentman husband. These socks ran about $8 at home, but were just under a dollar here, so I bought enough to last him a few cycling seasons.

"Did you find the socks and gloves you were looking for?" asked Hae-Kyun at the concert hall. I told her I had. "I not understand this. You not have socks and gloves in America?"

"Actually, we do," I said, "but I think they're all made here."

"Oh. So same thing then?"

I didn't know what to say. The socks and gloves in Korea were *so cheap*. I promised her that in Busan I would look at the items more unique to Korea like jade, amethyst and mother-of- pearl decorated items.

As promised, both concert performances in Seoul were full and well received. While I played the three new Korean ballads solo, I was told that in Busan, a well known opera singer would be singing two of them and I was to accompany her during her guest spot. I was scheduled to fly to Busan with Rosa so there would be time for me to rehearse with the diva. Hae-Kyun was taking the train and would meet us there.

The plane ride was only an hour in length. It surprised me that this commuter flight used such a large airplane and was filled to capacity. Rosa explained these flights ran frequently as businessmen needed to travel back and forth between Seoul and Busan often. As far as I could see, we were the only women on the flight, and surely I was the only foreigner.

Rosa and I checked into a hotel right on the sea; I could see the Busan Bridge outside my hotel room window. My room was 'American style', meaning its bed was not a futon on the floor, but a typical king-size bed to which we 'foreigners' were accustomed. The floors were a beautiful warm wood that looked brand new since guests were expected to remove footwear upon entering the room. I couldn't wait to go out and explore this city on the sea, but Rosa warned me that Hae-Kyun expected me to rest so I could be in "best optimal physical condition" for the next day's concert. Hae-Kyun was en route to Busan and would meet us for dinner.

I flipped through the television channels and checked out the dozens of QVC type channels. Although most all the Korean women I encountered were very slight in build and small-breasted, these shopping networks sold an inordinate amount of bras. The commercials were hysterically funny. I had never seen anything like them. Small-breasted women with sad faces were transformed into happy buxom women standing tall with chests out. Their padded bras changed their lives forever. And then there were the commercials for the toilets like the one in my hotel room. They did everything. They came equipped with heated seats with adjustable temperatures, a radio, several washing settings (including the one I call the Roto-Router setting), a seat vibrator, a reading light, telephone and adjustable seat heights.

That night's dinner in the traditional Korean restaurant was delicious. I had finally revealed to Hae-Kyun my distaste for spicy foods, something I was worried would offend her since this is the main characteristic of the country's best-loved dishes.

"Oh! I see. What a shame your system cannot do these foods," she said. "But no worries, we have other things for you." And with that Hae-Kyun managed to order wonderful Korean dishes for me without the spice. Heaven.

I could tell that there was a change in Hae-Kyun ever since she arrived in Busan. She seemed fragile, a bit tired, and a bit nervous, on edge. Often she and Rosa would embark on long animated conversations while I ate opposite them. It seemed they were disagreeing quite often. Hae-Kyun would raise her voice and give off a sigh of disgust. Rosa would then look at me and offer a polite smile. During one of these conversations I mustered up the courage to ask if there was a problem.

There was a long pause, and then looks at one another. Then Hae-Kyun started.

"Other people who sponsor concert give us problems," Hae-Kyun said.

"What kind of problems?" I asked. "Is there anything I can do to help?"

"You do not worry as we will resolve issues. Very delicate in nature. Has to do with CD sales. Record company that release your new CD should sell CD at concert, yes? And yet other concert sponsor said no, that cannot happen," said Hae-Kyun with a very distressed look on her otherwise serene face.

"Well, that doesn't make any sense," I began. "I mean, the whole reason for the timing of this tour is to coincide with the release of the CD."

"What you say?" asked Hae-Kyun.

"Coincide...same time. It is the idea we do CD release and concerts at the same time, right? You had said the record company was a sponsor of the concert."

"This is correct," said Hae-Kyun, "but promoter not reasonable and now what to do. Makes me angry."

It seemed to me at that point that a simple conversation between all parties would resolve the situation, but when I offered this Hae-Kyun pounced.

"No! We cannot show we are upset. We go along."

There was no more discussion.

The special guest on the concert bill in Busan was a plump soprano. I was sent the three songs she would be singing a few months prior; two were Korean pop ballads and the other a song I knew quite well having recorded it myself on my CD *Unchained Melodies*. The song was "Moon River". Her guest spot was top of Act II. The songs were all melodic and enjoyable enough to arrange. I wasn't worried.

The opera singer arrived after I had been practicing for about twenty minutes. She strutted on to the stage along with an entire entourage: publicist, agent, photographer, manager and wardrobe consultant. She handed her coat, white gloves and hat to an assistant and gestured for her crew to sit down in the audience. Without a word or nod, she simply pointed at me when she was ready for me to begin the introduction to the song. At least that was what I supposed she wanted, for me to start the song.

I didn't need to know this woman or comprehend Korean to

understand she was deeply unhappy during our brief rehearsal. She would sing and stop, sing and stop, point at me and then embark on a tirade to her entourage and my agent in loud angry Korean. This happened again and again. What was she saying? What was the problem? Other than her humorously bad English pronunciation of the English lyrics to "Moon River" I thought it all went quite well. The diva stormed off the stage after the last tirade, her publicist, agent, photographer, manager and wardrobe consultant following. Interesting. What had just happened? What was wrong? What did I do? My stomach began to turn. At my insistence, Rosa reluctantly translated the diva's last five-minute tirade. She managed to do it in one sentence:

"Singer thinks she will rest now in the dressing room, and piano player will stay here and practice more to become more good."

It was a mystery. My accompaniment was right on the money. It was the singer's pronunciation that needed a little work. *Moon River* sounded like *Moon Livah* and the line about being a huckleberry friend sounded like *my huckleweckky wend*, but what was an American gal to do? I stayed behind in the big empty hall and practiced through the songs a few more times while everyone else went to lunch.

The concert went without a hitch, except for the huckleweckky wend part, which no one seemed to notice but me. The audience loved it. The performance struck me as incredibly surreal and ridiculous and funny. I bit my cheek hard so I wouldn't laugh while I played. Here I was performing with a diva singing in Seoul who was singing in Korean and she was singing *Moon Livah* in English before a crowd of thousands. Did it get funnier than that?

A nice long CD signing line formed after the show and without a second to spare, Hae-Kyun appeared in the wings to hurry me out into the lobby. She began to run through the underground hallway and when we got to the grand lobby she yelled at me to keep up. "Don't keep audience waiting! They not like it! Lose sales!" she shouted as she continued to run. Faltering in my heels, I did my best to keep up with my spitfire agent who was yards ahead of me on the marble floor. She kept turning to me and shouting "Hoowie, hoowie...people wait!"

Many hands moved and adjusted tables and chairs. A seat was pulled out for me. I was practically lifted and situated into the chair while someone else placed a black Sharpie into my right hand. Because this was not my first concert in Korea, the scene was familiar. Friendly, happy faces with hands thrusting forward programs for signing and cameras at the ready for photos. And a happy surprise: the record label executive had her own table alongside mine and was happily selling the new CD offering. I never did find out how this all got resolved, but I'm glad it did.

My suitcase, filled with silk table-runners for friends, wallets to give as gifts, socks, gloves and Korean tea, and all my concert outfits, would barely close. By the time I was dropped off at the airport, my mind had left Korea. To my surprise, Mr. Kim, the music manager, was there at the ticket counter. He had been waiting for me. I did not expect to see him again. Mr. Kim was wearing a custom-made black suit, starched white shirt and blue tie. He was holding a long tube, about eight feet long, under his left arm.

"Hello Robin!" He could hardly contain his excitement.

"Hi! What a surprise! Are you traveling today too?"

"No, no," he said with a charming smile. "I came here to meet you and to surprise you with this." He put the tube down so it rested vertically on the floor like a pillar.

"What is it?"

"It is big poster of *you*! Very big. We all signed it after concert. All your friends who worked on concert. You take it home!"

My mind began to race. How the heck was I supposed to get this thing home? And what was I going to do with a giant poster of myself?

"Thank you! Thank you so much. That is so kind of you!"

"You are most welcome. And now I must go. I hope again we meet and maybe by then you have good cell phone and music player! You are a very good penis and you need these things!"

And with that, he turned on his heels and walked across the shiny white floor of the airport to the double doors that led into the sunny Korean morning. I had already checked my luggage and was carrying a rolling carry-on and large purse. I tried managing the tube under one arm but nothing doing. I tried balancing it on top of my carry-on bag. It fell off, time and time again. I struggled with what to do. I decided to trash the darn thing. It would never be allowed as carry-on luggage anyway. Half way down the corridor to the gate area, I regretted my decision. I felt rude, unappreciative. I went back. The tube was still standing where I had left it, by the trashcan near the ladies' room. I spotted a travel cart and decided to try that. It was awkward, and I think I knocked into a number of Korean travelers with the poster, but that gave me a reason to speak a little Korean. I said *Shil lyeh hamnida* as I walked to the gate, to no one in particular, knowing every few seconds someone would get jabbed with the darn thing. When it was time to board, the flight attendant, as I suspected, stopped me. I figured if the poster had to get thrown away, at least it would be Korean Air who made that decision, not me. But that didn't happen.

"Oh, this is a big package you are taking," said the beautiful Korean Airline attendant. All the attendants were beautiful. Their uniforms were classic navy wool worsted skirt/suits that were custom fit. Each attendant wore her black hair slicked back with a white silk orchid flower and had a small pink silk scarf around her neck tied into a square knot. They looked so refreshed and awake, this crew, and they looked like this after the flight landed too.

The attendant asked, "So what is in tube?"

"Well, it is a poster of...of me."

"Ah you! You musician?"

"Yes, I play piano. I was here for concerts."

"Oh yes, I know about. You did concerts in Seoul and Busan. Sorry I did not come. Okay, we will put in bottom of plane for you and then you pick up at end when you get off plane. Just wait for it, okay?"

"Thank you so much," I said as I boarded, and added, *"Kamsahmnida."*

They say the third time's a charm.

On my next and third trip to Korea I was paired with a percussionist who hardly spoke any English. It didn't matter. He was amazing. I had no idea what we would be doing together on stage, but by that time, I didn't waste my energy worrying. I knew that somehow, it would all work out. The percussionist was thrilled that I gave him an 8-minute solo to go crazy on stage, and that he did. He pounded his drumsticks on the piano, the floor, the bench, the music stand. He had the audience howling and screaming for more. By the time we played the love theme from the movie *The Godfather* ("Speak Softly Love"), the audience was insane. Next to the *Canon in D*, this song is my 2nd most popular arrangement in Korea. The drummer and I rehearsed it just once, and he followed along and hit the cymbals and used brushes on the snare just at the perfect moments to add drama in all the right places. It was as melodramatic as music can get and awfully fun to do, and I knew it was a one-time thing. That kind of over-the-top playing would never fly here in America.

I met Chiwoo again at a fashion show two nights later. I had no idea I was going to be playing at a fashion show in Korea when the tour was booked. I was told it was a benefit for a children's cause… and it was. But there was a fashion show too, and I followed the runway. The piano was placed on the runway and my music was accompanied by a slide show I couldn't see that depicted images of the children who would benefit from the evening's fundraiser. I was glad not to be mired with the details and glad not to have to understand what anyone was saying. I was there to play piano and that I did.

There was the death of a dignitary when I had first arrived in Korea and two of my concerts had to be cancelled as a result. In America you can still go to the movies or see a show or concert if someone in the government dies, but not in Korea. That would be disrespectful. All public performances in performing arts centers were cancelled for the week. I was paid the cancellation fee, but felt badly that Hae Kyun would lose money on my tour. On the other hand, it was nice to have unexpected free time to explore. So much for the Sock Man; I found the "real Korea" on this trip and shopped and dined where the foreigners did not go. The promoters of the concerts arranged for me to have my own little tour bus, which was extremely silly, and a staff I didn't need. I think one person's job was to make sure I had enough water.

At the third concert, all six staff members were stage right waiting for me to start the show. One gave me a tissue I didn't need.

Another handed me a cup of water when I wasn't thirsty. Someone else asked me if needed to lie down. What? And then, Hae-Kyun approached me moments before curtain.

"So Robin. Big discussion here about start of concert," she said to me in the darkness of the wings. We were at the LG Arts Center in Seoul. It was raining and I could hear the audience in the house and the slight pitter-patter of the rain on the concert hall ceiling. There was a black and white video monitor mounted in the corner of the wing, and all the staff members were now gathered around staring at it with concerned faces.

"What do you mean? You want me to change the order of the songs?" I asked.

It wasn't unusual for Hae-Kyun to change the order of the set, or select which dress I would wear. Unlike the "hands-off" agents in America, the agents here were very "hands-on".

"Well, I was talking with promoter and the manager of the hall, and we think that it would be best for you to play one song. Just one song. Then get up and take a bow and then we will have an intermission break."

"What?" I whispered to her incredulously. "That can't be what they want."

"Yes, yes. That would be best. That is what they want. Just go out and play one song. They will dim lights now. You go. Then get up and take bow and come back here."

"Hae-Kyun, that is so strange. Why?"

"No time for questions. We have to start. Please do as we say."

As I turned to face the stage entrance I saw Hae-Kyun being approached by several concert team members. I imagined they were asking her if I was going to comply. I nodded and smiled to them. I wouldn't let them down, but man, this was weird!

The lights dimmed and I made my way to the piano. As the lights came up on me, the audience applauded, glad I was there, but all I could think about while playing "Dreaming of Summer" was that I would be abandoning them for heaven's knew why in just a few minutes. I took my bow after the four-minute song as Hae-Kyun had instructed, and quickly exited stage right. I'm sure my face was flushed.

"Yes! You did great," she said. "Now let's go look."

I followed the stares of the staff members to the overhead monitor. The house lights faded up ever so slightly and in the monitor we could see people hurrying down the aisle to find their seats, programs in hand. There were hundreds of them.

"Okay, you see? We have latecomers. We do not want to embarrass them. You go out again and you will start concert again. Play "Dreaming of Summer" again. They will not know they were late."

It all came together. I had just honored those who were on time by starting the concert on time. For those who were late because of the rain, I would not embarrass them; they would not know the concert had begun. Brilliant. My experience told me that Koreans were so piano savvy that they would enjoy hearing "Dreaming of Summer" again and comparing the two renditions. I was just thrown because it wasn't really an "intermission break" that I had taken; it was just a false start. Hae-Kyun's meaning had been lost in translation.

"If this ever happens again, Helen," I said, calling her by her American name, "just tell me to do a 'false start'.

"Oh, that is what it is?"

"Yes, that is what we just did."

"I like it. False start. Like pretending to begin."

"Yes, pretending."

I did not come home with an enormously cumbersome poster, but the percussionist did sign a pair of maracas to give to my daughter manufactured by a company with whom he had an endorsement deal. It was an omen; she took up percussion the following year.

With Helen and her daughter after a concert in Korea

I THINK I'LL KEEP MY CLOTHES ON

I think I'll keep my clothes on. That was my first thought when I was told that clothing was optional at the Sweethollow Resort. I was scheduled to perform a concert at Sweethollow toward the end of my tour through Montana and Idaho.

Bebe and Chuck, my hosts during my first trip through Montana in 2004, were very enthusiastic about the nudist resort they would eventually own, and the lifestyle of "naturists". I knew this because within ten minutes of being inside their Ronan, Montana, home, I was shown vacation photos featuring life at Sweethollow.

"Isn't it great?" said Bebe as the vacation video played on their television while we sat on the sofa, a photo album spread across our laps. The photos were pretty atypical as far as vacation photos go and, well, quite shocking. I tried to take in what I was seeing without registering surprise or worse yet, too much interest. Bebe and Chuck were a married couple in their mid-fifties and admitted to having grown children from their previous marriages who found their parents' vacation preferences horrifying. I tried to stay neutral. After all, they were my hosts. I was their guest, having agreed to a good deal of "home hospitality" along the tour to save on the producers' expenses.

The photo album contained pictures of people of all ages, shapes and sizes. They were playing croquet, walking hand-in-hand, swimming, or just standing around...naked. They were wearing sunglasses, visors, and sneakers, but nothing else

"Oh! I know you have questions!" squealed Bebe. "Everyone does. Ask away!"

And so I thought, okay…if there was ever a time to learn about a nudist vacation, I suppose now was the time.

"Well," I said. "Umm".

I tried to think of a good question, but I didn't know where to start.

"Oh! I know what you are going to ask!" says Bebe. "I just *know*! Well, let me assure you, *nothing comes up*!" Bebe and Chuck burst into laughter and exchanged knowing glances.

Bebe repeated with a wink, "*Nothing* comes up!"

Chuck added, "You know, vacationing at Sweethollow is not a sexual experience. People don't go on a nudist vacation to gawk at one another. It's all about feeling free and easy in the skin you are in. By peeling away the clothing you are peeling away these layers that hide who you really are."

"Without clothing we're all about the same," he continued. "Nudism promotes self-esteem, acceptance of body image, clears social strata issues, and is really a lot of fun."

"Okay" I said. "What about…what about…hygiene? I mean what about sitting down and stuff?" I asked as I tried to avoid the image on the VCR now showing a pretty intense volleyball game at the resort.

"Oh. Well, everyone brings along a towel wherever they go and they sit on their towel. What other questions do you have? You must have more!"

I tried and tried, but I couldn't think of any.

"We wear sunscreen, and of course when it makes sense, a sweater. It's cold in winter!" said Bebe with great enthusiasm. I could tell she was looking for a sign to see if I was near conversion. Chuck was working on a fundraiser mailing and I offered to help seal the envelopes that were laid out on the table. The conversation was diverted for a while as we stamped, sealed and folded.

Agentman husband knew Bebe and Chuck were naturists and so when he called to check in on me we decided to take him on a little ride. I overheard Bebe telling Larry what a great sport I was being and how they turned the heat up nice and high so I wouldn't be uncomfortable. Then she stifled laughter as she handed the phone to me.

"What is she saying, Robin?" Larry asked, with just a slight amount of alarm in his voice. "Are you really all naked over there?"

"Well, you know what they say!" I said brightly. "When in Rome! I mean Chuck and Bebe are used to being naked in their home all the time and it seemed rude to make them wear clothes just because of me...so I decided, what the heck!" But then I burst out laughing and the jig was up.

Now it is several years later. Larry has booked another trip through Montana. It is coming up soon. Real soon. I am excited about this tour because I will be traveling to parts of the state I hadn't seen before, and this time I will have my own piano technician along with me. Clive Thompson will be driving the Steinway grand from Salt Lake City all the way to Glendive, Montana, which sits in the far eastern portion of the state. From there we will caravan through the state from concert to concert putting a few thousand miles on our vehicles. It promises to be a scenic adventure, and no small airplanes will be involved.

When Larry tells me that Chuck called to see if I would not only perform again in or around Ronan but also in Idaho at the Sweethollow Resort, I'm not sure the offer is serious. I recall a story I heard about a band that decided to play naked at the resort since their drums and guitars hid their privates sufficiently. It was a hot day and so they thought this was a practical idea, and they felt real hip, in proving they were flexible and cool, not "hung up". That feeling didn't last long though. Just moments into the second set one of the musicians got stung by a bee you know where.

Now Larry is asking me about the gig. Is this a dare?

"Maybe I'll do it," I say in his office while sitting in the one and only chair that is my favorite perch in his office. It is off-white, soft and cushy, and it gives a window view of the horse farm down the road. I sit here often while waiting for him to finish up a phone call so we can discuss business, what's for dinner, Valerie's homework or the roster booking schedule. I also sit here when I am just in need of a break. Somehow listening to Larry sell concert dates for our artists on the roster soothes me. When I've had enough, I retreat back to my office to carry on with contract work, bookkeeping and filling music orders.

"So what will it pay?" I ask.

"Well, you know it's typical of the tour. Pay is not great in the Wild West; you know that. It's an additional engagement for you that pairs nicely with the date the next day in Challis, Idaho."

"Okay," I say. "Whatever. Not a big deal. Just tell them I'm not playing naked."

I figure I will just do my best not to look at the audience, or if I do, imagine them with clothes on. After all, I don't have "hang-ups", do I? Maybe it will be a cold day and the audience will be wearing sweaters.

A tiny part of me wants to perform naked. If there was ever an environment appropriate for this fantasy, this is the one. I mean, what's the big deal? Why does everyone giggle and make fun of these resorts anyway? As Chuck explained it, he was hiking in the woods one day and realized that the trees were "naked"; that the woods were natural, the animals naked, and he was the only being hiding under layers of clothing. He felt "one with the world" and his environment when he peeled it all off. Makes sense. I try to convince myself.

I was naked in a co-ed sauna once. I was in Germany working on producing a recording for my best friend, Robin Meloy Goldsby. She took me to this incredible wellness center equipped with pools, saunas, and mineral baths. It seemed natural to disrobe in this environment. Men, women and children were enjoying the spa in the buff and to have clothes on would have been ridiculous in this situation. I sat cross-legged in the sauna and felt pretty relaxed amongst the strangers. It wasn't until the people in the room began passing a giant jar of honey and painting it on one another (for the health of the skin) that I felt a little out of my element. I mean, I could sit naked in a sauna with strangers just fine, thank you very much. But someone painting me with honey was another story. I tried to be nonchalant, but suddenly it dawned on me that here I was a Jew, naked in a German bathhouse. It was suddenly too much. I excused myself from the hot room and let the cold waters of the pool cool me down.

It was part of the hot sauna ritual to rinse with icy cold water after the honey absorbed into the skin. Goldsby went for it. I remember her having difficulty with the shower faucet and an older German man came over to assist. Despite her objection, he reached over her shoulder, turned on the faucet, snatched the hose from her hand and started spraying her with the ice-cold stream from head to toe. She screamed in horror, delight, surprise, I don't know what, but I saw the steam rise from her body as I doubled over in laughter. "He got me in the hoo-ha!" she yelled, after the man seemed satisfied that she was sufficiently cooled.

I had been naked many times at the Russian Turkish Baths on 10th Street in Manhattan. During my NYU days my friend Karen and I frequented the baths on Wednesdays, which was designated as "Ladies' Day". There we caught up on the week's events while breathing in the eucalyptus-scented steam, taking in the heat in the "HOT ROOM" or enjoying a drink from the juice bar while sitting in our robes and flip-flops.

The bathhouse is definitely an appropriate place to be naked. The concert stage is another story.

A week from the start of my tour I am told that my trip to Sweethollow will include a special "Meet and Greet Robin" dinner to help promote the weekend. In addition to the "clothing optional" dinner, there will be a Q & A session with about 12 guests regarding my creative process.

"This itinerary is getting interesting," I tell Larry as he shakes his head and smiles. He reminds me it was my decision to take the date and as my agent he simply "fields offers".

I call the Steinway dealer in Salt Lake to discuss this part of the tour, but the owner is on vacation. I reach Clive, my assigned technician and piano hauler, and tell him about the Sweethollow gig. I figure if he is upset about the circumstances this would give him a chance to back out and then get me out of the situation. I tell him that the resort folks promised he didn't have to see any skin during the moving of the piano; they would time the piano delivery and tuning accordingly… but Clive just laughs. He is not afraid of the naked people. Or so he says.

During a layover at an airport in Pittsburgh en route to Columbus, Ohio, I reflect on how I have felt about my body over the years. I have felt good, strong, athletic, fat, skinny, underweight, flabby, fit, sexy, unappealing. Certainly the people who go on naked vacations are, for the most part, not fitness freaks. I struggle with my issue. Am I fearful of others judging my body? Am I that uncomfortable with it myself? What I do decide is that I don't have to analyze any further. The purpose of my visit to this part of Idaho is to perform a concert and it is paramount I am prepared and comfortable. The next few hours of my flight delay are spent trying to figure out what does one *wear* to a performance at a nudist resort?

Just past the resort gates Clive and I are greeted by Chuck in all his glory, a beach towel around his neck. I recognize his face, of course, from my trip through Montana a few years prior, but not the rest of him. He puts his head inside Clive's piano truck and tells him where to park. Inside a naked Bebe at the front desk greets me. She shows me to my room. The "great room" that will house the concert is filled with guests both sitting around and milling about. They are reading newspapers, working on their laptops, chatting on chairs and sofas. Everyone sits on a towel and looks quite comfortable. The guests are in all shapes, sizes and ages. Several nod, smile and wave at me. I am given a tour of the exercise facilities, pool, hot tub and library. Everyone looks rather silly with their privates flopping about but within minutes the shock of it all dissipates. Clive busies himself with the moving of the piano on to the stage. I am given lunch and find that sitting down with some of the male guests at the dining tables is more comfortable than standing up. For a while I pretend they are in bathing suits since I can only see their chests and arms and heads. This works for a while.

"This is so freakin weird!" Clive says when we have a moment.

"I know, I know…but this is them and this is us and that's okay, right? I mean, they can do what they want and be how they want here…and we can be how we are…" I am struggling for the right words, but I am speechless, really. Clive has summed it up very well. It is freakin weird.

The "Dinner with Robin" guests number about 14 and I am being told stories of how some of the guests became nudists. I suppose many of them are hoping I will become a nudist between the time I have dinner and the time I take to the stage. I nibble at my dinner. I am seated next to Dick, an ophthalmologist here with his wife. Earlier in the evening Dr. Dick had challenged me to a game of Ping-Pong. Larry must have told Chuck about my ninja-like Ping-Pong skills. Dr. Dick turns out to be a good player and I win by only two points, but in the second game I win by a greater margin. Several times the Ping-Pong ball hits him in the testicles and bounces off them during play. I pretend I don't notice and so does Dick. Now we are sitting at dinner and everyone laughs at my joke, "I beat Dick's pants off in Ping-Pong," I tell them. The conversation switches to eyesight, contact lenses and Lasik surgery. It is freaking weird.

I perform the concert in black velvet pants and a silk top. I figure I might as well go for it. I enter the stage wearing a robe and take it off so I can say that I "disrobed" at Sweethollow. The audience is a friendly bunch, and they greet me with great enthusiasm when I take to the stage, but when I make a joke about the evening being a real "first" for me — that I had never played in pants before — a lady in the balcony row shouts out, "TAKE THEM OFF" and there is thunderous applause. I respond by telling the audience that I am naked before them; they will hear the very essence of my soul that evening through my music, and that while I am not a nudist, I thank them for their warm welcome. Nods and smiles, but I think they are disappointed in me.

The concert goes well, although it is hot in the room. Clive, while finished with his work, decides to sit in the first row and stay for the concert. I am glad that someone else from the outside world is experiencing this with me. I sell out of CDs and songbooks at intermission and do not have any left for the short remainder of the tour. I feel proud of myself for being a sport and I am proud of Clive too. Earlier in the evening Clive had volunteered to work on a dog of a piano belonging to the resort and the guests/members are very appreciative. It is at last playable. They are appreciative of me too, but I am relieved when the evening is over. I am exhausted from the drive, and the amount of energy it has taken to look every person I have spoken to directly in the eye.

After signing release waivers, the guests pose for a picture with me at the piano. It is the only thing I will have to remember the oddness of it all.

The audience loves my show, but unfortunately that means I receive a standing ovation, something I could have done without.

Afterward Chuck asks me if I regret playing with my clothes on.

"Not really," I reply. "I mean, you know, when you sit down at the piano, everything kind of spreads. It's not flattering, especially in the thigh area."

"Well," he says, "next time you come, we'll design special thigh covers just for you!"

I agree to that, but somehow I don't think there will be a next time.

After the piano is safely loaded on to the climate-controlled truck, Clive and I retreat to the quiet of the library near our rooms. We sit in wingback chairs and discuss religion, nudity and pianos. We come to the conclusion that the evening was somewhat of a letdown. The most fun part was the anticipation of coming to a nudist resort to play a concert. The jokes, the kidding, the curiosity, the shocked expressions on the faces of the people we actually told about this stop on the itinerary — these were the best part. The actual playing of the concert wasn't any different than any other place I have played…except the audience showed a lot of skin.

I was hoping that I would learn something new here — that the nudists had something to tell me that I didn't already know — but I found the opposite to be true. I learned that I could be comfortable in my own skin and still keep my clothes on. I learned that being nude in front of others doesn't mean you are necessarily sharing the essence of yourself. You can do this without taking off your clothes. In fact, I just had.

With a Song In My Heart **photo shoot**
Photo: Larry Kosson

PART VI
IT'S ALL IN MY HEAD

BEAUTIFUL DREAMER

They wouldn't let me see her. I still had a fever and could not be allowed into the neo-natal intensive care unit; it would be too risky for the babies, all of them fragile and most born prematurely.

Valerie's chances of survival were slim and I longed to hold her close. Larry went from NICU to maternity unit, maternity unit to NICU all day long, all night long. He reported to me hourly, assuring me constantly that our one-pound miracle baby would be okay and that my worry, my panic and sense of failure were all unfounded. The doctors' concerned faces and advice that we prepare ourselves for the worst told me otherwise.

I had already held one lifeless baby in my arms; Valerie's twin had succumbed to the infection that risked my life and that of the twins. I did not want to ever have to hold another lifeless baby, but my mind would wander there. It seemed that every minute I had to work to snap my thoughts back to a positive place, to a place of hope, to a place where there was a future.

On the fourth day Valerie began to slip away. Weighing 12 ounces, her under-developed lungs filled with air by an oscillating ventilator were becoming irritated by the very machine that was keeping her alive. Her heart, while healthy, had its PDA valve still open — a condition common in babies that did not take a breath on their own after birth. Her body, unable to maintain its own temperature, was in a constant state of flux. Born sixteen weeks early, she would need to develop outside the womb until she was full term. The neonatologists described this journey as a "roller coaster ride". There would be highs and lows. They had seen babies born weighing as much as four pounds who didn't make it; they had seen babies as fragile as Valerie come through. Some babies had grown to healthy weights only to succumb to necrotizing enterocolitis (NEC), a serious gastrointestinal disorder, days before their scheduled release. Because babies at this gestation could not run a fever, diagnosing an infection involved detective work, doctors' hunches and great observation. As we would see for ourselves, the NICU was a place where hearts were broken. It was also a place where miracles took place. Larry told me time and time again, our story would be the latter.

On day five I still had a fever and was beside myself. Confined to my hospital room, I only wanted one thing, and that was to see my baby. I asked Larry to bring some of my CDs from home. It occurred to me that perhaps he would be allowed to play them by Valerie's station. My music — it was "Mommy's Voice"; perhaps Valerie would be comforted to hear it.

The nurses gave Larry the okay. We didn't know it at the time, but they had assessed the situation and concluded that our daughter was not going to live much longer. What harm could it do to grant us this one silly wish?

The NICU was a bright noisy place. When I finally saw this for myself on day seven, I was shocked. I had pictured a quiet, low-lit room where doctors and nurses spoke in hushed voices. A place of healing for the most delicate of human beings, surely the atmosphere would be peaceful. But no. It was all hustle and bustle, a unit with the feel of a busy ER. The fluorescents burned brightly 24/7, the monitors and medical drips buzzed, chimed and chirped, doctors' beepers went off, the PA system beckoned medical personnel to come here, to go there. Even with the rule of parents and grandparents only as visitors, it felt crowded and over-populated.

"Larry," I cried from my wheelchair. "You lied to me. This is awful, just awful! You said it was all okay!"

"It *is* okay. All these tubes and wires and machines are a little confusing and upsetting at first, but once you understand what they are all doing and how they are helping Valerie recover, you won't be afraid of them. You'll be comforted by them."

What was he talking about?

Valerie's eyes were black and blue and sealed shut, closed like a newborn kitten. Her body was naked except for a diaper, no bigger than a pocket-sized tissue. Her mouth was bandaged to hold the intubation tube in place; heart monitor and blood pressure leeds covered her chest. Wires seemed to be coming from everywhere. An IV had been inserted into her ankle, but her wrists, arms and legs were all bruised from previous failed attempts at these locations. So fragile was she, that there was a sign on her resting spot that read "MINIMAL HANDLING PLEASE" in capital letters. Her skin, thinner than tissue paper, could not be touched. Too small for an incubator, she rested on a cotton padded rolling cart, and when she was weighed, she was lifted, cotton batting and all, on to the scale. Valerie had weighed 17 ounces at birth with a thumb on the scale, meaning the NICU nurse, knowing how much we wanted to save her, had weighed Valerie while exerting slight pressure on the scale with her thumb. This would insure that she was over the "saving weight" of one pound. Now, without the help of the thumb, Valerie weighed in at 12 ounces — the weight of a can of soda.

Larry had been right. After I learned the purpose of each procedure, instrument, monitor, and medicine, I felt more comfortable at our daughter's side. I learned how to read her vital signs on the screen. I knew when she had an episode of apnea before the siren sounded; I could tell when she was comfortable and when she was agitated. Unable to cry, perspire or suck, the clues to her well being could be told by the color of her skin, the numbers on the monitor screens, the chemistry of her blood tests.

After I had been officially discharged, my new home was this corner of the NICU where our daughter lay clinging to life. Larry and I went home only to shower and sleep. Very soon we were known as the experienced parents in the place, helping new parents learn how to scrub in properly, advising them on who was the best nurse for communication, where to eat on a break. Over those next weeks, we watched many couples who had come in with worried faces go home with happy ones, babe in arms.

Having a son or daughter in the NICU is always a traumatic event, even if it is only for a short time. To comfort the new parents who were particularly upset, a neonatologist would escort them over to the area where we were sitting. Often crying, sometimes sobbing, sometimes pale with fear, they would stand at a distance beside the physician within sight of our seats beside Valerie. In voices they thought we could not hear, the neonatologist would use Valerie, Larry and me to give them perspective.

"See *that* baby over there — that baby was born weighing just about a pound at 23 weeks. Her twin didn't make it. She is very very sick. She needs heart surgery, but her veins are too small to accommodate a pic line so who knows if she'll live long enough to get that surgery. See that machine next to her making all that noise? That is an oscillating ventilator. Her fragile lungs cannot handle a regular one; this one provides constant airflow as she does not have the ability to create blood pressure. A nurse must monitor that machine 24/7 to create it for her. She has had several life-threatening infections already, and is not responding to medication at present to fend off the latest one. Now *that* is a sick baby. *Your* baby weighs 5lbs and just needs bilirubin lights for a day or two. Then you will all go home and forget this place. But *that* family over there? That family could be here for months, or the baby could slip away in the night."

The couple would then cheer up, nod sympathetically in our direction if they caught our eye, but usually they would just walk back to their baby's incubator thoroughly humbled and incredibly grateful not to be us.

I often sat at Valerie's side working needlepoint. Larry read, sometimes aloud to Valerie. Unable to get to the two-pound mark, the neonatologists worried Valerie would not be able to get the much needed PDA surgery to close that heart valve. On October 22, 1999, exactly 4 weeks after Valerie's traumatic entry into the world, we arrived at the NICU to find a team of doctors staring at our baby.

"Today is the day," said Doctor Kamptorn, a short spitfire neonatologist who was the team leader for Valerie. "I dreamed all night about this situation," she said in her choppy Asian accent. "How do I get pic line in? Even the line the veterinarians use for kittens do not fit. She too small. Then I think of it! A big idea! I have Doctor DeCampli — heart doctor from Children's Hospital of Philadelphia — he is on the helicopter right now to come here and fix this heart valve. Without that, child will not live much longer. Must do this today."

"But, but...wait!" I objected. "We're not ready! I have to call the insurance company for clearance...and how will the pic line get in now? What's changed? She isn't two pounds yet. She's not ready!"

But I was taken by the elbow by Dr. Sun. He told me Dr. Kamptorn had an idea they all thought would work to get the pic line in. Once the line was in, the next hurdle would be moving Valerie to the OR. It would take a team of doctors walking a slow steady pace to the elevator, down the hall and into the Operating Room. She would be taken off the respirator and kept alive with manual air pumps and her blood pressure would be managed manually as well. The plan was in place. This was going to happen.

It took the better part of an hour for the team to roll the small cart containing Valerie the thirty feet to the elevator door. Counting together, breathing together, they moved along in synchronicity inch by inch with grace and intention to those elevator doors and then disappeared, leaving the two of us to wonder. It was a dance I will never forget — so purposeful, so intense, so slow.

After an hour on the nurse's station phone to the insurance company, Larry told me to just hang up. The surgery was happening, with or without their approval. Our bill, which was now in the hundreds of thousands of dollars, became meaningless to us, as did everything else like the world news, bad drivers who cut us off on the way to the hospital, the upcoming presidential election, food choices, the latest fashions, the buzz on the latest movies and electronics. Time was standing still and our entire life's meaning was our darling girl.

Why in the world did we love her so much? We hadn't exchanged glances. I hadn't held her close. I hadn't touched her save for an index finger across her forehead — a gesture permitted just this past week. We didn't know one another and yet she was all we knew. All our hopes, all our dreams, all our reasons for being were in this little baby. It was too late not to be attached.

The surgery took hours. Or minutes. Or days. It took forever. It happened so quickly. I don't remember.

In a rare lapse of sensitivity, the staff had us wait for our news in the maternity ward's waiting room. The room was filled with happy faces, balloons, food baskets, baby magazines, Proctor & Gamble and Johnson & Johnson samples of baby products. It was here that family and friends greeted new mothers who were departing the hospital with babies on their laps, balloons tethered to the arms of the wheelchairs.

Photos were taken, laughter was abundant. It seemed like one cruel joke, to be here among these people. I had nothing in common with them. These mothers had no idea. They had given birth to healthy babies and were on their way home. They didn't know what a NICU was. They didn't know about the babies that lie in there, sick and struggling for life. They didn't know about the heartbreak on the fourth floor, and they certainly didn't know why we were sitting there with long faces. The jubilance around us was too much to bear.

After an hour or so Larry and I wandered around the hospital aimlessly until coming upon a chapel. It was empty, so we went inside. And waited. And prayed. And waited. And prayed. I wrote a song in that chapel called "Turn the Page". My lyric had a happy ending and I left there feeling like we were all going to be okay.

Dr. DeCampli recognized Larry before we were formally introduced. In a small string of ironies that began with Dr. Kamptorn's treatment of Larry's sister's child many years ago, Larry had taken Dr. DeCampli's photograph for a medical ad. As a leader in the field of pediatric cardiology, he sometimes was asked to appear in ads in medical journals and magazines to endorse a medication, new technology, or medical programs. Dressed in blue scrubs, we could see the smile in his eyes before he removed the mask covering the smile across his lips. There was no need for words. I fell into his arms and breathed thank you, thank you, thank you while he reached out with his free arm to embrace Larry.

"She did great. Everything is fine. She's stable and strong and will be back in the NICU in a few hours. You two get something to eat and come back...but first wait..."

The surgeon reached down into a pocket and removed a small plastic rectangular case the size of a razor blade.

"I have a little token for you — something for you to show Valerie when she grows up."

He handed the case to Larry.

"Go on, open it. There's a tiny hinge there."

Larry opened the case, but we didn't understand its contents.

Dr. DeCampli explained. "These are titanium clips. I don't know why the company packs them this way. Once the box is open it's no longer sterile and I can't use the remainders. I only need one for a PDA surgery, so I give them to the parents. This is the clip that I used to close Valerie's heart valve. You can show her one day. As you can see, the clips are no bigger than a staple for one of those mini staplers."

"And how do you like that," said Larry. "Made of titanium, my favorite material. My bike is made of titanium. Light and strong."

"Well, that's also your Valerie. She's light and strong. The scar is small now, but it will grow along with her as she grows, and when she asks about it, you can show her this box."

After our thank-yous and several more hugs, Dr. DeCampli headed to change out of his scrubs and for the helicopter waiting for him on the roof of the building. Larry and I went to the diner a few blocks away and called our respective parents with the good news.

"SURPRISE!" shouted nurse Doreen, as we approached Valerie's side exactly one week after surgery. "See what's missing?"

I couldn't believe my eyes. The respirator was gone. Why hadn't anyone called us? Valerie was breathing on her own, with the help of a C-Pap giving her oxygen below her nose.

"She's 1 lb., 4 oz.; I think the smallest baby I've ever seen to come off the respirator!"

Doreen was excited. "And I have another surprise for you. This one is for you, Robin. Ready?"

I couldn't imagine there would be another surprise, but without a moment to guess at what it could possible be, Doreen lifted Valerie with her two hands and told me to hold out mine.

"I'm going to put her in your hands now. Just for a moment." And then she did.

My arms were extended outward as Valerie was placed into my two hands. She was warm and light. Her eyes were open and alert. My heart was so full it began to spill out of my eyes; tears rolled down my cheeks.

"Look at our sweetheart, Larry. Valerie," I cooed in a sing-songy voice, "We love you, we love you."

Doreen held her hands out and I placed Valerie back in them. Valerie was put back down on to the cotton batting.

"Next time it will be Dad's turn," said Doreen with a smile. Then she turned and left for her rounds.

We couldn't believe our good luck.

Valerie responded to the heart surgery well. She gained a few ounces. I held her in my hands for a few moments. It was all too good to be true.

Dorothy, who had triplets, but had lost the boy after a few days, was talking with her husband about baby announcements. Joining in on the conversation, we compared notes.

"It's just so awkward," she said. "I mean you can't exactly put a death announcement and a baby announcement in the same card, can you?"

"We're in the same boat. I want to honor Valerie's sister, but also celebrate Valerie. How do you do that? Plus there is the statistic thing. All the announcements have them. Height, weight…I can't exactly put Weight: 17 ounces, Length: 11 inches."

We all started laughing. Terri, a woman a few years younger than I with twin girls in the NICU born at 28 weeks, told us there was a Web site that dealt with these very issues. We all couldn't wait to get on when we got home and read the suggestions there.

When we were finally ready to send out our birth announcement, it read,

Our new love
Valerie Spielberg Kosson
September 22, 1998
Robin & Larry

Time moved strangely the next few months. Like Bill Murray's character in *Groundhog Day* it felt like I was awakening each day to the same day as the day before. I'd go to bed hoping and wishing for the next day to be different, but it wasn't, save for some mild variations. There might be new parents in the NICU one day; or it might be raining while we drove to the hospital. Valerie's regular nurse might be out sick; the hospital cafeteria might be out of pink lemonade. But we couldn't seem to get to the end of Valerie's birth; to the hour that we'd bring her home and start our lives as a family.

One evening we stopped by Larry's parents' house before heading back to the hospital for the evening visitation. They were entertaining company, all of whom were grandparents. They empathized with our situation, our worry. We heard accounts of this second cousin and that friend of a neighbor who also had "preemies" and they were all just fine now. Grown up and 6' tall, didn't you know. This one is in the gifted program in 6th grade and gained weight like crazy once she hit her fifth birthday.

While I understood these accounts were meant to make me feel better, they really didn't. When the anecdotes were all told, there was silence, and then someone changed the subject.

"Robin, have you been playing piano at the Hilton at Short Hills?"

"Ben!" his wife interjected. "Of course not. They've been living at that hospital. How could you play the piano in a time like this? The baby is in intensive care."

We said our goodbyes and from the car I called my agent.

"I'm ready to come back and play piano," I said.

"Oh, is the baby home?" asked Roger.

"No, not yet...but you know, the hospital is just five miles from the hotel. I could use a three-hour break each night playing the piano, you know?"

"Okay, I'll call the sub."

Larry agreed this was the best thing for me, and it was. Each night for three hours I poured my grief, my hope, and my fear into that piano. The job was a "background music" job, the perfect prescription. I was meant to disappear into the room and create atmosphere along with the candlelight, flowers, mahogany furniture and damask draperies. I was naked on the bench playing my heart out in a room full of businesspeople having cocktails, or restaurant guests waiting for their table to be ready. The piano rewarded me with melodic understanding that consoled my spirit and rested my mind. I floated away during those three hours, deep in meditation, the spell broken only by the occasional song request or a gentle reminder from the manager that it was time for me to take my contracted break.

On these evenings, I would stop by the NICU on my way home around 10:15pm and stay for a few hours. Given Valerie's precarious situation, no one minded my coming and going at all hours. The evening staff was humored by my visits in my formal concert wear.

"Ah, you're dressed up for your visit with your baby I see," said Marilyn, who was working a double shift. "You know, Valerie just looovvvves your music. She *loves* it."

"Well, how do you know? I mean it's certainly a nicer sound than all that beeping and alarm ringing, but do you think it calms her?"

"Do I think it calms her? Are you kidding? Of course it does. We have it all right here. Didn't Doreen say anything to you about this?"

"What do you mean?"

"Well, we…I mean, all of us nurses have noticed that Valerie really likes your music and we can tell because whenever we're playing it her vital signs improve. Her oxygen saturation levels increase, her breathing steadies, her blood pressure stabilizes. Just watch the monitor. You'll see."

And with that Marilyn began her rounds.

This was a "wow" moment for me and resulted in a turning point. I had received many letters and emails from listeners who told me that my music meant something special to them, and I was always happy to hear about couples using my music for their wedding procession, for massage, for romantic moments (sometimes in too much detail, I admit). I've heard from families who used my music during the hospice care of their loved ones, during funerals and memorial services, for life's important transitions.

But this was different.

How could a fetus, growing outside the womb, so underdeveloped, exhibit a preference for certain sounds? How could music have such a real physical impact on my baby? I understood musical preference, but physical, medical impact? Well, this was new. It astounded me. It intrigued me. It made me so so happy.

Before leaving that evening, I whispered into Valerie's ear. "My sweet, sweet girl, if we both make it through this, Mommy is going to make you your very own CD. I don't know if anyone will ever hear it but you, but that's okay. It will be yours. All yours." I ran my index finger slowly across her forehead until she fell asleep.

My search on Google for "music", "healing", "medicine" pointed me to AMTA, The American Music Therapy Association. Following the links to my area of interest, I found the work of Dr. Jayne Standley, a physician and researcher who spent the majority of her career studying the effects of music on the premature infant.

I couldn't stop reading about music therapy. There was something I could do besides sit, wait and pray. Medicine might save my child, but music would make her thrive. It had saved me time and time again, after all. Larry and I began to play my CDs at Valerie's station with intention in short increments. We sang to her in quiet voices. We made sweet melodic coo-ing sounds. Music from my early childhood came to me in my dreams, and when I awakened I wrote their titles on Post-It notes and stuck those notes to the Steinway. Late at night I would work on their arrangements. "The Itsy Bitsy Spider", "Row Row Row Your Boat", and one of the first songs I ever learned to play at age three on the Hammond Organ, Stephen Foster's "Beautiful Dreamer". These Post-It notes began to cover the piano, and when I could hardly find space for one more I knew it was time to book studio time.

With hope in my heart and a new musical dream, I began to heal as Valerie began to recover.

My recording contract with North Star Music was long over, so I released *Beautiful Dreamer: Lullabies for the Parent & Child* on my own newly formed playMountain Music label. Doing the project was enough for me. It was therapeutic. I was so immersed in being a new mom, I was not able to handle the business side of marketing the album properly, nor did I really care. North Star expressed interest in it and I ended up licensing it to them for the first few years. The reviews from magazines were gorgeous, but even better was the feedback I received from parents. Babies everywhere were calming down to *Beautiful Dreamer*. Letters of gratitude poured in. *Child Magazine, The Washington Post, Fit Pregnancy* — they were all champions of the recording.

When Andrea Farbman, Executive Director of the American Music Therapy Association, asked me if I would be interested in becoming a "Celebrity Artist Spokesperson," I said yes. It delighted me to no end that I would be in a position to learn more about this fascinating and growing field and work firsthand with music therapists during their workshops. My job was to observe, learn, understand, and eventually convey vital information to health care facilities, students and the general public about the benefits of music therapy. My first duties were appearing on panels where I simply told Valerie's story and how music played a vital role in our road to wellness. On November 20, 2003, I had the honor of being asked to perform for 1300 music therapists at the annual AMTA convention. It was my birthday, and the greatest gift I could receive was playing for this giving and special group of people. I also served on a panel at this conference along with my husband. It was called "The Effect of Music on the Premature Infant" or something like that, and yes, it was being led by Dr. Jayne Standley, my hero. When I met Jayne I couldn't contain myself. I just burst into tears and then apologized for my outburst while still sobbing. I explained as best I could how much her research meant to me during those months with Valerie in the NICU, how they gave me something to hold on to when all the medical professionals had the most pessimistic of outlooks.

When it was our turn to speak on the panel, Larry and I shared our NICU experience and the role music had always played in our lives and now, in the life of our darling girl. It was hard to re-live those memories with strangers, but it also felt good. Our audience consisted of music therapists, nurses, and students. Having a parent/musician perspective was important, and our listeners were kind, compassionate and grateful that we shared. That night we participated in a drum circle led by music therapist Christine Stevens. Valerie flew into the middle of the circle so she could dance and rejoice with the sounds and vibrations and positive energy swirling around her.

To this day I donate $1 from each sale of *Beautiful Dreamer* to music therapy research. My guess is that if I had known about this field as a college student, I might have been pulled in its direction.

The case studies, stories and work itself is incredibly fascinating and all of the therapists I've met have been the most grounded, remarkable people. The link between music and wellness is undeniable. I've witnessed it firsthand.

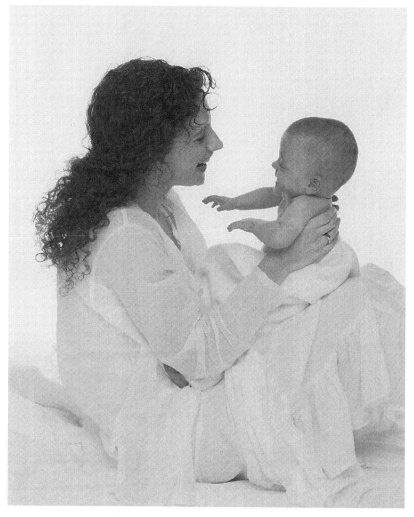

Larry took this photograph of me with Valerie during the photo shoot of *Beautiful Dreamer: Lullabies for the Parent & Child.* It's one of my favorites.

OUT OF THE MOUTHS OF BABES

I love the piano. I love my family. And while taking your toddler with you on a business trip might not be the first thing that comes to mind when someone says, "you can have it all", that is what came to mine. I figured that at least until Valerie was in kindergarten, I would take her along with me on tour so we could be together. This proved challenging at times, but it really was not all that difficult. I just had to have my act together on stage and off.

First there was the gear: portable crib, stroller, car seat, toys, snacks, stuffed animals and books. Then there were the CDs and songbooks for the merch table, my concert wear and our clothes, pull-ups and amenities. I could manage. Having a stroller allowed for almost everything to be one giant rolling cart, and the volunteers and staff at the concert venues were always so helpful and understanding. Except when they weren't.

At one show the babysitter hired by the venue didn't show up, and the box office manager was not willing to watch a little one. The show had to go on and I didn't want to seem difficult. I put Valerie in her "pack 'n play" portable pen off stage left. From the piano I could see her in the wings. I told her that Mommy was going to play piano for a little while just like I did at home. She had her favorite book to look at, *Pat the Bunny*, and her favorite stuffed animal friend, "Good Guy". She had teething rings and her "ba-ba" if she got hungry, and her favorite plastic mirror. After the first song, I smiled to myself as I saw her reach for her blanket and pull it over her head. She snoozed through Act I.

I remained stage left during Intermission and Valerie slept on. How lucky I was to have a child who was so *easy*. I couldn't wait to tell my relatives who thought I was crazy to take a baby on the road about this.

But Act II came and the tide turned. Valerie stood up in her Pack 'n Play and stared at me intensely while I played the first song. She looked mad. Wasn't I *done* yet? She had napped. She drank her bottle. She had read her book. What was next?

"MA!" she shouted. "MA!"

I played louder so no one could hear her offstage protest.

"MA-MA!"

In the next song introduction to the audience I mentioned I was traveling with my little girl and the audience might just hear her because she was watching the show from backstage.

There was a collective "Awwwww" as in "isn't that adorable", but what came next wasn't so adorable. In the middle of "Ireland", which is one of my longer pieces, Valerie decided to throw stuff to get my attention. At me. First came the *Pat the Bunny* book. She managed to launch it only a few feet so it barely made it on to the stage, but I got the message loud and clear, and a wave of panic came over me. On her face was a delightful, "See what I can do?" look. This was the toddler game of "toddler throws stuff, Mom goes and picks it up". But I wasn't practicing at home; I was on stage doing a concert in front of a sold-out house, so I kept playing.

Next came the bottle, or "ba-ba". It rolled across the stage, its pale blue color catching the stage light as it rolled toward the piano, stopping to rest at the piano leg farthest from me. It made a loud *clunk* when it hit the black stage floor. Did anyone notice that? My face grew hot. I played faster. I heard a few coughs from the audience. They could have been chuckles. I played louder. Oh dear.

The quiet section of "Ireland" seemed to calm Valerie. She sat back down and cuddled with Good Guy, no doubt looking to him for the comfort I was not giving. She wanted to be picked up. All the signs were there. My heart was breaking, but at least it seemed we were out of the woods. My heart stopped racing and I calmed into the song.

I finished the slow section of the song and just as the music transitioned to the re-capitulation, I saw Valerie's beloved Good Guy, who was part off-white bear, part blanket, arc through the air. He glowed in the light as he flew up high in the air, close to the lighting rig. The audience gasped. He landed smack center stage.

Giggles, laughter, confusion. Why was I not playing a shorter piece?

Next came the one-two throw of the plastic mirror followed by the binky. The throw of the mirror showed good aim and hit me in the head before landing on the piano bench. The rubber binky bounced off the lid of the piano and flew into the audience. It all happened so fast I told myself no one could have possibly noticed, or at least I prayed no one did. It was funny, humiliating, perfect, real and a crisis all at the same time. I pretended nothing had transpired.

Then, "MAMA!! BINK-YEEEEeeeeeeee!!!!"

There was one more song to play, but no matter, having no bink was nothing short of a sheer emergency. I took my bow after the final notes of "Ireland", made a quick exit and returned with babe in arms for my curtain call.

Valerie and I were met with thunderous applause and Valerie was smiling ear-to-ear, happy at last for our reunion. I sat at the piano so I could use the microphone and said, "I'd love to play one more song for you, but if the lighting tech in the booth could just raise the house lights for a moment?"

The house lights bumped up.

"I have a request," I said. Please take a moment to look under your seats and if you see a pacifier or binky, please bring it to the stage. Valerie seems to think it's out there somewhere." And then, to Valerie, "Did you toss your bink at Mama?" The audience consoled me with their applause. It was okay. I was a human being. A mommy pianist with a baby, trying to be both mommy and entertainer right in front of everyone, and I was almost achieving it, but not quite. They sympathized.

Turns out the binky made it to Row L. I thanked the man who returned it to the lip of the stage. He had it wrapped in a tissue. The audience cheered, whistled and applauded the man, our new hero. Good throw, Val, I thought. I handed Valerie and the binky to the stage manager stage right ignoring her look of surprise.

"Thanks. Just hold her for a sec. And wash the bink, please, before giving it to her." The audience heard my request. They laughed, giggled and applauded. How cute we were.

The encore was a blur. All I could think about was having just handed my child to a complete stranger backstage. It probably all looked "part of the act", but I was winging every moment.

Valerie sat happily in her stroller in the lobby after the show while I signed CDs and posed for photographs. She munched on Goldfish crackers, not a tear, not a sigh. The whole thing could have been a lot worse.

Notes to self: do not keep baby in wing space of theater. Do not give her things she can throw at you on stage.

The spring before kindergarten was to start, Larry was at a music conference and I was booked to perform in South Carolina. I was reluctant to go on tour with Valerie via plane —there was a lot to carry — but there really was no other choice. We boarded our flight, enjoyed our layover playing the card game War and reading *Amelia Bedilia*. On the second flight we both felt queasy on the descent and reached for the airsickness bags in the seat pockets in front of us at exactly the same time. We were in sync. We threw up in the same moment, and afterwards, we laughed about it.

The first venue was packed, but understaffed, and there was no one who could mind Valerie in the dressing room as I had been told. No longer worried she would throw things while I performed, I asked Valerie, "Do you want to watch the concert from the audience?"

"No," she said nonchalantly. "I want to color."

"Well, you can't stay here in my dressing room by yourself. How about I bring you to the audience and you can color there in a grownup seat?"

"I need something to lean on."

"Okay, we can get something."

Ten minutes before curtain, the house manager came to my rescue with a phone book.

Valerie and I were standing at the back of the house talking about where she would sit. I wanted her to be near the back in case she had to leave to go to the bathroom during the show.

Two elderly women approached us and said, "Is this your child?"

I told them yes, this was my daughter Valerie, and she was almost five.

"Would you like to sit with us?" they asked.

My daughter, who had never experienced "stranger aversion", was quick to respond.

"YES! Are you a grandma?"

The women were amused.

"We are both grandmas," said the woman with the white-haired bun. "Come, we'll find a seat nice and close so you can see Mommy play."

Oh dear Lord.

The grandmas were great. In my peripheral vision I could see them handing Valerie crayons and paper as needed. She was making rainbows and was happily amused. She was completely oblivious to the concert, and the stage lighting spilled off into the first rows, which gave her enough light by which to color. This was working out. And then I saw it.

A hand rose. Someone in the audience had a question. Valerie's hand.

I ignored it. Grandma One patted Valerie's hand down from the air when I began the next song, but at the song's end, during the applause, it shot up again. Higher, higher. Grandma Two whispered something in Valerie's ear. She shook her head. I had to make a decision. This could get bad. Before starting the next song I turned front and center on the bench and said, "I see someone in the audience has a question for me!" in an effort to make it part of the act. "Yes, young lady in the front. What is your question?"

"Mom, I have two questions. First, I can't find orange anywhere. And two, are you almost done?"

Outrageous laughter emerged. Valerie looked confused.

"Well, for now I suggest you color with red and then use yellow on top of it to get orange in the rainbow, and as for question number two, if you check the program you will see I have just a few more songs to play. In fact, this next one is for you!" And I played the song "Valerie" from *Beautiful Dreamer*. This one always made Valerie dance at home, but this time she just smiled and continued with her drawing, completely satisfied with my answer.

Note to self: Make sure you tell your kid that you really can't have a conversation during the show.

Despite my vast experience with traveling on tour with child in tow, I realize I don't have a lot of advice to artists hoping to do the same. All I can advise is: do it. Don't worry. It is great to have your family together as much as possible. Do your best. It's all in. I've been on stage with breast-milk-stained blouses, and stood in small radio studios reeking of throw up and diarrhea. There's nothing better.

We were on Cape Cod, Massachusetts, and Valerie started showing a bit more interest in my show. She was seven now, about to start piano lessons herself, and she wanted a job.

Larry gave her programs to hand out.

"Welcome to my mom's show," she said. "I hope you love it, although I think it is very very boring!"

At intermission she mimicked the hot dog salesman at the ballpark.

"CDs, get your CDs here!"

Valerie was fired from both jobs, but finally got a chance to shine in a job she invented. She drew rainbows on each CD bag and signed her name after the show. The rainbow design seemed to feature an inordinate amount of orange.

That pesky little rule about kids having to be in school prevented me from taking Valerie on tour with me in the coming years so touring became a bit more limited. I became more and more involved with our entertainment agency, handling payroll, taxes, contracts and press kits for our artist roster. One day Valerie came home from school and told us about a special event at her school during dinner. She said,

"So at school today we had Career Day."

"What did you do on Career Day?" I asked.

"Well, a few parents came in to talk about their jobs. There was a fireman, a policeman and a nurse. Camryn's dad is a fireman! Did you know that? Then we went around the room and told everyone what our parents did for work."

"What did you tell them about us?"

"I told them that Daddy sells Mommy."

"What? What did you say?" I had been only half-listening because I was draining pasta in the sink.

"I told everyone that Daddy sells mommy."

"Did anyone say anything about that?" I asked my daughter, who was already scooping butter into the bowl that would soon be filled with hot tri-color rotini. "Did the teacher ask you what you meant?"

"No. It was kind of quick."

Larry smiled at me. It was hard not to laugh.

That night at the kitchen table Larry and I talked about work with Valerie and tried our best to simplify the mission of our entertainment booking agency in terms any eight-year-old could understand.

"You know that Daddy is a booking agent for performing artists on tour, right?"

"Yes."

"And you know that Mommy is just one of those artists. I am one of the many artists on the *roster* of artists. The roster is the *group* of artists we represent or take care of. Daddy's job is to get booking dates for all these artists so they can make a living doing what they love, playing music. Mommy's job is to help with the contracts for all these artists, make sure they get paid, and of course, to play the piano when I have a date to play. Daddy books all those dates when I am out of town."

"I know that."

"Good then."

The next day Valerie came home and told us that she asked the teacher if she could say something to Mrs. Glover's class, and that Mrs. Glover said she could. She said,

"I made a little mistake yesterday and I wanted to fix it. It turns out that my daddy doesn't sell my mommy for work. That was the wrong way of putting it. It turns out that Daddy gets Mommy *dates*. Mommy likes to have a lot of dates, and when she doesn't have enough dates, she gets a little mad at Daddy."

Well, what are you going to do? That was completely true.

The next year a letter came home from school that was a call for volunteers for Career Day. Larry and I jumped at the chance. The other parents in attendance in our daughter's classroom were an ex-marine, a policeman, and a nurse. Larry fired up his PowerPoint presentation of artist pitches, which for the purpose of contrast, featured an opera singer we were representing at the time, a Scottish rock band known for its blue humor, and me. The kids loved the presentation. Hands shot up immediately afterward.

"I see what *they* do," said one boy. "But what do *you* do?"

"Well," Larry started, "I talk to people who run performing arts centers and festivals around the country about these wonderful performers, and I work to get them dates."

Indeed.

My turn to speak came, and I chose to talk to the kids about how music can unite us over generations. My examples were songs I had just played at a nursing home the week before: "Oh Susannah", "Home on the Range", and "Bicycle Built for Two". The kids all knew these songs and when I asked them how or why they knew them, they shrugged. "Church!" one boy shouted out. "My grandpa!" said another. My Americana mini-lecture ended with an epiphany of sorts. Why not record these songs so we don't lose them in future generations? It was pretty cool, I thought, that the 90-year-olds knew them *and* the nine year-olds. How many piano players were recording Americana arrangements anyway? Besides, I admit it bothered me that no one raised their hand in recognition when I sang the opening bars of "My Grandfather's Clock", my all-time favorite Americana song from childhood.

In Gerry's studio in New Hampshire, Kate MacLeod and I sat side by side. Kate sat on a stool with her guitar on her lap, and I sat on the bench close to the upper register of the Steinway. We improvised on "Oh Susannah" and it felt great. Valerie joined me in the studio for the recording of *Sea to Shining Sea*, bringing her talent with mallets to both bells and marimba. She had her own iPod now and she had practiced her parts at home while listening to the "practice tracks" I had recorded for her. They were somewhere on a playlist mixed in with her favorite pop songs, Japanese rock, some of the Americana music I had been researching, and the soundtracks to *Hairspray* and *Mary Poppins*.

Valerie nailed her parts in a few takes, but no thanks to me. After the first dry run, she insisted I take off my producer headphones and hand them over to Gerry, our engineer, because *he* was *official* and really knew what he was doing. *Sorry Mom, no offense, but you are just the piano player.* I wasn't offended; I was proud, and sometimes it is really great to "just be the piano player".

I took a break during her session and visited with my sister who had stopped by to see how things were going.

It was all going so beautifully, so on day three when doubt and panic swept over me upon waking it took me by surprise. I called Larry before heading out to the studio.

"Honey, I think I'm making a big mistake. I hired all the musicians, I booked the studio time, and we're halfway done, but really, who am I kidding? Who do I think I am recording Americana music? I'm no authority. I don't know what I'm doing. And even if I did, who is going to want to hear this? It's "Bicycle Built for Two" for Pete's sake!"

"Everyone," he said. "Everyone. Trust yourself."

As usual, Larry was right. The recording received beautiful reviews and I really loved the result. Kate MacLeod, cellist Catherine Bent and I joined together to tour it in the fall of 2011. The music brought back memories for so many. During each performance we could see people swaying to the music, and sometimes singing along to themselves, their minds adrift and filled with daydreams and memories. I had never been thanked so much after a concert as when I incorporated tunes from *Sea to Shining Sea*. People were moved.

As a gift to Valerie, I had arranged to record two songs I composed and often sang to her at night called "Look to Tomorrow" and "Lolly Lou, Lolly Lee" as bonus tracks. Her friend Brinkley sang backup with her on the first song. I remember thinking how perfect that moment was when the song wrapped. The expressions on their faces, the sincerity in their singing; it is all indelibly engraved in my memory. Wouldn't it be amazing if they grew up one day to sing these songs of comfort to their own children? Isn't that what song tradition is all about?

When the CDs were ready, I drove to Lancaster, PA, with

Valerie to pick them up from the manufacturer. I parked at the loading dock and, together, we loaded the boxes into the car. In keeping with my tradition, I opened the first box I touched, took out the first CD, unwrapped it and popped it into my car's CD player so I could listen to it on the way home.

We headed for home, the two of us, with our car full of CD boxes. The ride was going to take just about the length of the CD. Perfect. When "My Grandfather's Clock" came on Valerie began to cry in the back seat.

"What's the matter, sweetheart?" I asked in the rearview mirror. "You don't like it? Too loud?"

"No, Mommy. No. It's beautiful. So beautiful. I love these songs. I love that we recorded them. I love that I'm part of it. I love you."

"I love you too," I said, and then we both cried and laughed away our tears of joy.

There is great power in songs sewn in childhood. A wealth of emotional life is wrapped up inside of them, waiting for us, until we decide to sing them, hear them, and play them. And in doing so, a part of us reawakens.

"Mama?"

"Yes?"

"Can I listen to it again when we get home?"

Music to my ears.

Traveling with Valerie; Woodstock, Vermont 2000

MUSIC IN STRANGE PLACES

"It really is a very odd business that all of us, to varying degrees,
have music in our heads."
☒ Oliver Sacks, *Musicophilia: Tales of Music and the Brain*

The soundtrack to my life has been inspired by butterflies, friends, felines, lovers, history, the promise of world peace, birds, gardens, friendships, disappointments, my baby's eyes, my sister's smile, my best friend's laugh, men at war, Chekhov, Willa Cather, the house I grew up in, and the list goes on. Inspiration is everywhere.

But I never imagined one of the most active sources of inspiration would come from a space heater I used to keep under my desk in the winter.

The heater took a minute or so to warm up. Once it did, a string section began to play the most amazing music. At least that is what *I* heard coming out of the space heater. My husband said all he heard was a constant electronic hum. His loss. My gift. I heard beautiful new orchestral music. It was more than a little weird and perhaps disconcerting, but I found that, ultimately, I enjoyed listening to it while I paid bills at my desk. What could be the harm? And lucky me, it wasn't just the space heater that offered private concerts. I was lucky enough to be serenaded by the refrigerator, the dishwasher, air-conditioner vents in hotel rooms, and fans too. Amid their whirring, blowing and buzzing there was music. Always symphonic, and usually wonderful. I say just *usually*, because on occasion the most annoying bombastic music would come from these machines to torture me. I spent many nights alone in hotel rooms freezing or sweating out the night because of vents I had to shut off altogether that proved simply impossible musically. My physical discomfort was preferable to being assaulted by their truly terrible music.

The defroster in my old Nissan Altima produced violin and piano duets that were lovely. That imagined radio station only played when the defroster and the windshield wipers were on at the same time. I wasn't really bothered that I had imagined all this music; I was bothered that I couldn't share "the station" with anyone I knew because it was truly amazing. When that car died the music died along with it. No other automobile defroster ever produced a station quite like that one.

One night in New Hampshire, I decided to tell the concert manager about the buzzing theatrical lights. At intermission I found him and said, "The lights above the piano are really making a terrible noise. Can you fix them or just shut them off for the second half?"

"Oh really? I am so sorry! I didn't hear anything."

"Maybe you can't hear it from where you are, but from where I'm sitting it's terribly distracting. Normally something like that wouldn't throw me off, but the frequency keeps changing in pitch and it's almost musical, you know? So playing during that is like playing with a radio on or something."

"I'll check it out."

John got out the ladder during intermission and attended to the lights.

In the dressing room I changed my dress and touched up my makeup when there was a knock on my door.

"Robin, I got up there, right next to the lights, and nothing. I don't hear anything at all."

"What? You're kidding. Listen to that!"

"What?"

"Don't you hear *that*"?

"What? In here too? There's something in these lights too?"

I realized we were in the dressing room and the music was still there, coming out of the lights on the dressing room mirror. Oh no.

"No, no. Never mind. It's fine."

Confused, John went back to the stage to retrieve the ladder and put it away. I was left with a meandering etude in the key of D. It followed me from my dressing room to the stage. Blissfully, it only lived in that theater, and was gone as soon as I left the building. It wasn't beautiful or worth writing down, just long sustained F-sharps, D's, A's and tremolos that persisted and persisted, but led nowhere. Obviously those lights did not get the proper training to create anything worthwhile.

Recently, at my mother's apartment, I was nodding off but not quite able to sleep. Her appliances were singing to me from the other room. My mother, who had been reading next to me, noticed I had not fallen off to sleep.

"Robin, you had such a long drive. What's keeping you awake? I can tell by your breathing that you're still up."

I decided to confess the truth. She's my *mother*. This secret had gone on for too long.

"Well, Mom," I said, "I'd be asleep by now if it weren't for that damn music coming out of your refrigerator in the next room."

Silence. And then, "*Oh my God.* You hear it too?"

"What do you mean?" I asked my mother. I turned around to face her. "You actually hear something?"

What an epiphany.

"Yes," she said. "Yes I do! I thought I was crazy."

"We're both crazy," I said. "Because you and I both know whatever we're hearing is all in our heads."

My mother spilled, "I used to think the radio was on in the kitchen and I'd get up and check, and then it'd stop. Then it'd start again."

"Yeah, that's when the motor turns on and off. When the motor starts running to cool off the temperature inside, that is when you probably hear the radio music."

"How do you know that?" she asked.

"Because that's what happens with my refrigerator at home. What do you hear?"

"Well, nothing now," she said disappointedly.

"Me neither."

"What *did* you hear?"

"A pretty ballad with strings."

"Oh. Not me," she said. "I heard a waltz."

"Good night mom."

"Good night."

Parts of "Spirit in this House", "Dancing in the Quiet Rain", and "Ireland" came out of music I heard emanating from electrical appliances. Like I said, inspiration is everywhere.

TERRIFIC

My father spoke his last word to me in late October 2000. He was in a hospital bed. I had just received the CD proof of *Dreaming of Summer*. My dad loved my music and he has listened to it during his chemotherapy sessions often. I placed the headphones over his head, and pressed "play" on the portable CD player so he could hear the brand-new work. His eyes closed, he nodded as he listened to the first track. When it was finished, he whispered one word. The word was "Terrific."

I made up songs in my childhood. Songs about UFO's. Songs about the cats. Songs about getting lost. My father's reaction was always the same.

"That's terrific, Robin," he'd say. What are you going to do with that song?"

And then I'd get mad. What did he mean, what was I going to do with that song? Wasn't it enough that I wrote it?

"Nothing," I'd say. "Just play it now and then."

"Well, I think you should do something with that song," he'd say. Then he'd walk away, leaving me steaming mad and feeling unappreciated.

After I took the headphones off my father I told him of all the things I was going to do with those songs. His urging that I do something with my music worked on me over the years. It is probably because of my father that I like "doing stuff". Ours was not a relationship of ideas, feelings and philosophy. It was a relationship of action. It wasn't enough to just compose a song.

From the side of his hospital bed I told my father the songs of *Dreaming of Summer* were going to be published in a songbook folio so other piano players could play them. They were going to be aired on National Public Radio affiliates around the country. I was already scheduled to play a dozen garden-themed concerts. I was releasing a video for the title track that featured my husband's floral photographs. He nodded in approval at all of this and again whispered, "Terrific."

My father was discharged that afternoon so he could have hospice at home. He died the next day, my mother and I beside him, holding his hands, speaking our words of love and comfort.

A few years later, I was on stage about to play the song "Remembering You" from the *Dreaming of Summer* CD at a concert in Korea. I mentioned that my father had been stationed in Germany during the Korean War. After the interpreter conveyed this to the audience, the audience simultaneously stood up. It was the oddest thing, but I assumed it was a symbol of respect. They stood silently for five seconds before sitting down again. It was as though they had been counting, that's how precise their movements were from sitting to standing, to sitting again. I collected myself from that unexpected tribute and began the song. My heart was full. The song had been inspired by the loss of a romantic love, but now, on this day, the song was for my father and for the loss I felt years after his passing — loss that I didn't expect to feel. As I played, I remember wishing he could see me on stage in Korea. He would have thought it was pretty darn cool that I was performing so far from home. At the moment I completed the thought, the power in the concert hall went out. I kept playing. Sighs and gasps ensued, but I ignored them. If I didn't know where the keys were in the dark by now, I thought, I deserved any train wreck that was coming my way. But there was no train wreck. Just complete darkness, me, the piano, the melancholy phrases of

"Remembering You", and a meditation for my father, who, in this moment, felt oh-so-present at that concert. The darkness and the magic continued for the song's entirety, the power spontaneously returned a moment after the last note sounded. I bet my father would have thought the timing of that was, well, terrific.

**Age 9 with my Dad, the late Shel Spielberg in front of
our house in Maplewood, NJ**

ALREADY THERE

When I was an NYU student studying drama for the summer with the newly formed Atlantic Theater Company, playwright John Guare came up to Vermont to teach a master class. He promised at the start of his lecture that he would tell us the secret to success. I couldn't wait. We listened respectfully as he told us about the trials and tribulations of playwriting, getting plays produced, staying true to one's art, the history of his Lydie Breeze trilogy (we would all later act and produce one of those plays, *Women and Water*). At the very end of the class he told us the *big secret*. The one we were all waiting for. It was the secret to getting where we all wanted to go. The top. He was sitting down on a gray aluminum-folding chair at the front of the classroom. He leaned forward in his chair, and looked each of us in the eye before saying the three words that were supposed to change our lives. He had a glint in his eye. And then he revealed the big secret. He said, "You're already *there*."

That was it? That was the climax of his lecture? What a joke. He couldn't possibly mean that sitting in this hot classroom in August at Vermont College was "making it". I wanted to know how to get *parts*. How to win the hearts and minds of casting directors. How to make it on Broadway. My fellow classmates looked equally confused. We were students. We had so far to go. We were nowhere near where we wanted to be.

I eventually "got" what Guare was talking about — a few decades later. I bet the rest of the class eventually did too.

With all the attention we were paying to going, doing, achieving, we were missing where we were in the moment. That, in and of itself, was success to be celebrated. In our world, the goalposts were constantly moving and being set further and further away, and the irony was we were the ones moving them. Once we achieved something — like forming the Company, getting a play of ours off-Broadway, winning a coveted role — there was another goal to achieve that we were sure would make us *truly* successful. But then that thing would come and meant little if anything; we were on to the *next* thing.

I remember being in a dressing room of an off-Broadway play I was in. A girl in her early twenties, like me, was telling me of her longing for her big break. "You are so lucky," she said. "You got into the Atlantic Theater Company."

"Well, no, not exactly," I said. "I was in the class that started the Atlantic Theater Company. The company formed out of a few very unique workshops; there is nothing mysterious about it. You can start a company too."

"That's what I mean," she insisted. "You didn't even have to audition or anything. If only I could get into a good company or land the national commercial I just auditioned for, everything would change," she bemoaned.

But the commercial did come, and nothing really changed.

The same is true for the Grammy chasers (of which I was one) and the fame seekers I've encountered at recording studios, green rooms, audition waiting rooms, rehearsal studios and Internet listservs. I've heard the oddest of goals expressed in these settings. If musicians and artists were to "stand in their truth", a phrase I heard Suze Orman, the finance wizard use, we would see that all artists really want is to *connect*.

I don't know anyone in the arts who doesn't long for peer recognition and industry validation. That is what award ceremonies and golden trophies are all about. But it is clear to me that these kinds of accolades have to be achieved as a *by-product* of truthful day-to-day living in one's art. "Winning a trophy" or "becoming famous" as a stand-alone goal is a rather empty wish, and unlikely to leave any artist feeling fulfilled for long if attained without connectedness. I have known many musicians who have spent years building a network of industry voters instead of audiences. Composers who have worked on image more than content. Independent musicians spending more time pursuing a review in a prestigious publication instead of practicing their instruments. They don't seem very happy.

While on tour in rural Missouri, I was given the opportunity to play in a retirement home. I was scheduled to perform a public concert that same evening. I was newly appointed as an Artist Spokesperson for the American Music Therapy Association and was happy to have another chance to play piano. This particular concert event was for people who couldn't get out to the concert hall that night. It seemed like a nice thing to do.

As soon as I walked into the building I was accosted by a terrible odor. It was the odor of the sick and neglected. The retirement home wasn't really a retirement home after all. It turned out to be a run-down nursing home facility of the worst kind. State run, it experienced budget cuts year after year. The residents there rarely had visitors, never mind concert artists come to entertain them.

The director was a middle-aged woman who looked tired and overworked. She led me to an out-of-tune upright piano, her sensible black shoes clicking as she walked ahead of me on the white linoleum floor. The piano looked rather pathetic; it was so little in that big space, but I knew it would be there on its bench where I could make my escape from the sadness that was sweeping over me. I sat down and put my bags down to the side of the piano. I played a few chords. It was out of tune, but the action, I was happy to discover, was in pretty good shape.

Old people on stretchers and wheelchairs were rolled into the humid and dank "all-purpose room" to hear me play. Heads were drooped to the side. The residents were there, but not present. A microphone had been set up for me to tell my stories. I said, "Hello! How is everyone today?" There was no response, but I already knew the answer to my stupid question.

I managed to continue. "My name is Robin Spielberg, and I hope you will enjoy the music you are about to hear." Awkward silence. No applause. I began to play. I looked down at my watch. Only three minutes had passed. Fifty-seven more to go. I couldn't wait to get in my rental car and go back to my climate-controlled hotel room and forget about this morning, but as soon as my hands were on the keys I began to drift into the music my parents taught me. Music from yesteryear. That's what this occasion called for. "Moon River", "As Time Goes By", "Smoke Gets in Your Eyes", "Frankie & Johnny", "On the Sunny Side of the Street", "On Top of Old Smokey", "Stormy Weather," "Over the Rainbow". They were fun to remember and fun to play.

No one applauded after my first song; so I made a quick decision not to stop, to just thread the songs together continuously, like I did in my hotel gig days. I moved the mic stand away to the side. Funny, I had planned on talking about music therapy, about my grandparents and their connection to music. Just prior to walking into the facility I was thinking of *games* I could play with the residents like Name that Tune. I had brought along several large *fake books* for the occasion, but there would be no requests. Not today. There were no games here. Out of the corner of my eye

I could see a few feet tapping, a few hands moving to the music, but little else. It didn't get worse than this, I thought to myself. Just a day ago I was feeling on top of the world, packing to go on tour, and now look at me. Look at this gig.

When the hour was up I closed the piano lid with a sigh. It was a good hour of practice. The woman who had escorted me in had gone. There was no one to say goodbye to. Nurses appeared to roll the residents away, back to hallways, physical therapy, televisions and lunch trays. I gathered my things and found the way from which I came. I was walking down the hall to the nursing home lobby and then:

"Excuse me, excuse me, Miss Spielberg?"

A nurse was running after me down the hall. I must have forgotten something. My purse?

"Hi, Miss Spielberg. I just wanted to thank you so much for coming. It meant so much and the residents loved it so."

"Really?" I said quietly. "No offense, but how could you tell?"

"Oh my. You don't know, do you? Your music was so beautiful, so soulful. I could see — no, I could feel the spirits in the room lifting. Couldn't you?"

"Um. No. Not really. I guess I wasn't in tune; there was some distance between the piano and the residents because of the wheelchairs and stretchers. The setting was a little different for me. I couldn't really tell if anyone was listening."

"Oh they were listening all right. Did you know that Mr. Larson actually had a big break-through during your performance?"

"Who is Mr. Larson?"

"He was in the wheelchair to your left, with the full head of white hair."

"Oh yeah. I did notice him. He was enjoying "Moon River"

I think."

"That's right. But what you didn't know, what you couldn't know, is that Mr. Larson has not spoken in six months. Not a word."

The nurse's eyes began to turn red and tear up. She continued, "He was such a sweet sweet man, always joking, always kidding with the staff...but his wife died a while back and he became very low, very depressed. And there he was, just now, listening to you and singing along to "Moon River"! It was amazing. A miracle, really. He was tapping his foot too. Did you see? The Director wasn't here to show you out because she went to call his family to give them the news. Well, I have to get back to my station. I just wanted to thank you."

The nameless nurse angel hugged me. I couldn't return the embrace. My arms were weighed down at my sides with the tote bags filled with fake books and the CDs I thought I would sell to the residents. I just stood there with my arms pulled downward by the weight of the books. The nurse turned on her heels and left me there alone in the hallway, aghast. Everything I had thought I had just experienced was not true.

They *had* been listening. It *had* meant something, my being there. Applause or lack of it was irrelevant. Success here could not be measured in applause or standing ovation or paycheck. Those were the only tools of measurement I had when it came to performance. In fact, the greatest success of my life thus far had just been achieved. A stranger named Mr. Larson sang along to "Moon River" and broke his six-month self-imposed isolation. He came back. He came back, even for just a short while. He came back to the world of the living because he heard someone play a song that meant something to him, that connected with him.

It made him feel alive again.

I was already there.

The feeling I had of meaning, of worth in that moment, was a revelation. I began to actively seek opportunities to recapture it. As happy and glorious it is to receive standing ovations, to share the stage with somebody famous, or perform at Carnegie Hall, some of my proudest achievements have happened in places like that nursing home in Missouri, way under the radar where there was no applause. I never would have thought, back in the days when I thought I wanted to be a big Broadway star that I would feel this way, but it's my truth, and I am so glad I finally found it. It took me a few decades, but I found it.

My wish for all aspiring artists — actors, writers, musicians, painters — is that they realize their worth is in sharing their spirit, their art and their truth with others in positive efforts to connect through music, through the script, through their writing, through their orchestration, via their paintbrush or clay. Sometimes these efforts are not rewarded with award statuettes, popularity rankings, magazine covers or applause, and sometimes they just happen to be. Whatever the journey, perhaps it is wisest to start with the notion that we are "already there", and then proceed. It sure takes the pressure off, and for me, it has made the adventure a whole lot more fun.

ACKNOWLEDGEMENTS

Special thanks to my piano teachers: Rosemarie Zito, the late Jane Erickson, Richard Glasser, Alan Wolfe; you have all given so much of yourselves in your lessons and I am forever grateful. To my parents, Honey Spielberg and the late Sheldon Spielberg — they fostered music in our home, sang, whistled, hummed and encouraged expression through music every day. To my sister Eileen for her encouragement along the way. To my dear Valerie, playing music with you and being your mother are two of my favorite parts of being alive. To Robin Meloy Goldsby, the original Piano Girl: I couldn't ask for a better best friend; I am forever grateful for your encouragement, love, support, humor and help along the way. I love you. To my steadfast "Agentman" husband, Larry: you made my dreams your own, and have helped me stay the course. You believe in me always and you are the love of my life. To my encouraging and optimistic editor, Lauren Baratz Logsted: many thanks for your kind direction. Special thanks to Kenny Banyoun for your cover design, Kate MacLeod and Stephanie Winters for "playing along", and to Ariane for selling me on that Mac SE30. To my friends at Steinway & Sons (and especially Jenn Gordon, Betsy Hirsch, Eddie Krauss and Irene Wlodarski): the pianos you make help me realize my music to its fullest; there are no finer pianos in the world. To Cristori, inventor of the piano, I thank you. To Pachelbel, for that really great tune. To Dr. Jayne Standley, Dr. Andrea Farbman, and everyone at the American Music Therapy Association: for allowing me to be part of your mission of transforming lives through music. To every presenter who has ever hired me to play in a concert hall and to every audience member who listened, thank you. To Richard Waterman and Paul Mason: for taking a chance on me and releasing my very first CD on North Star Records. To the Atlantic Theater Company, and especially David Mamet, William H. Macy and Steven Schachter: for instilling in me fine work habits, giving me the chance to score those early plays, and showing me there is no finer thing than creating the theater in one's own heart. To Felicity Huffman: thank you for always opening your home to me and for always telling the truth. To Mary, Karen, Jordan, Neil and all my friends at Atlantic: thank you for your friendship through the years. Thanks to Scott Zigler, for encouraging me to go to Vermont that summer and to jump off that cliff; I am forever grateful. To Brett: for coming to the Grand Hyatt lobby every day during that difficult time and for being such a fine, fine friend. To Sarah, Meghan, Kelly, Tiffany, Laura and Mia, my interns over the years: thank you for listening to these stories and getting me ready for the road. To Sue & Bruce, I am so lucky to have you as friends. To Nada: Boo! I love gardening with you. To Tim, Kathy, Nancy, Regina and everyone at the Roots Agency, thank you for making sure I have more adventures to tell! To Gerry and Fran for your hospitality at Cedarhouse Sound during the making of the audio version of this book. To piano technicians everywhere: thank you. To piano lovers and listeners everywhere: I thank you.

ABOUT THE AUTHOR

Robin Spielberg is a pianist, composer, recording artist and entrepreneur. She has recorded fifteen albums of solo piano and piano-based instrumentals that have sold over a million copies and her music appears on dozens of compilation recordings around the world. Her compositions are published in several folios of piano music and are played by piano aficionados worldwide.

Robin is a celebrity artist spokesperson for The American Music Therapy Association. She is partner and Chief Operations Officer of The Roots Agency, an entertainment agency that books performing artists on tour. She is a founding member of the Atlantic Theater Company, a voting member of the National Academy of Recording Arts and Sciences, The Screen Actors Guild, The American Federation of Musicians, ASCAP and many other arts organizations.

Robin Spielberg is a Steinway Artist and brings her music and stories (and occasionally a Steinway) to music halls near and far.

Robin Spielberg resides in rural Pennsylvania with her husband, daughter and four fabulous felines. You can read more about Robin's life and work at www.robinspielberg.com

Discography
Heal of the Hand
Songs of the Spirit
Spirit of the Holidays
Unchained Melodies
In the Arms of the Wind
Mother

In the Heart of Winter
The Christmas Collection
American Chanukah: Songs Celebrating Chanukah and Peace
With a Song in my Heart
Beautiful Dreamer: Lullabies for the Parent and Child
Dreaming of Summer
Memories of Utopia
A New Kind of Love
Sea to Shining Sea: A Tapestry of American Music

Made in the USA
Lexington, KY
27 September 2013